T0139023

Citizen Empowerment through Digital Transformation in Government

Citizen Empowerment through Digital Transformation in Government

Edited by
Neeta Verma

CRC Press
Taylor & Francis Group
Boca Raton London

CRC Press is an imprint of the
Taylor & Francis Group, an **informa** business
A CHAPMAN & HALL BOOK

First edition published 2022
by CRC Press
6000 Broken Sound Parkway NW, Suite 300, Boca Raton, FL 33487–2742

and by CRC Press
2 Park Square, Milton Park, Abingdon, Oxon, OX14 4RN

CRC Press is an imprint of Taylor & Francis Group, LLC

Library of Congress Cataloging-in-Publication Data
Names: Verma, Neeta, editor.
Title: Citizen empowerment through digital transformation in government / edited by Neeta Verma.
Identifiers: LCCN 2021031768 (print) | LCCN 2021031769 (ebook) | ISBN 9780367628925 (hardback) | ISBN 9780367629014 (paperback) | ISBN 9781003111351 (ebook)
Subjects: LCSH: National Informatics Centre of India. | Technological innovations—Economic aspects—India. | Technology and state—India.
Classification: LCC HC440.T4 C58 2022 (print) | LCC HC440.T4 (ebook) | DDC 338/.0640954—dc23
LC record available at https://lccn.loc.gov/2021031768
LC ebook record available at https://lccn.loc.gov/2021031769

ISBN: 978-0-367-62892-5 (hbk)
ISBN: 978-0-367-62901-4 (pbk)
ISBN: 978-1-003-11135-1 (ebk)

DOI: 10.1201/9781003111351

Typeset in Palatino
by Apex CoVantage, LLC

Contents

Foreword

This is a highly relevant compilation of digital transformation journeys in government. Over the last three-and-a-half decades, no single organization has done as much, seen as much, and been a part of as many such efforts as the National Informatics Centre (NIC) of India. This collation of the evolution of several project initiatives cuts across several sectors and straddles both the central and state governments. Each chapter presents a distinct context, a different experience with varied learnings. Coming from actual implementers, who have spent years and often more than a decade in these projects, the insights afforded are deep indeed.

New and emerging technologies that are highly scalable, affordable, and quick-to-implement present attractive and unprecedented opportunities to use them to personalize government services. Consequently, the establishment of Centers of Excellence in blockchain, application security, artificial intelligence, micro services, and data analytics by the NIC and led by the editor, Dr. Neeta Verma, is timely and forward-looking. While charting the course toward this enticing future, it is important to appreciate not only where we stand today but also how we got here—which is what this anthology does. Every technology intervention needs to be tailored to the context and the need. At the end of the day, technology is merely a tool, and governance imperatives ought to drive adoption. Apart from that, the needs of the citizen merit greater importance than those of the government itself, because, in a democracy like ours, the government must serve the needs of the people. It is in this background that the emphasis on citizen services is particularly heartening. This was indeed the spirit and ethos of the successive National e-Governance Plan first launched in 2006. That technology can today be used not only to provide services to citizens but to also directly engage with them at a hitherto unimaginable scale is well brought out by initiatives like MyGov.

The pivotal role of technology in effective administration in diverse areas like treasury operations, tax collection, transportation, public distribution systems, and courts is evident from the relevant chapters. Yet another contribution that this compilation makes is in understanding the scope, successes, and challenges of technology interventions in the rural context, including agriculture, as well as in social sectors like healthcare and education. This is particularly important for a country like India, facing monumental challenges in achieving Sustainable Development Goals for its 1.3 billion population.

A sobering realization from these and many other instances of technology adoption in government is that technology is not an answer to all the deficiencies of governance. Technology cannot really compensate for poor governance, but it can certainly make good governance much better. Readers can draw their own inferences on such nuances from the detailed exposition on each project.

The editor, Dr. Neeta Verma, leads the NIC as the director-general at a time when new opportunities beckon, a strong foundation has already been built, and government policy lays strong emphasis on a digital India and a digital economy. She leads the NIC at an inflection point in its evolution as the country's principal technology support organization within government. Her transparent and infectious enthusiasm for exploiting technology to serve governance needs stands the NIC in good stead at this juncture when the future is discernible, and the past is known. As a professional, Dr. Verma is personally aware of both and has the onerous responsibility of connecting them. That is what makes this carefully selected compendium of project journeys so unique and relevant. It is simultaneously an opportunity to reflect on the transformations taking place outside of the government across sectors and to seamlessly integrate those systems and capabilities with government systems to benefit the entire ecosystem.

I do hope that all those engaged in or participating in the digital transformation journey of government that is taking place in real time before our eyes will benefit from the experiences shared in this book. I commend the editor, Dr. Neeta Verma, and the publishers for putting together this comprehensive collection of practical implementation trajectories, over an extended period, of many of the most important e-governance projects in the country. It is a must-read for any serious practitioner or analyst of e-governance in the country today.

R. Chandrashekhar
Former Secretary,
Department of Information Technology (now called MeitY),
Govt. of India

Preface

The government of India always believed in the power of technology and its potential to enhance efficiency and effectiveness in governance. It had set up National Informatics Centre (NIC) way back in 1976 to promote the use of technology in the government. The National e-Governance Plan was an important milestone in 2006 which focused on digitization in different sectors through Mission Mode Projects. Digital India Programme launched in 2015 focused on the pan–India Digital Infrastructure, Digital Services, and Digital Inclusion across the public and private sectors.

The NIC has played a pivotal role in the induction of technology in all tiers of governance across different sectors of socioeconomic development. In 2016, I was entrusted with the responsibility of leading the NIC as its director-general. While spearheading the development of digital platforms for citizen-centric initiatives of the government under the Digital India program, I came across young minds and quadranscentennial and semicentennial experienced practitioners at digital government, academia, and industry and realized the veracity and variety of tacit knowledge lying untold. I realized that the rich experience gained by these government practitioners over the decades must be compiled in the form of a publication, which will act as an important reference for future generations.

Digital transformation and growth are the top two priorities of governments worldwide. The Government of India is also aligned with global trends and priority areas of digitalization, citizen-centricity, data, and analytics to improve the availability of services through the use of new-age digital technologies. The roots of digital governance in India may be traced back to the early 1950s when Indian planners needed statistics and econometric modeling for economic planning. It was scientists like P. C. Mahalanobis and Homi Jehangir Bhabha, who pioneered the use of computers in India. Dr. N. Seshagiri, the founding director-general of the NIC and former Special Secretary to the Government of India, was always ahead of his time and spearheaded the information technology (IT) revolution in India. He laid great importance on inducting information and communication technology (ICT) in governance across the country.

India's digital journey has reached an eminent position globally as it empowers the citizens, ensures inclusive growth, and provides a framework for efficient and effective governance, all powered through technology. With the assistance of the NIC's pan-India infrastructure and digital solutions, government initiatives are now technology-enabled right from concept to commission, implemented at all levels of government services: local, state, national, and even international.

This book captures the technology-led transformation of various sectors and their evolution over a period. Right from the era of mainframe computers to cloud-based applications, this book presents the paradigm shift that citizens experienced while availing government services. This book is unique in the sense that it is written by practitioners in the digital government space. There is comprehensive coverage of case studies in various sectors, wherein ICT was used to deliver services to the stakeholders. The case studies covered in this book lie at the heart of digitally empowered India in which every citizen is given the power to access a variety of online services in an inclusive manner. This book also focuses on the stages of digital government across designing, delivering, and scaling while implementing critical and successful digital government projects.

The book will be of immense interest to (not limited to) policymakers, digital government practitioners, researchers, government training institutes, academicians, IT professionals, and students. The contributors of the chapters are senior digital government experts with an average experience of 25 to 30 years in informatics-led development programs. The chapters are the outcome of their research, practice, and experience in leading digital government initiatives in different sectors. It will also be a valuable resource for the countries that are at an early stage in their journey of digital transformation.

Dr. Neeta Verma

Acknowledgments

Bringing digital transformation in government requires the combined efforts of hundreds of people over the years. Not all the digital transformational initiatives could be covered in this book, but this compilation of leading case studies is the collective effort of many individuals since the conception of these initiatives. If I have inadvertently left someone out in the following, I apologize and would like to extend my gratitude to them. These are an outstanding group of people who have contributed to making this book possible, and I would like to thank all of them.

I am humbled to express my gratitude to my mentor and visionary founding director-general of National Informatics Centre (NIC), Dr. N. Seshagiri. It was his vision and leadership that contributed immensely to the information technology (IT) revolution in India. India's e-governance today is the outcome of the vision and hard work put in by Dr. Seshagiri through the 1980s and 1990s.

The NIC was truly blessed to have the support of visionary leaders through the years. My sincere thanks to Hon'ble Ministers for their guidance and emphasis to leverage the power of technology to empower the people of India. I would like to thank secretaries and senior government officers for their trust in the NIC and for providing the opportunities to build digital solutions in so many different sectors of the economy. My grateful acknowledgment to all former directors-general of the NIC for their leadership and commitment to leverage the best of technology for citizen services.

I am grateful to digital government researchers and practitioners in academia, industry, and ministries/departments of the central and state governments who helped me develop meaningful insights with each interaction. I would also like to thank Prof. M. P. Gupta (Professor, IIT Delhi), my PhD guide for his constant support and guidance. His pioneering work in the area of e-governance has motivated me to explore the innovative use of technology for governance.

I would like to thank my colleagues at the NIC who have authored these chapters. This book is a testimony to the rich experience they have in implementing technology solutions in diverse sectors.

This book is a long-drawn journey of many NICians who have dedicated their lives to this stellar organization and excelled in delivering citizen-centric projects in India. My sincere thanks and gratitude to every NICian who has contributed to this organization and made a difference in the lives of millions of people. It is through their hard work and commitment that we see the NIC emerging as a premier technology organization in India.

I would like to thank G. Mayil Muthu Kumaran and Pradip Kumar Upadhyay, who helped me put this book together. I would also like to thank Mohan Das Viswam for the exquisite cover design.

My special thanks to Shashank Mittal (Principal Consultant at PwC) for his tireless and continuous contribution right when this book was conceptualized to further research, transcription, compilation, consolidation, and refining the contents. His interest in digital transformation in government has contributed immensely to this book.

The NIC Library team was of immense help in providing all the latest relevant research articles, books, and reports, and I would like to thank them for their service.

This book would be incomplete if I don't mention my industrious team at the Director-General's Office. Thank you for keeping up with the late working hours and managing the schedule of my office so efficiently. I express my thanks to Sudarshan, Jasvinder, Deepak, Mohan, Amit, and Kamal for managing my office.

I would like to express gratitude to my husband, Dr. Lalit Verma, for supporting me over the years in all my endeavors. I would like to thank my children, Neha, Aastha, and Nitin for always inspiring me to do more. This book is a culmination of an idea conceived during one of the discussions with Neha. I am grateful to my parents and parents-in-law, who have selflessly supported me throughout my career.

Finally, I'm grateful to my publisher, CRC Press, for its help and patience despite the inconvenience caused due to the COVID-19 pandemic. I would like to thank Aastha Sharma and Shikha Garg for their support and guidance in finalizing the manuscript of the book.

Once again, thank you for making this book a reality.

Dr. Neeta Verma

About the Editor—Dr. Neeta Verma

Dr. Neeta Verma is Director General of the National Informatics Centre, a premier Technology organization of the Government of India. With a career spanning over three and a half decades, she has been instrumental in implementing high-impact digital initiatives across the country. In her current role as DG NIC, she is spearheading the digital transformation agenda of the government through the development of digital platforms for various initiatives of the government in different sectors of development. With the mobile revolution in the country, she is also ensuring a mobile-first strategy by focusing on delivering government services through mobile phones in ICT solutions built by NIC.

She has been an active proponent of leading citizen engagement through technology at various levels of governance. She was instrumental in setting up the technology platform for MyGov, which is a citizen engagement and crowdsourcing platform engaging over 14 million citizens. She brings an extensive experience in the field of open data and has led the launch of Open Data Platform to release government data in open for the public good. She has also been instrumental in formulating Government Open Data License. During the early years of her career, she provided consulting services to various government departments in India and abroad in establishing their web presence.

Under her leadership, the NIC established National Data Centers at various locations in the country and later launched the first National Cloud for Government in 2014 to provide state-of-the-art information and communications technology (ICT) infrastructure on demand to government departments for delivery of citizen services. She has aggressively worked toward the adoption of the cloud by government departments through a cloud-first strategy to provide scalability, agility, reduce time to commission, and attain a high order of efficiency in ICT initiatives of the government.

To leverage emerging technologies in governance, she led the establishment of its one-of-a-kind Centres of Excellence (CoEs) in blockchain, application security, AI, micro services, and data analytics. These CoEs are working toward exploring the applications of emerging technologies for agility in governance and delivery of services to citizens.

She has also played a key role in setting up of NIC CERT (Computer Emergency Response Team) in 2017. With her continuous contribution in the field of ICT, in

2019, she was featured among the top 55 inspiring women around the world who have showcased the prowess of technology in the government sector.

With her vision to transform government services, initiatives, and schemes through the application of technology, she has helped the NIC emerge as a trusted partner to the central government as well as the states governments in India. She oversees the 800-plus offices of the NIC, which are established right from central headquarters in Delhi to state and district offices in India.

Being the head of a premier technology institution of the government, she has interacted with government ministries, departments, and state governments, as well as government organizations, in realizing their digital transformation agenda. She has also worked closely with the Indian judiciary in its journey of digital transformation of the courts pan India.

She has also guided NIC teams in the productization of their popular solutions and has helped the NIC establish its own world-class software products such as eOffice, e-Hospital, eProcurement, eAuction, eTransport, and many more.

She holds a PhD from the Indian Institute of Technology, Delhi and an Executive Certificate in digital transformation in government from the Harvard Kennedy School. Her research interests include applications of emerging technologies in governance, cybersecurity, and data centers, among others. Apart from publishing her research in national and international journals, she has also coauthored books on the role of technology in governance. She is regularly invited at various national and international conferences and forums to provide thought leadership around technology in e-governance.

During the COVID-19 crisis, under her leadership, the NIC was entrusted with a wide range of responsibilities from the seamless provision of the network, cloud-to-messaging, and videoconferencing services to design, develop, and implement various technology solutions to help the government and its citizens during the time of distress. Under her leadership, the NIC developed several new mobile applications to cater to the specific needs of different departments in the central, as well as state, governments for managing home quarantine, containment zones, COVID hospitals, the issuance of passes during the lockdown, the digital transfer of subsidies to migrant labors pan India, and many more.

She was entrusted by the government to manage a mobile application, 'Aarogya Setu', which is enabled with the latest technology for contact tracing, to provision the safety of citizens from the pandemic. With more than 170 million downloads, the Aarogya Setu app became the most downloaded government application in India. Apart from Aarogya Setu, she also led the development of RT-PCR Mobile app to manage data related to COVID-19 tests pan India.

Under her guidance, the NIC has also worked closely with various national institutions such as the Indian Council of Medical Research, the Ministry of Health and Family Welfare, and the National Centre for Disease Control to extend necessary technical advice and support during the COVID-19 pandemic. She also supervised the establishment of the Central Data Hub to ensure the integration of various systems and the secure exchange of data among different IT systems of the government, which is currently being used by central and state government entities pan India.

Contributors

 Saba Akhtar, Scientist-F at NIC, is currently working as Head of Division for the School Education Informatics Division. He is also heading the Unified District Information System for School Education (UDISE+) project along with many other projects forschool education. Saba Akhtar holds a master'sdegree along with an MSc in operation research.

 Sunil Babbar, Scientist-E and Technical Director at NIC, has also been associated with the Open Data Initiative of India. He has coauthored various papers for the International Conference ICEGOV 2017, Web Accessibility Assessment of Government Web Solutions, and Open Government Data Policy and Indian Ecosystems.

 **Sunita Bennur** is Scientist-F andSenior Technical Director at NIC. She is currently working on eWaybill System, eInvoice System, and eWaybill Analytics System. She has worked on various successful eGovernance projects such as Bhoomi–Land Records Management System and Sakala–Karnataka Guarantee of Services to Citizens.

 **P.V. Bhat** is Scientist-G and Deputy Director General & State Informatics Officer at NIC and is handling a number of eGovernance projects for the last 31 years. He has a BE degree in computer science and an MBA in finance. He has been awarded the Prime Ministers Award for Excellence in Public Administration for his contribution totransforming the commercial taxes department in Karnataka.

 Suparna Bhatnagar is Scientist-E and Technical Director at NIC with over 31 years of experience. She has been involved in various projects under the National Health Mission—namely MCTS, RCH, and RCH 2.0 of Ministry of Health & Family Welfare. She has a master'sdegree in operational research from Delhi University, New Delhi.

Pradeep Kumar Garg, Scientist-F and Senior Technical Director at NIC, has 34 years of experience. He has worked on many important applications in the finance domain such as foreign investment monitoring andpsychotropic substances manufacturers' registration and monitoring in addition to providing support to various pay commissions and finance commissions.

Gautam Ghosh, Scientist-G and Deputy Director General at NIC, has over 38 years of experience in leading eGovernance projects for socio-economic development in various sectors such as transport, public distribution systems, and consumer affairs at the national level. He holds a master's degree in civil engineering from Jadavpur University and a master's degree in Computer Technology and Application from Delhi Technical University.

Rajiv Goel is Scientist-F and Senior TechnicalDirector at NIC. Withover 35 years of experience, he has played a key role in leading the information systems for the Panchayati Raj System and Land Records at NIC. He has a master's degree in science and a Post-Graduate Diploma in Computer Applications (PGDCA).

Tarun Kumar Goel is Scientist-F and Senior Technical Director at NIC with more than 26years of experience, particularly for the district administration and health sector. He has a bachelor'sdegree in computer sciences from Marathwada University.

Dr Piyush Gupta is Scientist-F and Senior Technical Director at NIC with over 25 years of experience. He has been involved in end-to-end management of various eGovernance projects for the transport and health sectors. He has a bachelor's degree in computer and systems sciences, a master's degree in engineering systems, and a PhD in computer science.

Rama Hariharan is Scientist-G and Deputy Director General at NIC. With over 35 years of work experience, she has led various projects for the Analytics & Modeling Division, Panchayati Raj, and so on. She has also worked as General Manager at NICSI and led the CoE for Data Analytics (CEDA). She has her master's in science (statistics) from Delhi University.

Pawan Joshi, Scientist-G and Deputy Director General at NIC,has more than 32 years of experience in leading various eGovernance projects for the government of India. Currently, he heads the eTransport Mission Mode Project, Quality Assurance & API Infrastructure Management Division, Nodal Centre for Mobile Application Development, User Experience Design Technology Division, and CoE on Microservices at NIC. He has an MCA from the Thapar Institute of Engineering and Technology, Patiala.

Mohd. Anwar Khan, Scientist-F, is currently working as Head of the Department for the eCounseling division at NIC. He has played a key role in the conducting of transparent e-admission services nationwide. He has been a part of the eCounseling services (examination and admission) which is developed by NIC and is being used by leading government entities and examination/counseling boards.

Manie Khaneja is Scientist-G and Deputy Director General at NIC. With over 27 years of experience, she has played a key role in leading the information systems for Panchayati Raj System and Rural Development at NIC. She has a master's degree in computer applications.

Naveen Kumar is Scientist-F and Senior Technical Director at NIC. He has more than 30 years of experience and is currently the Head of Division for the eHospital& ORS and CollabDDS projects. He has completed his BE degree in Computer Engineering from NSIT, New Delhi.

Sunil Kumar is Scientist-G and Deputy Director General at NIC. He is responsible for IT enablement in Health sector at national and state level and works closely with the Ministry of Health & Family Welfare in India. He has experience of 32 years in development and implementation of various e-Governance Projects. He has been State Informatics Officer of 3 states of India and managed various state-level IT projects such as land records, rural development, treasuries, food sector and courts.

G. Mayil Muthu Kumaran is Scientist-G and Deputy Director General at NIC and currently heads the Quality Assurance & API Management Infrastructure Division. He has more than 29 years of experience in the end-to-end computerization of the public distribution system andthe automation of turnkey projects for the Bureau of Indian Standards, Central Warehousing Corporation, Food Corporation of India, and Ministry of Food and Consumer Affairs. He has a BE degree in computer science & engineering and an M. Tech. degree in information technology.

Sitansu Sekhar Mahapatra is a new media and communication professional with over 16 years of experience in digital product management, content, policy, governance, service delivery, media convergence, and knowledge management. He has been associated with the Open Government Data Initiative of India since 2013.

Suresh C. Meti, is Scientist-E and Technical Director at NIC and has more than 22 years of work experience. He is currently involved in GST projects such as eWay Bill, eInvoice, and GST Prime, which are national-level implementations. He holds an engineering degree in electronics and communications.

Alka Mishra currently serves as Scientist-G and Deputy Director General at NIC. With more than 30 years of experience in digital governance, she is leading the NextGen Software Defined Cloud Platform, Open Data Platform, Guidelines for Indian Government Websites (GIGW), MyGov, National Portal of India, and various web technology projects for thegovernment of India.

Manoj Kumar Mishra, Scientist-G and Deputy Director General at NIC, has over 33 years of experience in leading key eGovernance projects. He currently leads the eCourts Informatics, Media and Protocol Division (NIC), Government eMarket place, and Legal Informatics. He also worked as Managing Director (NICSI) for three years. He holds a master's degree in computer applications from Aligarh Muslim University.

Deepak Chandra Misra, Scientist-G and Deputy Director General at NIC, has been associated with eGovernance for more than 35 years, particularly in the rural development domain. He has been involved in policy formulation, conceptualization, system development, and operationalization for many innovative eGovernance projects and has done projects for UNESCO, UNICEF, and World Bank. He has a master's degree in Computer & Systems Sciences from Jawaharlal Nehru University (JNU), New Delhi. He has published many articles and papers in national and international journals and has also been a reviewer for an international journal. He specializes in Enterprise Architecture, Low Code-No Code (LCNC) systems and Rural Informatics echo systems.

Durga Prasad Misra is Scientist-F and Senior Technical Director at NIC. He is Head of the Open Data Technology Division, Web Technology Division, and Cloud Technology Division at NIC and is the technical lead for the Indian Government Data Platform, National Portal of India, MyGov, S3WaaS, and NextGen Software Defined Cloud Platform.

Mala Mittal, Scientist-F, has been associated with NIC for more than 25 years. She currently headsthe Department of Agriculture Cooperation and Farmers Welfare (DAC & FW) and the Department of Agricultural Research and Education (DARE) Divisions. She is the project leader for IT projects associated with the agriculture sector and its affiliated organizations.

Prashant Kumar Mittal, Scientist-G and Deputy Director General, is currently Managing Director of NIC. With more than 32 years of experience in delivering ICT solutions consistently, he has contributed to numerous initiatives that resulted in improved efficiencies and delivery qualities in eGovernance. He has his MSc in physics with a specialization in electronics, Post-Graduate Diploma in Computer Applications (PGDCA), MS (software systems), and MBA in project management.

Dr Ranjna Nagpal is Scientist-G and Deputy Director General at NIC, where she heads the Agriculture-Informatics Division. She has more than three decades of expertise in conceptualization and implementation of multiple ICT initiatives, many of which have been awarded at various forums. She is also a renowned expert and thought leader on digital agriculture and upcoming technologies.

BVC Rao, Scientist-G and Deputy Director General at NIC, has been associated with eGovernance for more than 35 years, particularly for the Ministry of Corporate Affairs and the Ministry of Consumer Affairs, Food and Public Distribution domain in India. He has a master'sdegree in technology with specialization in instrumentation and computer science from Sri Venkateswara University, Andhra Pradesh.

Rajiv Rathi joined NIC in 1989 andis currently Scientist-G and Deputy Director General. He leads many projects and services including Aadhaar Authentication Platform of NIC, Biometric Attendance System, and Jeevan Pramaan (Digital Life Certificates) to provide services that are used by both citizens and government offices. He has a BSc (H) degree in physics and a master'sincomputer science and application (MCA).

H. L. Ravindra is Scientist-F and Senior Technical Director at NIC. He is currently working on GST-related projects such as GSTPro, GSTPrime, GST e-Waybill, and GST eInvoice. Prior to this, he worked at Central Excise, Belgaum,to implement the Central Excise Computerization project (SERMON) of NIC.

Dipankar Sengupta is Scientist-G and Deputy Director General at NIC. With more than 32 years of experience, he has played a key role in making Public Financial Management Systems (PFMS) the cornerstone of financial management as well other applications in the finance domain. He has also contributed to other national-level projects such as the e-way bill, e-invoice, and RT-PCR application for Covid detection.

Seemantinee Sengupta is Scientist-G and Deputy Director General at NIC. With over 31 years of experience, she has played a key role in leading the information systems for the Panchayati Raj System and Land Records at NIC. She has also worked as District Informatics officer at Silchar, Assam, and has a bachelor's degree in electrical engineering.

Varindra Seth, Scientist-G and Deputy Director General, has worked at NIC since 1996 and is presently working as Head of Division for Registrar General of India, Election Commission of India & Socio-Economic and Caste Census. He has his master's degree in technology from the Indian Institute of Technology, Roorkee.

Rajender Sethi is Scientist- G and Deputy Director General at NIC andleads the group of IT professionals working in the education sector at the national level. With more than 34 years of experience, he has worked on multiple platforms for design, development, and the nationwide implementation of IT systems in personnel andtraining as well as labor andemployment. He holds an M. Tech from Indian Institute of Technology, Delhi, and PG diploma from IIT Roorkee.

Kapil Kumar Sharma is Scientist-F and Head of Division for eOffice at NIC and has over 25 years of experience. He has been involved in end-to-end management of many eGovernance projects such as random generation and allocation of polling parties during elections, and so on. He has M. Phil degree in Operational Research from Delhi University and MBA(IT) from Bharati Vidyapeeth University.

Madhuri Sharma is Scientist-G and Deputy Director General at NIC. With over 36 years of experience, she has played a key role in leading various projects for education, rural development, fertilizers and more. She currently leads the e-HRMS project at NIC. She has completed her master's degree in technology from IIT, Delhi.

Dr Pramod Sharma is Scientist-F and Senior Technical Director at NIC with over 33 years of experience in eGovernance. He was involved in India's first news automation for Doordarshan News from NIC. He has his MSc in physics from Agra University, Agra, and has a PhD in physics from the same university.

Nagesh Shastri is Scientist-G and Deputy Director General at NIC and has over three decades of experience. He played a major role in transformation of Union Budget computerization beginning in 2008. He has led many eGovernance initiatives for the Ministry of Finance and has been part of national-level projects such as the e-way bill, e-invoice apart from the applications in finance domain. He has also contributed to setting up CoEs in emerging technologies such as artificial intelligence and blockchain at NIC.

Joydeep Shome is Scientist-G and Deputy Director General and heads the eTransport Mission Mode Project at NIC. He has been instrumental in the successful adoption of flagship applications in the transport sector such as Vahan, Sarathi, echallan, mParivahan, and so on by states across the country. He is an engineering graduate in electronics and telecom from NIT Silchar and has more than 32 years of experience.

Ashish J. Shiradhonkar is Scientist-F and Head of Department of the eCourts project at NIC. He has been involved in the conceptualization, development, and operationalization of the eCourts mission mode project across all sub-ordinate courts and high courts of the country for the past 26 years. Ashish holds a BE from Marathwada University, an MS in software systems from BITS Pilani, and an LLB from University of Pune.

Shyam Bihari Singh, Scientist-G and Deputy Director General at NIC, has over 34 years of experience as IT Change Leader in the government sector. He has successfully led nationwide ICT projects such as the National Scholarship Portal (NSP), eCourts-MMP, and various other key projects. He is a recipient of the Prime Minister's Award for Excellence in Public Administration 2006–07, the e-Governance Award from DoPT, and several other awards from the Government of India.

Dr Yogesh Kumar Singh, Scientist-F at NIC, has 31 years of experience. He is the Head of Division for the Department of Higher Education at NIC. He has been leading various projects at the national level including AISHE, the UGC–National Academics depository,and so one. He holds a master's degree in physics from IIT Roorkee and a PhD from the National Physical Laboratory, New Delhi.

Anand Swarup Srivastava is Scientist-F and Senior Technical Director at NIC with over 25 years of work experience. He is currently the Head of Division for the IVFRT project. He has a master's degree in computer applications (MCA) and has been appreciated on several platforms for his contribution in establishing a virtual communication platform in government departments for the Prime Minister's prestigious project 'PRAGATI'.

Rachna Srivastava is Scientist-G and Deputy Director General at NIC and is a member of the NICSI board. She has more than 30 years of experience and has been involved in the conceptualization, system development, and operationalization of many national eGovernance projects such as AISHE, National Employment Service Project, e-Office Project (NIC) and so on. She has a master's degree in computer applications from Jawaharlal Nehru University, New Delhi.

Pradip Kumar Upadhyay is Scientist-F and Record Officer at NIC. His research area includes digital library in government and digital records management. He has earned his MSc in Physics from University of Delhi and master's degree in library and information science from University of Delhi. He was also the Fulbright Scholar (2002–2003) at the University of Illinois, Urbana-Champaign, and winner of the SIG III International Paper Contest 2006 for the paper 'e-Granthalaya: Moving Towards Rural Digital Library for Sustainable Rural Livelihoods'.

Dr Neeta Verma is the Director General (DG) of NIC and has over 35 years of work experience in leading and implementing high-impact digital initiatives across the country. In her current role as DG NIC, she is spearheading the government's digital transformation agenda through the development of digital platforms for various initiatives.To leverage emerging technologies in governance, she led the establishment of Centers of Excellence (CoEs) in blockchain, application security,artificial intelligence, micro services, and data analytics. She holds a PhD from the Indian Institute of Technology, Delhi, and an Executive Certificate on Digital Transformation in Government from the Harvard Kennedy School.

Jitender Kumar Yadav is Scientist-G and Deputy Director General at NIC. He leads the application of technology in theImmigration & VisaDivisionand has experience in the implementation of multi-stakeholder national-level ICT projects and flagship schemes for thegovernment of India. He has a strong technical academic background and holds anMSc, MTech-CS, and PGDCA.

Abbreviations

AI	Artificial intelligence
APAR	Annual Performance Appraisal Report
API	Application programming interface
APMC	Agriculture Produce Marketing Committee
ASHA	Accredited social health activist
BPL	Below the poverty line
CBO	Community-based organization
CBSE	Central Board of Secondary Education
CGHS	Central Government Health Scheme
CIS	Case information system
CLF	Cluster-level federation
CMAT	Common Management Admission Test
CPAO	Central Pension Accounting Office
CPSMS	Central Plan Scheme Monitoring System
CRISP	Computerized Rural Information Systems Project
CSC	Common service center
DARPAN	Dashboard for Analytical Review of Projects Across Nation
DAY-NRLM	Deendayal Antyodaya Yojana—National Rural Livelihood Mission
DBT	Direct benefits transfer
DDO	Drawing and disbursement officer
DDU-GKY	Deen Dayal Upadhyaya Grameen Kaushalya Yojana
DISHA	District Development Coordination and Monitoring Committee
DoRD	Department of Rural Development
DRDA	District Rural Development Agency
EPIC	Election photo identity card
eTAAL	Electronic Transaction Aggregation and Analysis Layer
EVM	Electronic voting machine
FCI	Food Corporation of India
FOSS	Free and open-source software
FPS	Fair price shop
FRO	Foreigner Registration Office
FRRO	Foreigner Regional Registration Office
FTO	Fund transfer order
GIS	Geographical Information System
GPAT	Graduate Pharmacy Aptitude Test
GPF	General Provident Fund
GST	Goods and Services Tax
GSTIN	Goods and Services Tax Identification Number

GSTN	Goods and Services Tax Network
ICP	Immigration Check Post
ICT	Information and communications technology
IFMIS	Integrated Financial Management Information System
IIFT	Indian Institute of Foreign Trade
IIIT	Indian Institute of Information Technology
IIM	Indian Institute of Management
IIT	Indian Institute of Technology
IoT	Internet of Things
IRMA	Institute of Rural Management Anand
IT	Information technology
JEE	Joint Entrance Examination
KMS	Knowledge management system
LGD	Local Government Directory
MCTS	Mother and Child Tracking System
MGNREGA	Mahatma Gandhi National Rural Employment Guarantee Act
MoHFW	Ministry of Health and Family Welfare
MSP	Minimum support price
NCERT	National Council of Education Research and Training
NCHM	National Council for Hotel Management
NDSAP	National Data Sharing and Accessibility Policy
NEET	National Eligibility Entrance Test
NeFMS	National Electronic Fund Management System
NeGP	National e-Governance Plan
NFPP	National Food Procurement Portal
NFSA	National Food Security Act
NIC	National Informatics Centre
NICNET	NIC Satellite Network
NIOS	National Institute of Open Schooling
NIT	National Institute of Technology
NJDG	National Judiciary Data Grid
NKN	National Knowledge Network
NPA	Nonperforming assets
NPCI	National Payments Corporation of India
NPTEL	National Programme on Technology Enhanced Learning
NREN	National Education Research Network
NSAP	National Social Assistance Programme
OCR	Optical character recognition
OGD Platform	Open Government Data Platform
OGPL	Open Government Platform
OMR	Optical mark recognition
OTP	One-time password
PaaS	Platform as a Service

PAO	Pay and Accounts Officer
PDS	Public Distribution System
PFMS	Public Financial Management System
PIMS	Personnel Information Management System
PMAY-G	Pradhan Mantri Awaas Yojana-Gramin
PMGSY	Pradhan Mantri Gram Sadak Yojana
PM-KISAN	Pradhan Mantri Kisan Samman Nidhi
POS	Point of service
PPP	Public–private partnership
PSC	Phyto-Sanitary Certificates
PUCC	Pollution Under Control Certificate
RTO	Regional Transport Office
SaaS	Software as a Service
SBM	Swachh Bharat Mission
SDG	Sustainable Development Goal
SECC	Socio Economic Caste Census
SHC	Soil Health Card
SPARROW	Smart Performance Appraisal Report Recording Online Window
SWAN	State-wide area network
TPDS	Targeted Public Distribution System
UDISE+	Unified District Information on School Education Plus
UGC	University Grants Commission
UGC-NET	University Grants Commission-National Eligibility Test
UIDAI	Unique Identification Authority of India
UIP	Universal Immunization Programme
UMANG	Unified Mobile Application for New-Age Governance
UNDP	United Nations Development Programme
UPI	Unified Payments Interface
USAID	United States Agency for International Development
VAT	Value-added tax
VO	Village organization
VSAT	Very Small Aperture Terminal
VVPAT	Voter Verifiable Paper Audit Trail

1

Digital Transformation in Government—A Case Study of India

Neeta Verma and G. Mayil Muthu Kumaran

1. Introduction

The Government of India has been at the forefront in the use of technology to strengthen governance. To promote the use of technology, the Government of India established an IT organization—the NIC—way back in 1976. The government has also focused on the growth of a vibrant IT industry in India by adopting progressive policies at the right time.

The initial use of computers in government was focused on data digitization, processing, and analysis, resulting in the development of the Management Information System (MIS), which has helped the government in gaining insights for planning and decision-making. Furthermore, with the advent and proliferation of communication networks, IT systems were enabled to assist with the implementation and monitoring of social development schemes in the domains of poverty alleviation, health, education, and agriculture. IT systems were also used to digitize tax systems right from excise and customs to income tax for enhancing efficiency and accuracy.

The advent of the World Wide Web shifted the focus to delivering information to citizens in an easy and inclusive manner. Every government organization was encouraged to have its web presence, with a focus on citizen-centric information that was previously difficult to obtain.

Taking the e-governance a notch higher, the NeGP ushered in a paradigm shift by using technology for the delivery of services to citizens. Through Mission Mode Projects (MMPs) in every sector of the economy, the NeGP led to the end-to-end digitization as well as the development of integrated systems catering to the needs of different stakeholders. The national portal and state portals came into existence intending to provide single-point access to information and services. Massive digitization across the government and the online delivery of services to citizens led to an enhanced demand for resources that resulted in enhancing the capacity of National Data Centres managed by the NIC as well as the establishment of State Data Centres in

DOI: 10.1201/9781003111351-1

every state. Another key objective of the NeGP was to take the services to the district level, which was made possible by a country-wide communication network of the NIC that used both terrestrial as well as VSAT links depending on the geography of the districts. The NKN provided multigigabit network connectivity to government and academic institutions pan India. Today, it acts as the NERN of the country.

Digital India is an important landmark in the digital transformation of government. It focused on the empowerment of people and inclusive governance through the power of technology and digital enablement of citizens through various schemes. The mobile and broadband revolution in the country helped the government extend its reach directly to the people of India by cutting across its geography, both urban and rural. Mobile-based governance led to the development of several mobile applications for government services from availing subsidies and scholarships to applying for certificates and licenses. It also promoted the engagement of citizens with the government through the MyGov platform, giving citizens a real feel of participative governance, which enabled them to provide inputs regarding important policies of the government.

Due to the proliferation of IT systems and the resultant growth in data, recent years have unleashed the potential of data and led to the emergence of an entire industry around it, paving the way for a data-driven economy. The availability of cloud infrastructure and data analytics capability within the government accelerated the use of data analysis within various IT systems of the government, thus inculcating the culture of data-driven governance. The significance of data was further amplified during the management of COVID-19, and it also led to the widespread use of data analytics and modeling to generate insights and influence decision-making. With the increased span of digitalization, the spectrum and sophistication of cyber threats have increased manifold. Therefore, there is a need to be aware of such threats and build a defense mechanism appropriately. To address the ever-increasing threat of cyberattacks in terms of their magnitude as well as their sophistication, the Computer Emergency Response Team (NIC-CERT) was set up in the NIC to analyze, monitor, and respond to cyber threats on government cyber infrastructure like websites, emails, and digital solutions. The NIC-CERT works under the close guidance of CERT-In, which is the national nodal agency for responding to computer security incidents as and when they occur.

The mainstreaming of AI tools and technologies can be a truly transformative journey. The acceptance of AI across the value chain, namely, government organizations, Public Sector Undertakings (PSUs), the private sector, start-ups, and academia, will unlock the potential of AI by creating a righteous cycle of supply and demand. The government has started engaging with the start-ups in a big way to promote innovation in inclusive delivery of services and Make in India software products under its Atmanirbhar Bharat Abhiyan.

The following sections shall take us through the journey of technology-led initiatives in the Indian government over the last four decades which commenced with modest beginnings by use of MISs.

2. National Informatics Centre (NIC)

It all began in 1963 with the creation of the Electronics Committee, also known as the Bhabha Committee, which developed a 10-year road map for Indigenous computer and component production. The aim was to reduce dependence on imported technologies and increase reliance on domestic goods. The establishment of the Sarabhai Committee, chaired by Vikram Sarabhai, a prominent leader of India's space program, bolstered the electronics industry even more. The committee was tasked with providing strategic guidance for in-house production, allowing for faster capacity development. These two committees' recommendations culminated in the creation of a self-sufficient industry, resulting in the establishment of the Department of Electronics in 1970 and a new Electronics Commission. While the new commission was tasked with formulating policies and providing oversight, the department was tasked with putting them into action [1].

The NIC, a small program started as an external stimulus of a UNDP project in the early 1970s, became fully operational in 1976. The NIC has had a significant influence on the Indian digital economy and has evolved into a think tank for the government in this regard [2]. By effectively using its country-wide network, the NIC was able to 'Reach the Unreached' well before the internet was launched in India. The NIC is currently embedded in Indian geography, encompassing all states, union territories, and districts. Dr. Narasimhiah Seshagiri's vision for the establishment of the NIC was to lead the digitization movement in the right direction and at the right time. Dr. N. Seshagiri believed that harnessing the power of technology for efficient public service delivery was critical and that ICT culture should be visible in all sectors of the economy [3].

2.1. National Informatics Centre Network (NICNET)

The Indian government's use of information technology during the IX Asian Games in 1982 was an important milestone. The Asian Games Special Organizing Committee tasked the NIC with implementing the Results Information System. The instant display of games results across different stadia brought the potential of network technologies to the front and culminated with the concept of a government communication network to be set up by the NIC.

The NICNET was designed to be a pan-India computer communication network using satellite communication. Initiated in 1983, the NICNET was envisaged to support more than 50 ministries/departments in the central government, 32 states/union territory governments, and more than 500 district administrations [4]. Besides communication among different government entities, the NICNET was extensively used for the flow of data from the ground through its district nodes for further processing and analysis using mainframe computers set up by the NIC.

3. Policy and Promotion of IT

India's digital transition has opened up whole new possibilities of innovation in governance. Computer use was limited in the early 1980s to just a few organizations through mainframe computers. The setting up of the NICNET was a landmark event during this decade. The digitization of data collected through various surveys, the implementation of programs, and its processing and analysis to generate insights for decision-making were the primary objectives of the use of computers those days. Government agencies gained direct access to a computer with the advent of personal computers. Personal computers were initially used as a productivity tool by agencies across the central and state governments. During this decade, the government also announced policies to promote the production of hardware and software within the country.

3.1. Computer Policy and Software Policy

The growth of the IT industry needed the required emphasis from the leadership as well. In view of the same, the government announced the first computer policy in 1984 and software policy in 1986. These policies provided the required impetus for the manufacturing of computers, peripherals, and allied products having the latest technologies. These policies were intended to leverage the low-cost expertise available within India and avoid the expenses incurred in traveling abroad [5].

After the launch of computer policy in 1984, the production of computers went up by 100% in physical terms and by 65% in monetary terms, with a reduction in price by 50%. In view of this growth, a need was realized to formulate a comprehensive policy for the long-term sustenance of the software market as well [6]. As a result of that, a software policy was announced in November 1986, with the objectives of promoting software exports for capturing sizable share in the international software market as well as the promotion of integrated development of software in the country for domestic and export markets.

3.2. Technology for Poverty Alleviation

ICTs had made in-roads in the development in the rural sector during 1986, with the launch of CRISP by the Ministry of Rural Development (MoRD) to assist DRDAs. As part of this project, each district was provided with computers and software called CRISP for supporting development in the rural regions. The program assisted DRDAs with information processing regarding poverty alleviation schemes at the district level. The objective of this initiative was to facilitate monitoring and planning exercises of the MoRD and related departments.

3.3. Monitoring of the Universal Immunization Programme (UIP)

Launched in 1985, the UIP was a national program under the Ministry of Health, intending to immunize 85% of newborns and 100% of expectant mothers by 1990 against six diseases, that is, pertussis, neonatal tetanus, measles, tuberculosis, polio, and diphtheria. As part of this program, the mission was to achieve a reduction in mortality and morbidity; an increase in the capacity of domestic production of vaccines; the establishment of cold-chain, phased implementation across all districts; and the implementation of a monitoring and evaluation system. The extensive use of technology was made during the implementation, reporting, monitoring, and evaluation of the Immunization Programme [7].

3.4. Computerization of Land Records

It is important to ensure the availability of accurate and timely data of basic land records for effective implementation of the Land Reform Programme and its related projects. To achieve the same, the Government of India had launched the initiative on the Computerization of Land Records (CoLR). The objectives of CoLR were computerization of ownership and plot-wise details for the issue of a timely and accurate copy of the Record of Rights (ROR) to the landowners, store the records with the latest digital technology for a long time, provide fast and efficient retrieval, and provide a database for an agricultural census. The computerization of land records includes the computerization of both spatial and nonspatial data. This initiative later evolved into the Digital India Land Records Modernization Programme (DILRMP) to provision real-time landownership records available to the citizens [8].

4. Connected Government

4.1. Teletext

Teletext was one of the advanced communication technologies of that time, which provisioned the transmission of pages of information as digital signals through the television network. Introduced by Doordarshan in 1985, INTEXT (the teletext service of India) utilized blank lines in video signals for transmission of information in the form of pages of a magazine. The data was organized into pages, which consisted of text and graphic symbols. By using a decoder, the viewer could view these pages. The NIC provided software services for teletext, which helped Doordarshan in editing the teletext pages. Down the lane, Doordarshan revised the teletext services by adding stock quotations from major exchanges, Air India flight information, and railway ticket confirmation. In 1993, a telecast of about 10 pages of stock reports, updated every half hour, was also started.

4.2. Election Results

In a democratic country, a political representative governs effectively only if their electoral victory is deemed credible by citizens. So, with vote casting, vote counting should also be fair. This implies round-to-round reporting of the results of each constituency to citizens at large. To achieve this, a result information network was built in which television was a medium to show results collated using the NICNET, thus combining the information-collecting power of satellite data network with the nationwide broadcast capability of Doordarshan. The election result network success was an example of the online information capturing and dissemination capability of the NICNET. This has paved the way for the use of computer networks for nationwide online information collection during the implementation and monitoring of flagship programs of the government.

4.3. Education: Computerization of Seat Allotment

To have centralized control and impart greater knowledge regarding seat matrix and reservation policies, the entire process of counseling was shifted to reporting centers equipped with internet connectivity. Students had to report to these centers to register and lock the preferred choices in the presence of a curating official. Demand draft was the integrated mode of payment.

Due to the centralized counseling process, the counseling board could administer greater control over the counseling process and candidate management. The allocation of seats was done as per merit, reservation policies, and preferences of institutions and branches exercised by the candidates. The NIC provided the requisite infrastructure and network connectivity at reporting centers. In 1993, computerized allotment of seats was conducted for Bachelor of Medicine and Bachelor of Surgery (MBBS)/Bachelor of Dental Surgery (BDS) courses with a teletext display of seat allotment status on multiple television monitors.

4.4. Rail Ticket Reservation

The Indian Railways system is one of the largest railway networks in the world, with 13,169 passenger trains and 8,479 freight trains, plying 23 million travelers and 3 million tonnes (MT) of freight daily from 7,349 stations built across the length and breadth of the country [30]. Only a few years ago, booking a train ticket was a challenging task for Indian citizens. It usually involved long waiting times and endless queues at ticketing centers run by the railway staff with no guarantee of anything. In the late 1980s and early 1990s, Indian Railways moved to computerized reservations. In 1999, when the Indian Railway Catering and Ticket Corporation (IRCTC) was created, the idea of the online booking of tickets was a revolutionary initiative. Indians were spending hours in queues to get just a single ticket. But providing convenience was not the only concern of the government. It also wanted to introduce efficiency in customer services. When the IRCTC project was launched in 1999, the infrastructure was already in place, and interestingly, the railways had a computerized backend that was developed in the 1980s with centralized databases. The IRCTC launched online passenger reservation systems in 2002.

4.5. IT in Judiciary

The Supreme Court of India had introduced computerization way back in 1990. The List of Business Information System (LOBIS) was developed and implemented by the NIC primarily for the scheduling of cases and the generation of cause lists. The successful implementation of the LOBIS software in the Supreme Court encouraged the replication of the same software in the High Courts. By 1993, many High Courts had taken initiative to implement the LOBIS system. With the introduction of COURTNIC over NICNET, the status of the case in the Supreme Court was made available to the litigants and advocates from the NICNET node in the High Court or the nearest district headquarters [9]. In March 1995, the chief justice of India launched the Judgement Information System—a nationwide case law information system for the Supreme Court of India. In 1997, the Supreme Court of India and the NIC launched the 'The Computerization of District Courts' project. This was the first nationwide implementation in which courts from all 430 district headquarters were selected [10].

4.6. District Information System—DISNIC

In order to offer proper consideration to the micro-level demands and potentials in decision-making, the Indian Planning and Development Process was heading toward a more decentralized approach. 'DISNIC—a NICNET based district government informatics programme' for enhancing planning and development, spanning 28 areas, such as agriculture, animal husbandry, irrigation, industry, education, environment, rural development, and the like, was launched with the establishment of NICNET nodes in all 500 districts of India, which are the basic administrative spatial units at the substate level and consistent with the Government of India's decentralized planning notions. Because it is critical for planning and development, an integrated approach to database creation across several industries was established. Using NICNET facilities at 500 district nodes, the DISNIC-PLAN Programme has established a distributed database on village-level information for about 600,000 villages across the country. Project efforts have included connecting these databases to a spatial database in the form of maps to perform effective spatial analysis in a GIS environment [11].

5. National eGovernance Plan (NeGP)

The NeGP is one of the landmark initiatives taken to mainstream ICT in governance at both central and state levels in 2006. The NeGP focused on establishing the right governance and institutional framework in the country, creating the core IT infrastructure, and implement several Mission Mode Projects at the central, state, and integrated levels. The original vision of NeGP was to 'make all government services accessible to the common man in his locality through common service delivery outlets and ensure efficiency, transparency, and reliability of such services at affordable costs to realize the basic needs of the common man'. The plan originally consisted of 31 MMPs and eight components [12].

MMPs under NeGP included central as well state-level projects across various sectors, including education, health, agriculture, social empowerment, post, police, finance, taxes, banking, insurance, finance, passport, and visa, among others. It also focused on the internal automation of the functioning of the government through projects such as eOffice and eProcurement. While components of the NeGP focused on infrastructure, standards, and policies, the popularity of the web and access to web browsers among citizens encouraged government entities to establish their presence on the web for dissemination of information about programs and schemes as well as services offered by them. Efforts were made subsequently to consolidate these websites to provide one-point access to citizens for government information as services. The India Portal and state portals became quite popular in those days. The e-District project was designed to consolidate the district-level services for citizens. The e-District System, coupled with citizen delivery systems, brought a lot of convenience to citizens in rural areas for accessing government services. Figure 1.1 represents the 31 Mission Mode Projects under the NeGP ecosystem.

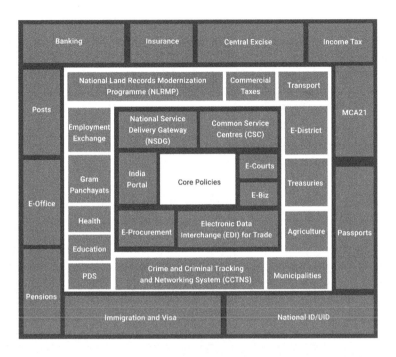

FIGURE 1.1
The NeGP Ecosystem.

5.1. Public Private Partnership (PPP)

Realizing that the government departments can partner with the other stakeholders and inculcate a spirit of partnership to handle these large, complex, and voluminous projects, the NeGP adopted the PPP route. This partnership not only helped in private investment but also made it possible for the long-term sustainability of these projects, in terms of both assured service delivery and commitment.

Project MCA-21, one of the first large-scale e-governance projects commenced in the PPP mode. It facilitated the online filing of returns and the reporting of financial results and enabled citizens to report investor grievances [13]. The Passport Seva Project (PSP), another MMP of the government, was converted to a PPP mode as part of the NeGP [14].

5.2. Common Services Centers (CSCs)

CSCs are the access points for the delivery of different e-services to the remotest corners, thus enabling a digital and financially inclusive nation. They are a single-stop solution for provisioning facilities for multiple services at a single location. More than just service delivery points, CSCs have been able to promote rural entrepreneurship and build rural capacities and livelihoods. With a key focus on the rural population, these centers have enabled community participation and social inclusion by catering to the regional, linguistic, geographic, and cultural diversity of the country [15].

5.3. NREGASoft: Web-Based System for the Rural Employment Guarantee Act

Through the National Rural Employment Guarantee Act 2005 (NREGA), the Government of India aims to secure the livelihood of rural households, by providing at least 100 days of guaranteed wage employment to an individual in each financial year. With this objective, the NIC, in consultation with the MoRD, implemented a web-enabled system, known as NREGASoft in 2006. The application ensured the planning and monitoring needs of the scheme. NREGASoft is a workflow-based system, available in both online and offline mode, for capturing various activities under NREGA at the central, state, district, block, and panchayat levels. Through NREGASoft, the government has strengthened record keeping, assisted gram panchayats in scheme implementation, and provided all documents—job cards and the like—related to worker's information in the public domain [16].

5.4. Central Public Grievance Redressal and Monitoring System (CPGRAMS)

Redressal of public grievances is a barometer to measure the effectiveness of the administrative processes and policies. The persistence of these public grievances is a worrisome situation for any government. In view of this, a web-based CPGRAMS was implemented by the NIC, under the guidance of the Department of Administrative Reforms and Public Grievances (DARPG), to facilitate speedy redressal through efficient monitoring of grievances. Operational till today, this system has evolved in terms of technology as well as its geographic coverage.

5.5. eOffice, eProcurement, eSamiksha, and PFMS

Many IT systems were built and deployed at a large scale to support the functioning of the government. Some of the notable ones that have pan-India adoption across hundreds of agencies are eOffice, eProcurement, PFMS, eVisitor, and eSamiksha. eOffice provides a digital workplace to government employees, wherein all the files can be created and processed digitally. eProcurement provided a self-service digital platform to government agencies to handle their procurement end to end digitally. eSamiksha provides summaries and action points that emerged from government meetings and their follow-ups. eVisitor is a digital solution for managing the reception of any government office.

Starting with the initial objective of providing an MIS to track funds and support decision-making, the PFMS altered the landscape of the central government's payment, receipts, and accounting functions dramatically and enabled the complete tracking of funds—up to the end beneficiary—and a reduction in funds parked with downstream implementing agencies by adopting the just-in-time transfer of funds. To facilitate the above objectives, a PAO module for capturing all releases and expenditures of Central Civil Ministries, a centralized Human Resource MIS and a NTRP were developed as key components of the PFMS.

6. Digital Infrastructure for Government

One of the important mandates of the NIC was to provide state-of-the-art digital infrastructure to the government at the central, state, and district levels. Setting up a common infrastructure shared across all entities of the government has resulted in huge savings and helped in applying common standards and security policies across the entire infrastructure. Over the years, the NIC has set up pan-India network (NICNET), videoconferencing network, data centers, messaging services, geospatial infrastructure, the NKN, cloud infrastructure, and cybersecurity teams as a shared resource for the whole of government. The infrastructure efforts of the NIC were further augmented by state governments in the form of State Data Centres and SWANs under the NeGP. Figure 1.2 represents the various components of Digital Infrastructure ecosystem in India.

6.1. National Knowledge Network (NKN)

The NKN is a cutting-edge multigigabit pan-India network connecting leading research and educational institutions of the country. The government has leveraged a strong digital infrastructure with a holistic approach. It has extended high-speed connectivity to government offices and research and academic institutions of the country.

With the availability of multigigabit network connectivity from a robust and resilient network, the NKN accelerated the digital transformation within the government's functioning from program management, files management, procurement to human resources, and financial management besides giving an impetus to videoconferencing and messaging for government communication and interaction.

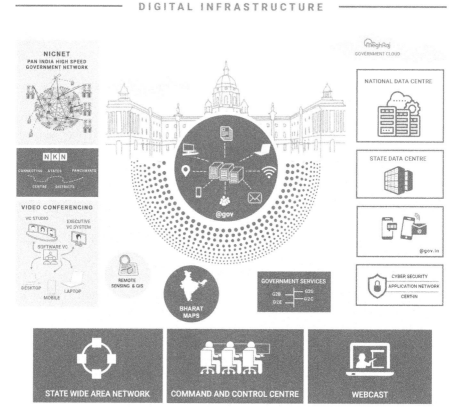

FIGURE 1.2
Digital Infrastructure.

The NKN brings together scientists, scholars, and students from various backgrounds and regions to collaborate on research in different domains. International tie-ups of the NKN have facilitated research institutions in India to collaborate with foreign research institutes as well. Within a short period, the NKN has made significant advancements by connecting more than 1,700 institutes and 50 million students, researchers, and faculty in the network. It has contributed immensely to enhancing research and collaboration in key sectors like health, agriculture, nuclear, space, and weather, among others [17] [18].

6.2. Government Data Centers

With an emphasis on e-governance, access to timely information, and the e-delivery of services, the need was felt to provide scalable services, which require setting up a scalable, reliable, and resilient infrastructure. Data centers became the foundational block to host IT systems of the central and state governments for high availability, reliability, business continuity, and multilayer security with round-the-clock monitoring and technical support. The NIC had set up its first Internet Data Centre in 2002. Over the years, the NIC has established National Data Centres in Delhi, Hyderabad, Pune, and Bhubaneswar. Later, these data centers also supported setting up multizone government cloud. These data centers provide the facility of shared hosting and co-location services. State governments augmented the data centers' capacity by setting up State Data Centres under the NeGP.

6.3. National Cloud (Meghraj)

In order to utilize and harness the benefits of cloud computing, the Government of India initiated a government cloud initiative 'Meghraj' in 2014. Before the advent of the cloud, the arrangement of a digital infrastructure was an exceedingly time-consuming process for every individual project; however, setting up a secure cloud infrastructure across government data centers has significantly reduced the time taken for provisioning of digital infrastructure. The availability of on-demand services and the scaling up of infrastructure during peak loads have also been made possible by cloud infrastructure. A cloud-based service delivery platform set up by the government has also helped in meeting several other objectives, including the optimum utilization of existing infrastructure, manageability and maintainability, rapid deployment and reusability, scalability, ease of first-time IT deployment, efficient service delivery and agility, security, cost reduction, and standardization. Over a period, several government programs and schemes, such as the SBM, MyGov, e-Hospital, National Scholarship, e-Transport, and PM-Kisan, among others, have been successfully launched due to a robust and agile cloud infrastructure. To augment cloud capacity, the government has also empaneled public cloud service providers complying with government guidelines on the cloud.

7. Digital India

The Digital India program, launched by the Hon'ble Prime Minister in July 2015, is a flagship program of the government with a vision of transforming India into a digitally empowered society and knowledge economy. The Digital India initiative is aimed at improving the lives of the common citizen. The program focuses on three key vision areas, namely, digital infrastructure as a utility to every citizen, governance and services on demand, and the digital empowerment of citizens [15]. Figure 1.3 showcases the three key vision areas and the nine pillars of the Digital India Program in India.

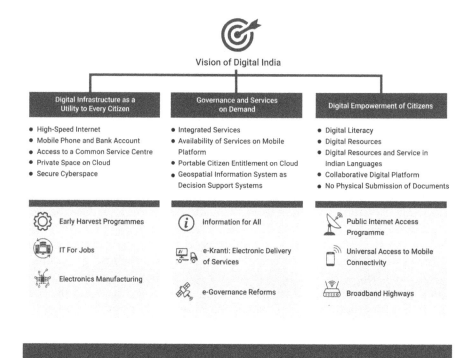

FIGURE 1.3
Vision of Digital India Program.

Since the launch of the Digital India initiative, digital has been making inroads nearly into all aspects of our lives be it education, health, banking, payments, transportation, entertainment to communication. We have witnessed the mobile and broadband revolution in the country. It has accelerated the pace of digital transformation across the public and private sectors, thus empowering citizens across rural and urban in many ways. The emergence of India Stack is another significant development leading to cashless, paperless, and faceless delivery of citizen services with Aadhaar, Mobile, and UPI being its important components.

Digital technology is bridging the gaps in social and financial inclusion with initiatives such as DBT. With digital, citizens can now apply for a license online and instantly receive updates on the status of their application. People can apply for an appointment with a doctor online or view laboratory test results on their devices. Since the launch of Digital India, students are applying for scholarships online, and pensioners are availing their pensions from the comfort of their home without having to spend time in a queue. Some of the building blocks of the digital transformation of government services are discussed next.

7.1. Mobile Governance

We have witnessed the mobile revolution in our country with 1.2 billion mobile connections and more than 700 million smartphone users spanning rural and urban India. India is going digital and mobile-centric due to the increasing population and increased usage of smartphones. This has also led to an exponential rise in mobile applications in the country providing multilingual interfaces, including languages such as English, Hindi, and many other Indian languages. Mobile has become the primary channel for the government to engage with the citizens, be it for information dissemination or the delivery of services.

There has been a lot of focus on the development of mobile applications for every digital service. Mobile applications are an integral part of any new IT system developed today. In fact, in some cases, service is delivered only through the mobile app. Mobile apps can offer a more personalized, localized, and convenient mode of access to service. A large number of mobile apps are developed by government agencies in the last few years leading to mobile governance [19].

7.2. Digital Identity (Aadhaar)

Aadhaar is a digital identity of individuals for availing various government benefits under various schemes, subsidies, and social and public welfare benefits. It is the biggest and largest publicly owned biometric technology platform to establish the digital identity of an individual anytime anywhere. Aadhaar is a verifiable 12-digit identification number issued by the UIDAI to approximately 1.22 billion residents in India from newborn to senior citizen.

Through Aadhaar, it is ensured that the benefits of schemes directly reach the actual beneficiaries without any middlemen, forgery, or duplicity. Various government services are being delivered using Aadhaar-based DBT, such as the PDS, rural employment guarantee, cooking gas subsidy, scholarships, health insurance, pensions, and the like [20] [21].

The eSign service is an innovative service to facilitate the signing of electronic documents in an easy, efficient and secure way, using Aadhaar e-KYC (electronic Know Your Customer) services. Legal sanctity to eSign is provided by Information Technology Act 2000 [22]. Many citizen services and applications are using eSign such as DigiLocker, birth certificates, marriage and income certificates, account opening in banks, vehicle registrations, and so on [15].

7.3. DigiLocker

DigiLocker is a flagship initiative of the Ministry of Electronics and IT (MeitY) under the Digital India Corporation (DIC). DigiLocker aims at the 'digital empowerment' of citizens by providing access to authentic digital documents to citizen's digital document wallets. The issued documents in the DigiLocker system are deemed to be on par with original physical documents as per Rule 9A of the Information Technology (Preservation and Retention of Information by Intermediaries providing Digital Locker Facilities) Rules, 2016 notified on 8 February 2017, vide G.S.R. 711(E). Over a period, many government services have started delivering documents (certificates, marksheets, driving licenses) through the DigiLocker.

7.4. Unified Payments Interface (UPI)

UPI is a payment system launched by the NPCI and regulated by the Reserve Bank of India, which facilitates an instant fund transfer between two bank accounts on the mobile platform. UPI is built over an Immediate Payment Service (IMPS) for transferring funds using a virtual payment address (a unique ID provided by the bank), an account number with the Indian Financial System (IFS) code, a mobile number with MMID (Mobile Money Identifier), Aadhaar Number, or a one-time use Virtual ID [23].

UPI seeks to make money transfers easy, quick, and hassle-free. The proliferation of smartphones, the availability of an online verifiable identity, universal access to banking, and the introduction of biometric sensors in phones will proactively encourage electronic payment systems for ushering in a less-cash society in India. The demonetization of November 2016 was arguably the major catalyst in digital payments in India [24].

7.5. One Nation One Platform

The availability of cloud services and high-speed networks has led to a concept of One Nation One Platform, whereby a single platform caters to the implementation of a government scheme in a digital form across the country. Schemes like the SBM, Housing for All, SHC, Fertilizer Subsidy, and PM-Kisan are built on a single platform on which the stakeholders across the central government, states, districts, and subdistrict levels interact to perform their respective roles. This has brought in a lot of efficiency, efficacy, and resource-saving in the implementation and monitoring of a program. Such systems also facilitate data analysis to generate insights.

While new programs under Digital India were designed this way, some of the old programs have also been migrated to this concept over the years. A classic example is the e-Transport Mission Mode Project under the NeGP, which has evolved into a comprehensive digital platform, facilitating all transport-related services through a single web-based system operational across the country. This has successfully transformed the service delivery mechanism of various transport-related activities (vehicle registration, driving license, enforcement, taxation, permit, fitness, etc.). This platform was further enhanced to connect to other stakeholders to offer a new set of services such as eChallan (enforcement solution), PUCC (pollution compliance system), virtual courts, and the like. The GST is another classic example of a single platform whereby multiple agencies from the government and the private sector interact to provide a variety of tax services.

8. Emerging Technologies

Technology is developing at a fast pace, and every new development opens up new opportunities. Due to the proliferation of IT systems and the resultant growth in data, recent years have unleashed the potential of data and led to the emergence of an entire industry around it, paving the way for a data-driven economy. The availability of cloud infrastructure and capability of data analytics within the government and the accelerated the use of data analysis within various IT systems of the government thus introduced the culture of data-driven governance.

The mainstreaming of AI tools and technologies can make things possible like never before. It can help us overcome barriers of language and literacy in providing access to people at the bottom of the pyramid by using AI for the social good. We have also witnessed the emergence of a vibrant start-up ecosystem in India, demonstrating innovation by leveraging emerging technologies. To help government departments leverage emerging technologies, the NIC has set up Centres of Excellence across the nation in data analytics, blockchain, AI, API management, and microservices. These centers are building various proof of concepts using emerging technologies to demonstrate innovation in the delivery of services inclusively and equitably.

8.1. Data-Driven Governance

The government has always been using all this data to have a comprehensive view while formulating policies. What has changed now is the way the data is being collected, processed, and analyzed and the technologies available to do so. The digitalization of government data was the necessary catalyst to ignite the move toward data-driven governance, which has further been strengthened by the availability of a plethora of data-related technologies and infrastructure. Data-driven governance is an approach to governance in which data are central to performance improvement and for steering and informing policy decisions. In a data-driven government, data are treated as a strategic asset, on par with financial and human resources. The availability of timely and robust data supported by technological capabilities that enable analysis and strengthen decision-making can have a transformative effect on the overall quality of governance.

8.1.1. DARPAN

DARPAN has been supporting the governance ecosystem, through an As-a-Service model, by providing a data analytics dashboard and tools to various ministries as well state governments and district administrations by ensuring real-time and dynamic project monitoring. The platform has enhanced analytical capabilities by consolidating the data from multiple data sources and provisioning a single source of truth through a centralized dashboard [25].

8.1.2. PRAGATI (Pro-Active Governance and Timely Implementation)

PRAGATI is aimed at monitoring and reviewing the critical programs and projects of the government. The platform is a unique combination of digital data management, videoconferencing, and geospatial technology. The platform connects secretaries and chief secretaries of the states with the Hon'ble Prime Minister for discussing key issues and understanding the ground-level situation. As of May 2021, 36 PRAGATI sessions have been held to review and monitor more than 350 projects [26].

8.1.3. PRAYAS

To provide a technology solution for data-driven management of the flagship programs of the government, an integrated platform titled 'PRAYAS—Pursuing Excellence in Governance' was built under the guidance of the Prime Minister's Office. PRAYAS envisions to be a platform to provide an integrated and consistent view of the performance of government programs and schemes, thereby encouraging a culture of data-driven governance. More than 100 flagship programs have been incorporated in PRAYAS for review by different stakeholders [27].

8.2. AI for the Social Good

NITI Aayog, a think tank of the government, released a document titled 'National Strategy for Artificial Intelligence' in 2018. With the overarching theme of 'AI for All', the strategy document highlights the potential of AI to solve social challenges faced by citizens in areas such as agriculture, health, and education vividly explained through use cases across different domains. The strategy document also made broad recommendations for supporting and nurturing an AI ecosystem in India under four heads, namely, promotion of research, skilling and reskilling, and facilitating the adoption of AI solutions and the formulation of guidelines for responsible AI [28].

The large-scale usage of AI for the social good requires government to overcome bottlenecks and mitigate risks especially around data accessibility and a skilled workforce. In most cases, data that could have societal implications either are owned by a private organization or are commercially available or have not been collected yet. Moreover, it is important to meet the supply–demand gaps by investing in the right talent having high-level AI expertise who can develop AI models in a shorter span. While a lot of initiatives are being taken by the government, academia and industry to build an AI ecosystem in the country, the Ministry of Electronics and IT, Government of India is working on a national program on AI to guide and support these initiatives.

9. Technology Initiatives during COVID-19

The onset of the COVID-19 pandemic and associated lockdowns have brought technology to the center of our deliberations. The pandemic has made videoconferencing an integral part of the government's functioning and has played a vital role in virtual communication from the office workplace and those working from home (WFH). The NIC has supported government officers in WFH with platforms and services like eOffice, videoconferencing, and messaging. The integration of digital payments and DBT in many government schemes has helped the direct transfer of benefits to people in need. Software systems were also developed for testing, tracing, quarantine, treatment, and hospital management to the issuance of passes for movement of essential goods and delivery of critical services.

In addition to this, several new mobile applications were developed to cater to the specific needs of COVID-19 management. Mobile applications such as the Aarogya Setu app have proved to be important instruments in our fight against COVID-19. The Aarogya Setu App [29] provides a technology solution to data-driven contact tracing and alert the citizens with their probable risk of infection. This helps prevent the spread of the coronavirus and keeps people safe. With over 185 million downloads (*numbers as on July 2021*) [29], it is also the most downloaded government application in India. In addition to the CoWIN platform, the Aarogya Setu app has also become an important channel for citizens to register and schedule for vaccination and receive their Vaccination Certificate.

10. A Way Forward and Conclusion

e-governance and citizen-centric services have given a significant boost to citizen empowerment, resulting in a significant shift in government service delivery, greater transparency, decentralized planning, improved efficiency, and accountability to the citizens of India. There are continuous efforts to make government services faceless, cashless, and paperless so that the need for citizens to visit government offices can be eliminated.

India's digital transformation story is one of citizen empowerment and inclusion focused on accessible, inclusive, and equitable technology. Technology has been an important enabler of transformational change and a disrupter in both the public and private sectors around the world. The use of emerging technologies to educate and empower citizens is being recognized as a game changer in India's narrative. Technologies, when combined with digital strategies, do play a key role in the transformation of any organization.

As emerging technologies progress and become more advanced, the emphasis is turning to creating strategies that incorporate these technologies and provide comprehensive solutions to society's long-standing issues. Moving forward, these new technologies, also known as key technology drivers, are expected to interconnect and converge while greatly enhancing interoperability, resulting in an environment capable of responding to user behavior, predicting their needs, delivering solutions, and executing them with limited human interaction.

References

[1] MGK Menon and Electronics Commission, *Perspective Report on Electronics in India*, Bombay: Department of Electronics, 1975.

[2] United Nations Development Programme, "UNDP and India: A Partnership for Sustainable Development," 2016. [Online]. Available: www.in.undp.org/content/dam/india/docs/undp-and-india-a-partnership-for-sustainable-development.pdf.

[3] National Informatics Centre, "Tribute to a Great Visionary: Dr N. Seshagiri," *Informatics: An eGovernance Publication from NIC*, July 2013. [Online]. Available: https://informatics.nic.in/uploads/pdfs/f3ebf7bc_Lead%20Story.pdf.

[4] N. Seshagiri, et al., "NICNET: A Hierarchic Distributed Computer Communication Network for Decision Support in the Indian Government," [Online]. Available: http://repository.ias.ac.in/85175/1/39-a.pdf.

[5] Biswajit Dhar and Reji K. Joseph, "India's Information Technology Industry: A Tale of Two Halves," in *ARCIALA Series on Intellectual Assets and Law in Asia*, Singapore: Springer, 2019, pp. 93–119, 7 September. [Online]. Available: https://link.springer.com/chapter/10.1007/978-981-13-8102-7_5.

[6] Software Technology Parks of India, "Emergence of Software Policy," [Online]. Available: http://bengaluru3.stpi.in/stpi-bengaluru-emergence-software-policy.

[7] Ministry of Health and Family Welfare, "Universal Immunization Program," [Online]. Available: https://main.mohfw.gov.in/sites/default/files/5628564789562315.pdf [Accessed 10 April 2021].

[8] National Informatics Centre, "Land Records Computerization Catching on," *Informatics: Quarterly Newsletter from National Informatics Centre*, vol. 1, no. 4, April 1993. [Online]. Available: https://informatics.nic.in/uploads/pdfs/fecf274c_scan-vol-1-no-4-Apr-1993.pdf.

[9] National Informatics Centre, "CourtNIC: Verdict of Computerization," *Informatics: Quarterly Newsletter from National Informatics Centre*, vol. 2, no. 2 October 1993, p. 4. [Online]. Available: https://informatics.nic.in/uploads/pdfs/d2cd8e0a_scan-vol-2-no-2-Oct-1993.pdf.

[10] National Informatics Centre, "JUDIS: For a Just Cause," *Informatics: Quarterly Newsletter from National Informatics Centre*, vol. 3, no. 4, April 1995, pp. 4–5. [Online]. Available: https://informatics.nic.in/uploads/pdfs/ebfbdb4d_scan-vol-3-no-4-Apr-1995.pdf.

[11] M. Moni, "DISNIC-PLAN: A NICNET Based Distributed Database for Micro-level Planning in India," Proceedings of 22nd Very Large Databases Conference (VLDB'96), Mumbai, India, 1996, p. 586. [Online]. Available: www.vldb.org/conf/1996/P586.PDF.

[12] Ministry of Electronics and Information Technology, "National e-Governance Plan," [Online]. Available: www.meity.gov.in/divisions/national-e-governance-plan [Accessed 10 April 2021].

[13] Murali Patibandla and Rupal Sethi, *An Analysis of Public-Private Partnerships in Infrastructure of Provision of Public Goods through E-Governance in India*, Working Paper No. 564, Bangalore: India Institute of Management, March 2018. [Online]. Available: www.iimb.ac.in/sites/default/files/2018-06/An%20Analysis%20of %20Public-Private%20Partnerships%20in%20Infrastructure%20of%20Provision %20of%20Public%20Goods%20through%20E-Governance%20in%20India%20 564.pdf.

[14] Press Information Bureau, "Passport Seva Project," [Online]. Available: https://archive.pib.gov.in/4yearsofnda/hComprehensive-Materials/MEA.pdf.

[15] Ministry of Electronics and Information Technology, "Report: India's Trillion; Dollar Digital Opportunity," 2019. [Online]. Available: www.digitalindia.gov.in/ebook/MeitY_TrillionDollarDigitalEconomy.pdf.

[16] Ministry of Rural Development, "NREGASoft: Strengthening National Rural Employment Guarantee Scheme (NREGS) implementation," [Online]. Available: https://nrega.nic.in/netnrega/iceg.pdf.

[17] V. S. Prasad, et al., "Assimilation of Satellite and Other Data for the Forecasting of Tropical Cyclones Over NIO," *MAUSAM*, vol. 72, no. 1, January 2021, pp. 107–118.

[18] National Informatics Centre, "National Knowledge Network," [Online]. Available: https://nkn.gov.in.

[19] Vaishali Kadu, Vijaya Mahesh Bagret and Abhishek Verma, "Transforming from e-Governance to M-Governance," *International Journal of Advanced Research in Computer and Communication Engineering*, vol. 4, no. 2, February 2015, pp. 1021–2278. [Online]. Available: https://ijarcce.com/wp-content/uploads/2015/03/IJARCCE-103.pdf.

[20] Unique Identification Authority of India, "My Aadhaar," [Online]. Available: https://uidai.gov.in [Accessed 10 April 2021].

[21] Ajay Bhushan Pandey, "Aadhar: The Digital Identity to New India," *Yojana*, December 2018, pp. 21–24.

[22] Ministry of Electronics & Information Technology, "Information Technology Act 2000," [Online]. Available: www.meity.gov.in/content/information-technology-act-2000.

[23] National Payment Corporation of India, "Unified Payment Interface: API and Technology Specifications," February 2015. [Online]. Available: www.mygov.in/digidhan/pages/pdf/sbi/NPCI%20Unified%20Payment%20Interface.pdf.

[24] Press Information Bureau, "Digital Transactions Registered Tremendous Growth," 9 November 2018. [Online] Available: https://pib.gov.in/PressReleseDetail.aspx?PRID=1552364.

[25] National Informatics Centre, "DARPAN: NIC Dashboard Services," [Online]. Available: https://darpan.nic.in.

[26] Richa Chauhan and Neelni Goswami, "An Initiative by Government of India 'PRAGATI': Ensuring Proactive Governance and Timely Implementation," *SSRN*, 1 July 2020. [Online]. Available at https://papers.ssrn.com/sol3/papers.cfm?abstract_id=3638932.

[27] P. K. Mittal, Anjali Dhingra and Ashutosh P. Maurya, "Prayas: Pursuing Excellence in Governance," *Informatics: An eGovernance Publication from NIC*, April 2021, pp. 23–26. [Online]. Available: https://informatics.nic.in/uploads/pdfs/c64f94ef_23_26_eps_prayas.pdf.

[28] NITI Aayog, "National Strategy for Artificial Intelligence," June 2018. [Online]. Available: http://niti.gov.in/sites/default/files/2019-01/NationalStrategy-for-AI-Discussion-Paper.pdf.

[29] Aarogya Setu App [Online]. Available: https://www.aarogyasetu.gov.in/

[30] India Brand Equity Foundation, Indian Railways Industry Report [Online]. Available: https://www.ibef.org/industry/indian-railways.aspx.

2

Digital Empowerment of Indian Agriculture

Ranjna Nagpal and Mala Mittal

1. Introduction

Agriculture is one of the oldest and most important professions in the world that is critical for human survival. The oldest evidence of agriculture being taken up as an organized profession has been found in various ancient civilizations on the Indian subcontinent. However, the agriculture sector experiences a diverse set of challenges throughout the world. Globally, the area under cultivation is shrinking due to the spread of cities and industries, the depletion of water resources, changing and unpredictable climate patterns, and falling farm incomes. Considering all the foreseen challenges, it is essential that the food production be doubled to feed the world population, which is expected to rise from the current 7 billion to 9.6 billion by 2050 [1].

1.1. Agriculture in India

Agriculture plays a vital role in India's economy. Of the total workforce in the country, 54.6 percent is engaged in agricultural and allied sector activities (Census 2011) and accounts for 16.5 percent of the country's gross value added for 2019–20 (at current prices).

India has the 10th-largest arable land resource in the world and has a wide variety of soil types. India is also the largest producer of spices, pulses, milk, tea, cashew, and jute and the second-largest producer of wheat, rice, fruits and vegetables, sugarcane, cotton, and oilseeds. Food-grain production in India is estimated to be a record 295.67 million tonnes (MT) [2] during the 2019–20 crop year and is slated to grow to 298 MT [2] during 2020–21.

Production of horticulture crops in India is also growing and has reached a record 320.5 million metric tonnes [2] in 2019–20. In allied sectors, India has the largest livestock population of approximately 535.78 million, which is about 31 percent of the world's livestock population.

Agricultural exports from India have grown over the years and now stand at US$35.09 billion in fiscal year (FY) 2020. The Agriculture Export Policy, 2018

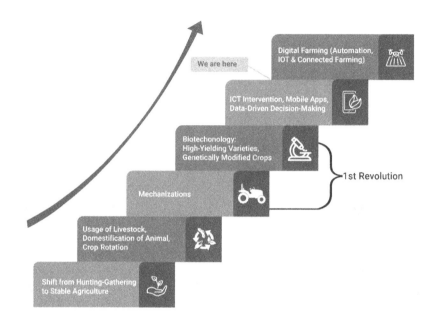

FIGURE 2.1
Evolution of Agriculture.

aims to increase India's agricultural export to INR 4,193.4 billion (US$60 billion) [2] by 2022.

The Government of India has introduced several schemes and programs to improve the growth of the agriculture sector. As per the Union Budget 2020–21, INR 2,830 billion [3] (US$40.06 billion) has been allocated to the Ministry of Agriculture and Farmers' Welfare.

1.2. Challenges in the Indian Agriculture Sector and the Need for a Technology-Based Response

India, in addition to the global challenges, also faces distinct challenges that are domestic in nature. Most of the agricultural decisions regarding sowing, choice of crops, amount of fertilizer and irrigation, and harvesting, among others, are still not based on data analytics inputs.

The mechanism of issuing farming-related advisories (weather, rainfall, pest attack, etc.) also remains in the nascent stage. The cost of cultivation, whether it be the purchase of inputs (seeds, fertilizers) or farm machinery or transportation remains high and needs to be supplemented by the government via direct and indirect incentives and subsidies.

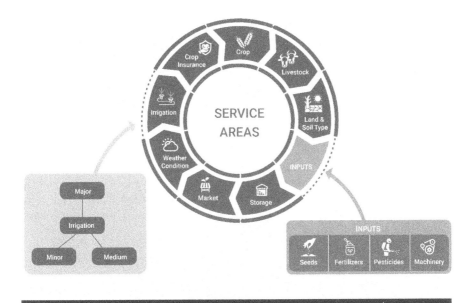

FIGURE 2.2
Stand-Alone ICT Systems.

The farm mechanization levels and the usage of modern farming techniques are low, and consequently, the productivity is lower than the global standards. Furthermore, the post-harvest facilities are inadequate and not modern, and hence, the post-harvest losses are also a cause of concern. A lack of information regarding prices and markets hinders the optimum price discovery for the agri-produce.

The Government of India had implemented relevant policies and programs at various times to improve farm productivity and incomes. Many ICT initiatives have been implemented by the government to address these challenges and to further support the rollout and adoption of agricultural policies and programs. ICT initiatives started with stand-alone systems implemented in earlier days in selected agriculture sectors as shown in Figure 2.2 and have moved to advanced web-based pan-India systems, and now the focus is moving to advanced technologies like AI, IoT, and others in addition to the conventional ICT solutions.

2. Global Scenario and Trends

The UN Food and Agriculture Organization predicts that the agriculture industry will need to produce 70 percent [4] more food than the current

availability. This implies that there will be a requirement of approximately 1 billion tonnes more wheat, rice, and other cereals and 200 million more tons of livestock per year, on almost the same agricultural surface area. This increased demand along with the growing environmental and regulatory pressures presents a daunting challenge for the global farming industry. Since a majority of the land suitable for agriculture is already farmed, this growth must come from higher yields.

Digital agriculture can provide the solutions to the problem of feeding the world sustainably. Digital farming technologies originated in the 1980s, with the rise of precision agriculture technology, and have since grown to be applied across millions of acres across the globe. As mentioned in Figure 2.3 various digital technologies are being applied in different agriculture sectors for increase in productivity and benefit to farmers and common citizen.

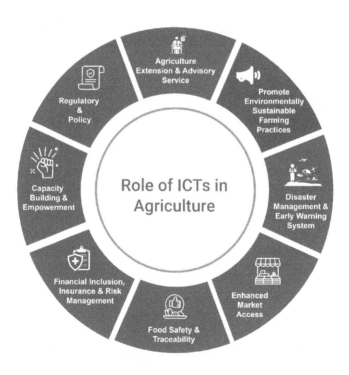

FIGURE 2.3
Role of ICTs in Agriculture.

2.1. North America [5]

In the 1990s, the adoption of precision agriculture practices grew rapidly, particularly in Canada and the United States, with the use of satellite imaging, GPS-enabled 'auto-steer tractors', and early versions of yield monitor technologies. The accelerated adoption of precision agriculture in North America is attributed to a combination of factors including increasing size of crop farms, appetite for entrepreneurship and innovation in agri-food, the accessibility of loans and financing options for farmers, and the relative economic stability of large industrial farming operations. The uptake and evolution of digital farming stalled in the early 2000s, but in the past decade, adoption increased, alongside advances in robotics, the decreasing costs of sensor technology, and computing capabilities for collecting and analyzing massive volumes of data.

2.2. Australia

Australia is a land of climatic extremes that have brought numerous challenges to farming. These have led to inventions and methods of production that have often put Australia at the forefront of world agricultural development. The gains in production made by Australian farmers over the decades have been impressive. An increase in productivity has occurred due to a combination of factors, including innovative farming techniques, scientific developments in areas such as plant and animal breeding, and improvements in the management of crops, livestock, land, water, and pests. These innovations are further supported by the increased availability and use of sophisticated machinery and information technology that allow farmers to work smarter. An increasing number of farmers, for example, are using the internet and IT to monitor international market trends, communicate and interact with suppliers throughout the agriculture supply chain, access weather forecasts, and use satellite imagery in developing farm plans [6]. In line with other developed countries, Australia is pushing for digital agriculture by providing AUS$7 million [7] Digital Farm Grants for last-mile solutions for agriculture.

3. Journey of ICT Initiatives in Agriculture in India

The Ministry of Agriculture & Farmers' Welfare is the coordinating agency of the central government for all agriculture-related matters specially issues concerning agriculture, horticulture, animal husbandry, dairying, fisheries, training and skill development, research and career development in the agriculture sector, and farmers' welfare. The ministry is constituted of three departments, that is, the Department of Agriculture, Cooperation & Farmers Welfare (DAC&FW); the Department of Agricultural Research and Education (DARE); and the Department of Animal Husbandry and Dairying.

In 2019, the Ministry of Fisheries, Animal Husbandry, and Dairying was formed, which consists of the Department of Animal Husbandry and Dairying and the Department of Fisheries. Other related ministries of the agriculture sector are the Ministry of Water Resources for large-scale irrigation management and the Ministry of Chemicals and Fertilizers.

To meet the vast requirements of agriculture development for different crops, varied agro-climatic regions, implement regulations, research and education, and participatory growth, there are multiple agencies associated with the Ministry of Agriculture and Farmers Welfare.

A road map for mainstreaming ICT in the agriculture sector started with the concept of Digital Network for Farmers, which was brought in as the recommendation of the National Conference on 'Informatics for Sustainable Agriculture Development' (ISDA-1995) organized by the NIC. It proposed AGRISNET—an infrastructure network up to block-level agricultural offices facilitating agricultural extension services, AGMARKNET—to network Agricultural produce wholesale markets, and rural markets, ARISNET—Agricultural Research Information System Network, SEEDNET—Seed Informatics Network, HORTNET—Horticultural Informatics Network, PPIN—Plant Protection Informatics Network, FERTNET—Fertilizers Informatics Network, and VISTARNET—Agricultural Extension Information System Network, among others.

After small-scale automation in few domains, the real ICT journey in the agriculture sector started in 2001 with a project called DACNET. DACNET's key criteria included ease of use, increased speed of information delivery, low incidence of errors, reduction in malpractices, and affordable services for all. The project emphasized a systematic approach to the creation, usage, and capacity building in IT in the agriculture sector. It involved networking of directorates, regional directorates, and field units for internet and intranet access with the central DACNET resources; establishing a local-area network throughout Department of Agriculture field locations; and empowering employees through specialized system training programs.

Various web-based applications at the directorate, regional directorate, and field units such as Plant Quarantine Information System, Crop Weather Watch, Market Prices Analysis, Computerized Registration of Pesticides, and Farm Machinery Informatics Online were developed under DACNET. The DACNET project promoted ICT culture in the directorates.

To increase the reforms in the agriculture sector concerning farmers' welfare, the DAC&FW launched the NeGP in Agriculture (NeGPA) in FY 2010–11 in seven pilot states [8]. This scheme was subsequently extended into a second phase to cover all the states and two union territories from FY 2014–15 with the aim of (1) bringing farmer centricity and service orientation to the programs, (2) enhancing the reach and impact of extension services, (3) improving the access for farmers to information and services throughout the crop cycle, (4) building on enhancing and integrating the existing ICT initiatives of the center and states, (5) enhancing the efficiency and effectiveness of programs through process redesign, more effective management of schemes of DAC, and promoting a common framework across states. The following service clusters were identified under NeGPA:

Service Clusters
Information on pesticides, fertilizers, and seeds
Providing information on soil health
Information on crop, farm machinery, training, and Good Agricultural Practices (GAPs)
Information on forecasted weather and agro-met advisory
Information on price, arrivals, procurement point, and providing interaction platform
Electronic certification for exports and imports
Information on marketing infrastructure
Monitoring implementation/evaluation of schemes and programs
Information on fisheries
Information on irrigation infrastructure
Drought relief and management
Livestock management

As a part of the NeGPA initiative, the DAC&FW developed the One Stop Window-Farmers Portal [9] for the dissemination of information on the various agricultural-related matter including seeds variety, storage godowns, pests and plant diseases, GAPs, a package of practices, watershed, Mandi details, and the like.

The department also developed and implemented the SMS/mKisan Portal [10] for sending advisories on various crop-related matters to the registered farmers through SMSs. Mobile telephony has also transformed the tenor of farmer's life. In mKisan portal more than 50 million [10] farmers are registered for receiving crop advisories through a short message service (SMS).

Various mobile applications have also been developed to facilitate the dissemination of information to farmers on the critical parameters, namely, the weather, market prices, plant protection, agro-advisories, extreme weather alerts, input dealers (of seed, pesticide, fertilizer, farm machinery), SHC, cold storage and godowns, soil testing laboratories, veterinary centers and diagnostic labs, crop insurance premium calculators, and the government schemes.

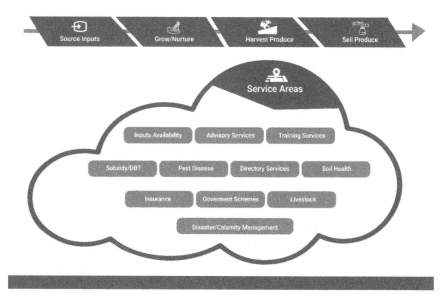

FIGURE 2.4
Service Areas in the Agriculture Value Chain.

The agriculture value chain mentioned in Figure 2.4 consists of preproduction input supply, production, postproduction, industrial processing, distribution, and marketing involving various stakeholders. A farmer needs various inputs while performing the activities of sowing, growing/nurturing, harvesting, and selling his produce, and thus, various IT applications have been built around these services areas.

3.1. Soil and Crop Disease Management

Advisories are essential for farmers to enable them to make data-driven decisions rather than acting on intuitions. With the changing weather and climate patterns, availability of new varieties of farm inputs (seeds, fertilizers, pesticides), changing consumer demands, and market dynamics, the dependency on traditional wisdom is not always bearing fruit. IT intervention is essential for delivering on-time, localized, and relevant advisories to the correct set of recipients.

Few notable IT initiatives in respect of soil and crop disease advisories are discussed in the following.

3.1.1. SHC: Empowering Farmers to Improve Soil Health for Enhancing Agriculture Productivity

Soil is one of the most important components determining plant growth and the quantity/quality of agricultural produce. To increase soil fertility and productivity, it is important to assess the nutrient status of soil and ensure an appropriate dosage of fertilizers and micronutrients. The SHC Portal is an IT platform that empowers farmers to improve soil health for enhancing agricultural productivity. It provides the soil nutrient status of a farmer's holding and advises him on the correct dosage of fertilizers. It contains the status of soil concerning 12 parameters: N, P, K (macro-nutrients); S (secondary nutrients); Zn, Fe, Cu, Mn, Br (micro-nutrients); and pH, EC, and OC (physical parameters) [11] [18]. Currently, SHCs can be generated in 22 languages in India.

Under the SHC program, the soil sample collection and testing are planned once every two years, whereby one soil sample is collected for 2.5 hectares of land in irrigated and 10 hectares [12] in rainfed conditions, thus covering multiple farmers' lands in each soil sample.

Two cycles of soil testing and issuance of the SHC have been undertaken. During cycle I, from 2015 to 2017, 25.3 million samples were tested and 107.3 million SHCs were issued. During cycle II, from 2017 to 2019, 27.7 million samples were tested and 117.5 million SHCs were issued, indicating the volume of transactions being handled in the portal [13]. The server and network infrastructure have been set up to meet this ever-increasing demand.

The Soil Health Card (SHC) Portal uses dynamic dashboards and GIS technology to display soil maps. The software uses complex scientific algorithms to provide fertilizer recommendations for different crops being grown in different soil types under irrigated or rainfed conditions.

3.1.2. Crop Doctor: Crop Disease and Health Advisory

Crop Doctor is a mobile app to which farmers can send queries along with the image about a particular concern and can receive information about nutrient deficiency, disease, insects affecting the crop, and so on. It covers almost all major crops such as paddy, vegetables, pulses, and oilseeds and has been successfully implemented in Chhattisgarh.

3.1.3. CROPSAP: Crop Pest Surveillance and Advisory

The efficient eradication and management of pest diseases are crucial factors for ensuring sufficient crop production. If pests and disease problems are not managed in time, it may result in economic losses to the farmer.

To avoid crop losses due to pest and disease recurrence, the Government of Maharashtra implemented CROPSAP in 2010–11. It was the first time in the country when ICT was widely used for plant protection. Pest scouts and pest monitors collect and feed pest data through their mobile. The data are processed and scientifically interpreted for identifying an epidemic area of a particular pest. Real-time detailed and short advisories are issued by the experts at the State Agricultural University (SAU) and sent through SMSs to

5 million registered farmers, displayed at gram panchayats, and published in local newspapers and other print and electronic media.

Apart from this, the correlation of weather parameters vis-à-vis pest population dynamics is carried out and superimposed on GIS maps to develop pest forecasting modules.

3.2. Farm Inputs (Seeds, Fertilizers, Pesticides)

The availability of farm inputs at the right time and the right price is vital to the quality and quantity of the harvest. From the government's perspective, monitoring such inputs and ensuring timely availability at the correct price are essential yet very complex tasks, which are difficult to carry out without an efficient IT system running in the backend.

Fertilizer subsidies in India are the second-largest government transfer, with a yearly outlay of more than INR 700 billion [14]. The DBT Policy in the fertilizer sector is a pathbreaking initiative of the Government of India to support the target beneficiary, that is, the farmer, with a timely and adequate supply of fertilizers at subsidized prices. The scheme focuses on tracking the movement of fertilizers through the supply chain and the final sale of fertilizers to the farmers.

3.2.1. e-Urvarak—Integrated Fertilizer Management System for Ensuring Adequate and On-Time Delivery of Fertilizers to the Farmers

e-Urvarak is a technology solution for the scheme 'DBT in Fertilizers' for managing fertilizer subsidy disbursement by the government and covers all functionalities in the entire fertilizer supply chain for capturing transactional data starting from the procurement of raw material, the production of fertilizers, imports at different ports, the movement from plant and ports by rail or road to district warehouses in accordance to the monthly supply plan, and sales from district to wholesalers and from wholesalers to retailers. A broader view of e-Urvarak integrated technology solution is shown in Figure 2.5. The POS-based application enabled with Aadhaar-based biometric and contactless OTP-based authentication is used to capture fertilizer sales from retailers to farmers. Home delivery of fertilizers to the farmers has been implemented as a pilot project in Andhra Pradesh where farmers after biometric authentication can place their orders through RBK (Rythu Bharosa Kendra) located in their villages and the fertilizers are then delivered at their doorstep. The system is used for the generation and paperless processing of subsidy claims of about INR 740 billion for 2019–20 (later revised to INR 799.96 billion) [15] for their payment to fertilizer companies through the PFMS.

The system has helped in making the fertilizer supply chain more efficient, minimizing leakages and diversions, and ensuring adequate and timely availability of fertilizers to the target beneficiary, that is, the farmer at subsidized prices. The system tracks the real-time availability of fertilizer stocks at the

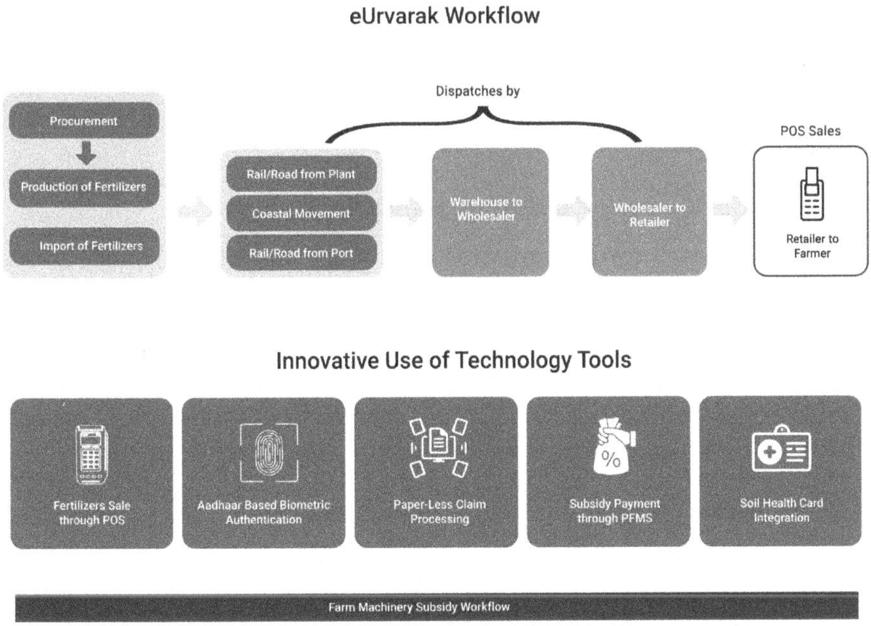

eUrvarak Workflow

FIGURE 2.5
e-Urvarak—Integrated Fertilizer Management System.

plants, ports, warehouses, rake points, wholesalers, and retailers. Moreover, the DBT subsidy payment system is completely paperless. As a result of these efficiencies in DBT, the government was successful in saving an estimated amount of INR 100 billion on fertilizer subsidies during 2018–19 [16].

As a part of the system, a dynamic dashboard is available [15]. This graphical user interface provides an updated view of the key performance indicators. It serves as a monitoring and analytical tool for central and state governments to assess the overall demand and supply position, plan fertilizer movement in advance, and address any shortages on time.

3.2.2. Automation System for Seed Certification, Traceability, and Seed Supply Chain—Ensuring Quality Seeds to Farmers

The seed supply chain is a complex ecosystem involving various stakeholders with several challenges in validating important criteria such as the origin of the seed, stages in production, conformance to quality standards such as genetic purity, germination rate, and the like. Spurious and low-quality seeds enter the seed supply chain at various stages. Therefore, it is required to assure that good quality seeds reach the farmers. Furthermore, the seed traceability is important to track the seed to its origin to ascertain its pedigree and quality.

Online seed certification systems have been implemented by Odisha, Uttarakhand, Uttar Pradesh, and Telangana. To realize the true potential of this IT-enabled system, a seed certification and traceability system is now being considered for pan-India usage, incorporating the best practices and advanced technologies like blockchain, among others.

3.3. Farming (Growing, Nurturing, Harvesting)

Farming involves growing and nurturing crops and plants using various irrigation facilities and machinery. The Pradhan Mantri Krishi Sinchayee Yojana (PMKSY) has been formulated by the government with the vision of extending the coverage of irrigation 'Har Khet Ko Pani' and improving water use efficiency 'Per Drop More Crop' in a focused manner with an end-to-end solution for source creation, distribution, management, field application, and extension activities. PMKSY has the following program components:

1. **Accelerated Irrigation Benefit Programme**—To focus on faster completion of ongoing major and medium irrigation including National Projects

2. **Har Khet Ko Pani**—The creation of new water sources through minor irrigation (both surface and groundwater), repair, restoration, renovation of water bodies, construction, and rainwater harvesting

3. **Per Drop More Crop**—To promote efficient water conveyance and precision water application devices like drips, sprinklers, pivots, rain-guns in the farm (Jal Sinchan)

4. **Watershed (Command Area) Development**—The effective management of runoff water and improved soil and moisture conservation activities such as ridge area treatment, drainage line treatment, rainwater harvesting, in situ moisture conservation, and other allied activities on a watershed basis

A web-based application to facilitate project-wise data entry, the generation of various reports, and the monitoring of the status of completion of various components of these projects have been implemented. A dashboard has also been developed with visualization and presentation for the various components of all these projects.

3.3.1. Farm Mechanization

Farm mechanization plays a critical role in increasing agricultural productivity and is one of the important elements of modernization of the agriculture sector. The government is helping farmers by providing subsidies to procure machinery to improve farming efficiency and farm power availability. There are about 22,000 Custom Hiring Centers (CHCs)/farm machinery banks and high-tech hubs established in villages under various schemes of DAC&FW to provide agricultural machinery on a rental basis to small and marginal farmers who cannot afford to buy high-value machinery and equipment.

To ensure the quality of agricultural implements and tools, performance testing is being done for various types of farm machinery and equipment at the four Farm Machinery Training and Testing Institutes (FMTTIs), designated SAUs, and Indian Council of Agricultural Research (ICAR) institutions. The subsidy provided for the purchase of farm equipment is available only for such equipment that meets the prescribed quality standards. To ensure this, manufacturers need to get their farm equipment tested before their sale.

To facilitate the previously mentioned schemes, a digital platform [17] has been built. The platform proposes to seamlessly integrate all the services being offered by the government to various stakeholders and provide a single window for the same.

The following digital solutions are being offered on this platform.

3.3.2. Agri-Machinery DBT Portal

As shown in Figure 2.6, Agri-Machinery DBT Portal facilitates the automation of farm machinery subsidy workflow and implementation of DBT. This portal was implemented to provide an end-to-end online workflow for all stakeholders so that the scheme can be operationalized simply and effectively.

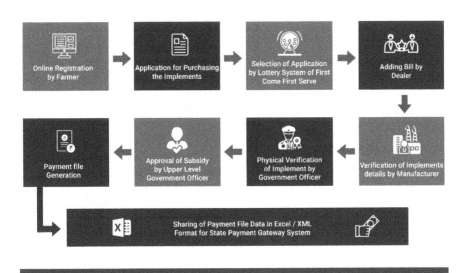

FIGURE 2.6
Farm Machinery Subsidy Workflow.

3.3.3. Centralized Farm Machinery Performance Testing Portal

This portal is used for monitoring the testing of farm machinery by FMTTIs involving manufacturer registration, online submission of application and fees, sampling of equipment, testing, and uploading of test reports.

FARMS is a mobile app connecting farmers with CHCs, which has been developed to benefit small and marginal farmers by the timely availability of farm implements on competitive hiring rates from CHCs. It also allows the sale and purchase of used farm equipment.

3.4. Post-Production Logistics (Transport, Marketing, Export/Import)

A major challenge in Indian agriculture has been the postproduction losses due to inadequate postproduction logistics availability. Even when the facilities are available, a lack of awareness leads to underutilization. Several IT initiatives have been undertaken in this regard to ensure availability and promote the usage of these facilities.

3.4.1. AGMARKNET

Agricultural Marketing Information Network (AGMARKNET) links about 7,000 agricultural wholesale markets in India with the state agricultural marketing boards and directorates for effective information exchange. It provides price and commodity arrival information from the APMC's mandis to users and reduces the information asymmetry in agricultural prices.

3.4.2. e-NAM (National Agriculture Marketplace)

eNAM is an electronic trading portal that networks the APMC mandis to create a unified national market for the online sale of commodities. The solution is currently implemented across 800-plus regulated markets for 100-plus commodities.

3.4.3. Kisan Rath Mobile App

Kisan Rath Mobile App as mentioned in Figure 2.7 for hiring and a transport facilitates farmers/Farmer Producer Organizations (FPOs) and traders to hire transporters for agri-produce. It ensures smooth supply linkages among the farmers, warehouses, FPOs, APMC mandis, and intra-state and inter-state buyers and helps in the reduction of food wastage by ensuring timely transport.

The Fruits and Vegetable Module of Kisan Rath enables the sale and purchase of horticulture produce by directly connecting farmers and FPOs with the traders.

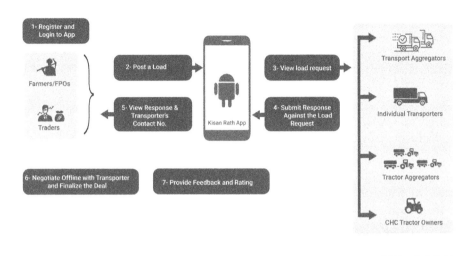

FIGURE 2.7
Navigation and Flow for Hiring a Transport Vehicle in Kisan Rath.

3.4.4. FARMAP

FARMAP is an IT platform that captures data of the cost of cultivation from farmers of 20 states and generates state-level cost estimates to be provided to Commission for Agricultural Costs & Prices (CACP) for the fixation of MSPs of principal crops. It uses complex algorithms for generating estimates.

3.4.5. PQIS (Plant Quarantine Information System): Enabling Safe Global Trade in Plant and Plant Material

PQIS is a workflow-based system to bring efficiency and effectiveness in the functioning of plant quarantine (PQ) stations. It helps in the speedy processing of applications for Import Permits, Import Release Orders, and PSCs. It provides online registration of importers and exporters and facilitates online application submission and processing.

It also ensures the availability of country-specific and plant material-specific searchable information on import and export procedures to PQ officers, thereby ensuring easy monitoring at all levels. The PQIS system is operational across 87 locations in the country and is being used by 45 PQ stations and 145 PSC-issuing authorities.

3.5. Financial Support Systems

The government is working toward relieving the financial distress of the Indian farmers by providing financial support in the form of crop insurance and supplementing farm incomes with direct income support. This involves beneficiary registration, determination of eligibility, processing of claims, stakeholder coordination, and crediting of money to the end beneficiary which is not possible without a robust IT system.

3.5.1 PM-KISAN: Supplementing Financial Needs of Farmers by Direct Income Support

The PM-KISAN scheme was launched in February 2019, to augment the income of small and marginal farmers by direct payment of INR 2,000 for every four months into the bank accounts of eligible farmers.

To operationalize a scheme of this magnitude, a technology-enabled PM-KISAN portal was developed. This system integrates with various state systems, supports bulk upload and processing of records, validates them by integrating with Aadhaar and PFMS, and thereafter transfers the benefit via DBT into farmers' bank accounts. The data upload and processing functionality was designed in such a way that no development or customization effort was required at the states' end, thereby enabling faster enrolment in the scheme.

The portal provides an end-to-end mechanism for capturing the details of beneficiaries under the scheme and transfers the benefits directly to their accounts after various levels of validation. It also provides tools for monitoring at various levels in the form of drill-down reports and analytical dashboards. The portal has linkage to the PFMS for transfer of scheme benefits.

To further increase the beneficiary coverage, the portal provides facilities to farmers for self-registration, name correction as per Aadhaar, and checking the beneficiary status. Also, it provides access to CSCs across the country for farmer registration, correction of records, and status verification.

To broaden the reach further, a **PM-KISAN Mobile App** was developed which enables farmers to view the status of their application, update or carry out corrections in their Aadhaar cards and check the history of credits to their bank accounts. A 24x7 IVRS-based helpline for status verification is also available.

As of January 2021, PM-KISAN has benefited more than 107.5 million farmers. Since its inception, the PM-KISAN ICT system has enabled the disbursement of direct cash benefits of approximately INR 1,128.27 billion directly to the verified beneficiaries.

3.5.2 Pradhan Mantri Fasal Bima Yojana Comprehensive Crop Insurance

PMFBY aims to provide a comprehensive insurance cover against failure of the crop thus helping in stabilizing the income of the farmers. The scheme covers all food and oilseeds crops and annual commercial/horticultural crops for which past yield data are available and for which requisite number of Crop Cutting Experiments (CCEs) are being conducted under the General Crop Estimation Survey (GCES). The scheme is implemented by empaneled general insurance companies. Selection of the implementing agency is done by the concerned state government through a bidding process. The scheme is being administered by the Ministry of Agriculture & Farmers' Welfare and is compulsory for loanee farmers availing Crop Loan/Kisan Credit Card (KCC) account for notified crops and voluntary for others.

An IT portal is developed to enable farmers' registration, calculation of insurance premiums, reporting crop losses, tracking the status of an application, and raising grievances, if required. It also aims to promote awareness and provides an interactive dashboard for efficient monitoring of the scheme.

3.5.3 *Rythu Bandhu Scheme—Farmers' Investment Support Scheme*

It is a welfare program to support farmer's investment for two crops a year by the Government of Telangana. The government is supporting the farmers by providing an assistance of INR 5,000 to every farmer, per acre per season, to support the farm investment, twice a year, for the Rabi and Kharif seasons. This is the first direct farmer investment support scheme in India in which the cash is paid directly to the farmers. An IT system with a dashboard has been developed to monitor the scheme.

Apart from the above, other IT initiatives for DBT include **AC&ABC** (Agri Clinics and Agri-Business Centres scheme for setting up agri-ventures), **ATMA** (Agricultural Technology Management Agency for providing training to farmers through extension workers), and **HORTNET** (a workflow system for disbursement of subsidy for horticulture crops).

3.6. Animal Husbandry/Livestock Management

Livestock rearing is one of the most important economic activities in the rural areas of the country contributing significantly to the national economy. The government has initiated various schemes to bring further improvement to increase the availability of genetically improved livestock, poultry, control of diseases, and so on.

The Livestock Census has been conducted quinquennially throughout the country. So far, 19 Livestock Censuses have been conducted. The 20th Livestock Census was successfully conducted throughout the country using tablet computers and facilitated breed-wise data entry of various schedules. Two hundred sixty million records on livestock have been collected by enumerators at the village level. A web-based application is developed for the supervisor, scrutiny officer, and state administrator to scrutinize the data entered by the enumerator at the subdistrict, district, and state levels, respectively. Online and offline mechanisms are developed to capture the data in a tablet.

3.7. Umbrella App for Farmers—Kisan Suvidha

Kisan Suvidha is a smart app for farmers that aims to bring all the agricultural schemes and services under one umbrella for access by the farmers via a single interface, obliterating the need for multiple apps and web portals. As of March 2021, farmer-centric services of various focus areas such as PM-Kisan, fertilizers, Kisan Rath, crop insurance, agri-marketing and procurement, soil fertility, organic farming, seeds, farm machinery, horticulture, PM-KMY, training and extension services, government schemes, directory services, advisory services, animal husbandry, and so on have been integrated with Kisan Suvidha. The app can be accessed from a mobile, desktop, laptop, or tablet.

4. Agriculture and Use of Emerging Technologies

Agriculture in India can take advantage of emerging technologies like IoT, AI, data analytics, blockchain, remote sensing, and GIS, which can contribute to the growth of the sector. AI systems can be used for the identification and control of pests. Information on symptoms and pictures of pests and diseases can be fed into the system. Based on the picture posted of the insect and the disease, the system can match and identify the disease and suggest remedial actions. AI can also be used for identifying patterns and factors affecting market dynamics and making predictions about prices, sending alerts in case of scarcity or paucity of a particular commodity or a sudden increase or fall in the prices. Similarly, the IoT can send signals and triggers about the precise input requirement for precision farming. It can be used for water management as well. Blockchain technology can be used for tracing agricultural inputs such as seeds, fertilizers, and organic products. The application of data analytics has already demonstrated significant value and can be used to analyze market trends, usage of fertilizers, distribution of inputs and availability, and the like.

Furthermore, remote sensing and GIS are very crucial technologies, having a wide range of applications to tackle issues related to soil, climate, and topography. These technologies have manifold applications in agriculture including crop differentiation, crop growth monitoring, stress detection, crop inventory, soil moisture estimation, precision agriculture, crop acreage estimation, and yield prediction.

5. Digital Agriculture Platform—A Way Forward and Conclusion

The farmer is at the core of any agricultural activity. All the agricultural services and schemes are aimed to ensure benefits to multiple stakeholders with farmers being the topmost priority. Numerous efforts are being done in the country by the government, international agencies, nongovernmental organizations, the private sector, and start-ups. Currently, there are disparate systems, each delivering unique functionality to address a particular need. Better services can be delivered to the farmer by collaborating and integrating with other systems. Besides, policy planning and strategy formulation for a region is interlinked with the demographic/climatic parameters of the region. Accordingly, the latest technological developments are moving toward building up a digital agriculture platform. A conceptual diagram is given in Figure 2.8 for incorporating latest technologies and building up a digital agriculture ecosystem for all stakeholders.

This platform is envisaged to be an ecosystem of stakeholders of the government and private players focused on the farmer and other beneficiaries. It proposes to enable seamless interoperability of various ICT domains of agriculture using common standards and allowing data exchange between them. It is also envisaged to provide role-based comprehensive delivery of information/services to all beneficiaries and stakeholders through a common identity or a single window. The platform endeavors to promote active collaboration among all the stakeholders of the ecosystem for better planning and policy formulation specific to each region.

The creation of the platform requires the identification of a farmer. A nationwide, database of verified farmers is currently being developed which shall keep a unique record of farmers of India. The Farmer Database shall provide a unique farmer ID to identify a farmer in various schemes related to the agriculture sector ensuring their smooth implementation.

The Government of India has introduced several initiatives to assist the various domains of the agriculture sector including soil health, seeds, markets, horticulture, and fertilizers, among others. The government has also come up with different expert systems that will help in determining marketing alternatives and optimal strategies for farmers. The sustainable benefits of these initiatives, coupled with the innovative use of emerging technologies, will help in achieving the vision of doubling farmers' income in the future.

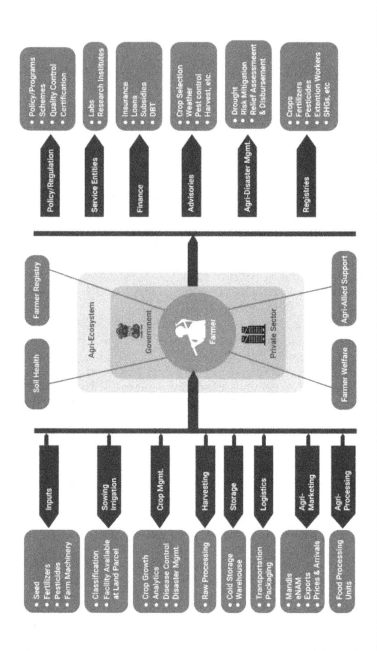

FIGURE 2.8
Approach for IT Initiatives in Agriculture.

References

[1] Food and Agriculture Organisation, "The Future of Food and Agriculture-Trends and Challenges," 2017. [Online]. Available: www.fao.org/3/a-i6583e.pdf [Accessed 14 November 2020].

[2] India Brand Equity Foundation, "Agriculture in India: Information About Indian Agriculture & Its Importance," November 2020. [Online]. Available: www.ibef.org/industry/agriculture-india.aspx [Accessed 14 November 2020].

[3] "Budget 2021: Next Green Revolution," *Business Today*, 2021. [Online]. Available: www.businesstoday.in/budget/agriculture/ [Accessed 10 March 2021].

[4] The Guardian, "UN: Farmers Must Produce 70% More Food by 2050 to Feed Population," 2011. [Online]. Available: www.theguardian.com/environment/2011/nov/28/un-farmers-produce-food-population [Accessed 14 November 2020].

[5] Sarah- Louise Ruder, "A Digital Agricultural Revolution: Ontario Grain Farmer Perceptions of Digital Farming and Big Data," University of Waterloo, Canada, 2019. [Online]. Available: https://uwspace.uwaterloo.ca/handle/10012/14878 [Accessed 10 March 2021].

[6] Australian Government Productivity Commission, "Trends in Australian Agriculture: Productivity Commission Research Report,' 2005. [Online]. Available: www.pc.gov.au/research/completed/agriculture/agriculture.pdf [Accessed 10 March 2021].

[7] Govt of Western Australia, "Media Statements," 2020. [Online]. Available: www.mediastatements.wa.gov.au/Pages/McGowan/2020/10/Round-Three-of-Digital-Farm-grants-to-boost-connectivity.aspx [Accessed 14 November 2020].

[8] Press Information Bureau, "Nationale-Governance Plan in Agriculture (NeGPA): Towards the Mission of Digital Agriculture," 2021. [Online]. Available: https://pib.gov.in/PressReleseDetailm.aspx?PRID=1697526 [Accessed 24 February 2021].

[9] Department of Agriculture Cooperation and Farmers Welfare, "Farmer's Portal: One Stop Shop for Farmers," [Online]. Available: www.farmer.gov.in/.

[10] Department of Agriculture Cooperation and Farmers Welfare, "mkisan—A portal of Government of India for Farmer Centric Mobile Based Services," [Online]. Available: http://mkisan.gov.in [Accessed 14 November 2020].

[11] National Portal of India, "Soil Health Card," [Online]. Available: www.india.gov.in/spotlight/soil-health-card#tab=tab-1 [Accessed 24 February 2021].

[12] Department of Agriculture Cooperation and Farmers Welfare, "Operational Guidelines for implementation of Centrally Sponsored Scheme Soil Health Card," 11 February 2015. [Online]. Available: https://agricoop.nic.in/sites/default/files/GSHC3.pdf [Accessed 14 November 2020].

[13] Department of Fertilizers, "Annual Report 2019–20".

[14] Vartika Singh and Patrick S. Ward, "Challenges in Implementing India's Aadhaar-Enabled Fertilizer Management System," Cereal Systems Initiative for South Asia (CSISA) Note 11, International Food Policy Research Institute (IFPRI), April 2018. [Online]. Available: https://csisa.org/wp-content/uploads/sites/2/2018/04/Fertilizer-DBT-Research-Note-12-April-18_FINAL.pdf.

[15] Department of Fertilizers, "iFMS Dashboard," [Online]. Available: https://urvarak.nic.in.

[16] Government of India, "Direct Benefit Transfer," [Online]. Available: https://dbtbharat.gov.in/estimatedgain.

[17] Department of Agriculture Cooperation and Farmers Welfare, "Digital Platform for Farm Mechanization and Technology," [Online]. Available: https://agrimachinery.nic.in/.

[18] Department of Agriculture Cooperation and Farmers Welfare, "Soil Health Card," [Online]. Available: https://soilhealth.dac.gov.in/.

3

Healthcare for All through Policies, Platforms, and Innovations

Sunil Kumar, Naveen Kumar, Piyush Gupta,
Tarun Goel, and Suparna Bhatnagar

1. Introduction

Healthcare has become one of the largest growing sectors in the country, in terms of both revenue and employment. Healthcare comprises hospitals, medical devices, clinical trials, outsourcing, telemedicine, medical tourism, health insurance, and medical equipment to name a few. The healthcare sector in India is growing at a brisk pace due to its strengthening coverage and services and increasing expenditure by public, as well as private, players.

Indian healthcare delivery system is categorized into two major components—public and private. A three-tier structure encompassing the primary, secondary and tertiary healthcare facilities has been established to bring healthcare services within the reach of the individuals. The primary tier includes three types of healthcare institutions, namely, a Sub-Centre (SC) for a population of 3,000 to 5,000, a Primary Health Centre (PHC) for 20,000 to 30,000 people, and a Community Health Centre (CHC) as a referral center established for every four PHCs, which covers a population of 80,000 to 120,000. The district hospitals operate as the second tier for the rural population and as the primary tier for the urban population. The tertiary healthcare is provided by healthcare institutions in urban areas that are well supplied with sophisticated diagnostic and investigative facilities such as the All India Institute of Medical Sciences and government medical colleges.

2. Evolution of Healthcare in India

2.1. Health as a State 'Subject'

Public healthcare in India witnessed an upsurge in 1983 when the Parliament endorsed the National Health Policy. However, as India was already

DOI: 10.1201/9781003111351-3

establishing different healthcare initiatives for specific target groups, in 1975, Integrated Child Development Services was launched to improve the nutrition and health status of children in the age group of 0–6 years. India also established National AIDS Control Organization, National Leprosy Eradication Programme, Mission Indradhanush (immunization program), and Pulse Polio, among others. Over a period, the anti-HIV and the anti-polio campaigns have been significantly successful. In India, the success of various healthcare initiatives has been at different levels since health is a state subject in India and various states have a diverse set of challenges, healthcare initiatives have also displayed different levels of success.

2.2. Streamlining Alternate Medicines

The Department of Ayurveda, Yoga and Naturopathy, Unani, Siddha and Homoeopathy, abbreviated AYUSH, has been integrated into the Indian national healthcare delivery system to strengthen public health in rural India. The department was created in March 1995 as the Department of Indian Systems of Medicine and Homoeopathy under the Ministry of Health [1]. AYUSH received its current name in March 2003.

In 2005, the Indian government launched the National Rural Health Mission (NRHM) to improve healthcare delivery in the rural areas of the country, in which AYUSH was integrated as an important element. This was done with the objective of offering multiple treatment options to people as well as promoting alternate forms of medicine. It became a full-fledged ministry in November 2014.

2.3. Strengthening Community Health

ASHAs, introduced by the NRHM in 2005, are the key cadre in India's community health programs that focus on improving maternal and child health. The ASHAs have played three major roles: They function as a 'link worker', between the underserved population and the health service centers. Second, they are also trained and provided with a kit that comprises condoms, oral contraceptive pills, delivery kits, and simple lifesaving drugs. They are also 'health activists' who create awareness on health and mobilize the community toward health planning.

2.4. National Health Mission (NHM)

The NHM [2] encompasses its two Sub-Missions, the National Rural Health Mission (NRHM) and the National Urban Health Mission (NUHM). The key components include health system strengthening; reproductive, maternal, neonatal, child and adolescent health (RMNCH+A); and communicable and noncommunicable diseases. The NHM envisages the achievement of universal access to equitable, affordable, and quality healthcare services that are accountable and responsive to the needs of the citizens. The NRHM was launched by the Hon'ble Prime Minister on 12 April 2005 to provide accessible, affordable, and quality healthcare to the rural population, especially the vulnerable groups. On 1 May 2013, the Union Cabinet approved the launch of the NUHM as a sub-mission of an overarching NHM, with NRHM being the other sub-mission of the NHM.

2.5 Ayushman Bharat

Ayushman Bharat is an endeavor to move from the sector-based segmented approach to health service delivery of a comprehensive needs-based healthcare service in India. This scheme aims to undertake pathbreaking interventions to comprehensively direct the healthcare system (covering prevention, promotion, and ambulatory care) at the primary, secondary and tertiary levels. Ayushman Bharat adopts a continuing care approach, composed of two interrelated components.

2.5.1. Ayushman Bharat—Health and Wellness Centers (AB-HWCs)

In February 2018, the Government of India led the conception of 0.15 million (150,000) health and wellness centers (HWCs) [3] by remodeling the existing SCs and PHCs. These centers are focused on delivering comprehensive primary healthcare closer to the homes of people. They cover maternal and child health services and noncommunicable diseases, including free essential drugs and diagnostic services.

HWCs are delivering an expanded range of services to address the primary healthcare needs of the entire population in their area, expanding access, universality, and equity close to the community. It also focuses on engaging and empowering individuals and communities to adopt healthy behaviors and make changes that reduce the risk of developing chronic diseases and morbidities.

2.5.2. Ayushman Bharat—Pradhan Mantri Jan Arogya Yojana (AB-PM-JAY)

The second component under Ayushman Bharat is the Pradhan Mantri Jan Arogya Yojana or PM-JAY [4] as it is popularly known. On 23 September 2018, PM-JAY was launched by the Hon'ble Prime Minister of India in Ranchi, Jharkhand.

The AB-PM-JAY has emerged as the largest health insurance scheme in the world, aiming to provide a health cover of INR 0.5 million (500,000) per family per year for secondary and tertiary care hospitalization to more than 107.4 million poor and vulnerable families (approximately 500 million beneficiaries) that constitute the bottom 40 percent of the Indian population [3]. The beneficiaries included are based on the deprivation and occupational criteria of Socio-Economic Caste Census 2011 (SECC 2011) for rural and urban areas, respectively.

3. Institutional Structure

Since the Constitution of India makes the provision of healthcare the responsibility of state governments, healthcare in India is a state subject. With this, every state is responsible for providing nutrition and uplifting the standard of living of the citizens by delivery of good public health services.

Figure 3.1 presents a broader view of institutional structure for health sector in India. The overall health and well-being of the citizens are managed by the MoHFW [5] and the Ministry of Ayurveda, Yoga and Naturopathy, Unani, Siddha and Homeopathy (MoAYUSH) [1]. These central ministries formulate the health policies for India. The MoHFW is composed of the Departments of Health and Family Welfare (DoHFW) and the Department of Health Research (DHR). The MoHFW provides funds to the state governments for various health schemes in the hospitals under the Program Implementation Plan (PIP) of the National Health Mission (NHM). PIP facilitates the planning, approval, and allocation of budgets of various programs under the NHM. PIPs help in standardizing and institutionalizing the planning and implementation of programs under NHM funding. The monitoring of PIPs

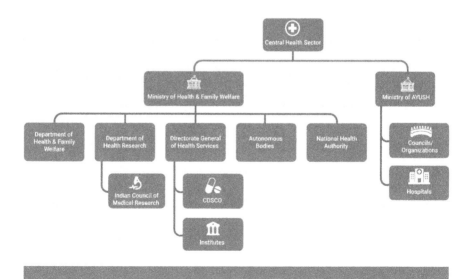

FIGURE 3.1
Institutional Structure Demonstrating the Health Sector in India.

also enables the measurement of physical and financial progress made by the states against the approved PIPs.

4. IT-Enabled Transformation in Healthcare

There have been broadly three components in the health sector, namely, patients, health providers, and health systems. Technology has been playing a crucial role in integrating these components for monitoring health schemes as well providing services to the patients. Users of smartphones and the internet are growing at a very fast pace in India, and it is proving to be of use for patients to access health-related information and getting healthcare services. In the last 25 years, there have been lots of transformations concerning the use of technology in the health sector. Some of the transformational technological initiatives and evolution in health sector in India are shown in Figure 3.2. A major impetus for technological intervention was the Government of India's policies and directives related to the use of technology in the health sector. The initial focus of using technology in the health sector was to monitor the schemes such as the UIP, the Pulse Polio Programme (PPP), the Target Free Approach, and family welfare programs by using a health management information system to monitor various indicators. Previously, the government made use of technological infrastructure and applications for monitoring health schemes and programs. Initially, databases were created at state and district levels as NICNET was the only available option reaching the district level. The transmission of data from districts to states and further to the national level was through emails with data as an attachment. These data were manually downloaded and then put into the database for compilation and generation of reports for monitoring various health schemes. The major challenges during that time were a lack of clarity on usage of ICT, non-clarity of requirements, infrastructure limitations, and weak internet bandwidth, to name a few. The UIP was launched in 1985 [6]. The monitoring of UIP was among the first IT-enabled application implemented by the MoHWF, the Government of India in 1990. In the UIP IT application, the number of children being vaccinated under different age groups was captured against the target given to the states. Based on the UIP experience, in 1995, special focus was given to the PPP, and a technology-powered application was developed to monitor this program up to the district level. Data capturing was done at the district level, transmitted through email using text files at the national level, and then extracted to be put into the database. After this, the compilation was done, and reports were generated for monitoring of the program at the state and district levels.

This phase of ICT intervention helped administrators and planners in getting the data for the monitoring and future planning; however, robust ICT

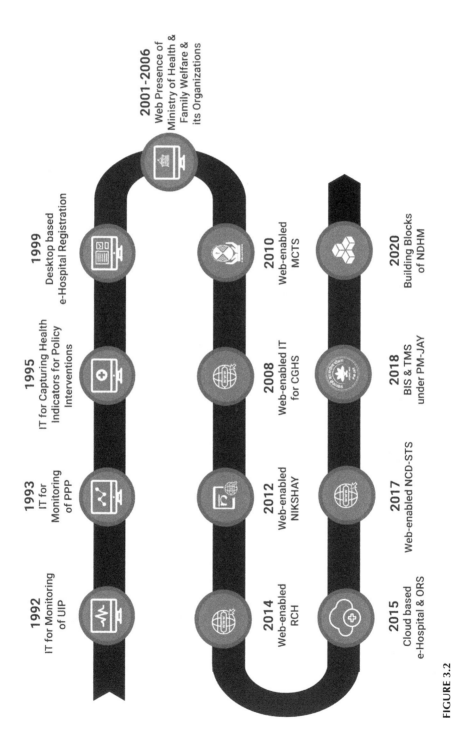

FIGURE 3.2
Transformational Journey of Health Sector in India.

support was not available to health facilities, health services providers and patients. In 2000, the development of websites by various ministries in the Government of India and state governments started. The MoHWF and its organizations also started developing their websites. The online presence of the ministries and departments through websites helped the citizens of India in getting appropriate information about the various schemes and initiatives openly and transparently. Earlier, this information was available in the form of books only.

Over a period, internet connectivity in India also improved and reached up to the block level. This also increased mobile penetration signifi-cantly. A paradigm shift was experienced from websites to web applica-tions, which also led to the development of patient-centric applications. Initially, the development of two kinds of web applications was started in general. One is vertical IT health applications, whereby health infor-mation of the beneficiaries is captured pertaining to specific health pro-grams such as the MCTS, TB Patients Tracking System (NIKSHAY), and the Non-Communicable Disease Screening and Tracking System, among others. The other is horizontal IT health applications, whereby the health information of any patient is captured such as through a hospital man-agement information system (HMIS; e.g., e-Hospital, e-Sushrut, e-Sanje-evani, etc.), patient portals such as the Online Registration System (ORS) and providing health information to citizens through the National Health Portal. Vertical health applications are target-oriented and monitored for either the eradication of disease or the improvement of services to the ben-eficiaries. Normally, the government approaches beneficiaries to achieve the objective. However, horizontal IT health applications are generic solu-tions, and patients approach the health facilities to avail themselves of the services, whenever required. These applications are patient-centric, based on health systems, and support to health services providers. These digital solutions enabled us to move toward prevention-focused and outcome-driven healthcare.

In 2013, it was realized that many of the web-based health applications are operating in silos. Sharing health data across health applications was a challenge. The MoHFW released its first report on electronic health records (EHRs), which described the standards to be adopted by IT-based health applications so that the EHR for each citizen of India could be generated. Although its initial implementation was slow, later it picked up as software development agencies started realizing the importance of these standards. These standards were revised in 2016 based on the feedback received from the public and private sectors along with healthcare professionals. The Central Bureau of Health Intelligence has been imparting training to health professionals and statisticians on the International Classification of Diseases 9 and 10 Standards for disease classification.

The Government of India released the National Health Policy in 2017 [5]. In this policy, the Digital Health Technology Ecosystem including applications of digital health and leveraging the digital tools for AYUSH, has been envisaged. Taking this policy initiative forward, the MoHFW released National Digital Health Blueprint (NDHB) [7] in 2019, and to implement this NDHB, the National Digital Health Mission (NDHM) was established in 2020 with the objective to provide the necessary support for the creation of integrated digital health infrastructure of the country.

The NDHM [8] has recently launched five building blocks, namely, HealthID, Digi-Doctor, Health Facility Registry, Personal Health Record App, and Consent Management. The HMIS of the e-Hospital platform has been integrated with these building blocks and released in production for three hospitals initially, paving the way for all the hospitals that have already implemented the e-Hospital platform for the integration of health records.

5. Major Health IT Initiatives in India

Various IT applications were developed during the period from 1990 to 2020. These applications have brought changes in the life of patients, health providers and health systems, planners, and administrators. Case studies of some of the information systems, which helped the government and the public at large in an effective way, are being presented in the following.

5.1. IT-Based Monitoring of the PPP

The PPP was launched in India in 1995. Children in the age group of 0 to 5 years were administered polio drops during the national and subnational immunization rounds (in high-risk areas) every year. About 172 million children are immunized during each National Immunization Day [9]. Monitoring such a massive program became easier due to an IT-based PPP application. This was a time when there were no web applications. A local server–based application was developed, and implementation was done at the national, as well as at the state, level. Data were transmitted using email and compiled for national reports for progress monitoring. This helped the MoHFW in reviewing the progress and facilitated the faster implementation of the program in the states. The implementation of IT to monitor the progress of the PPP between 1995 and 2012 helped the MoHFW in achieving the objective of polio eradication from India.

5.2. HMIS

In order to monitor the health indicators for service delivery related to reproductive, maternal, and child health; immunization; family planning;

vector-borne diseases; tuberculosis; morbidity and mortality, outpatient department (OPD), inpatient department (IPD) services, data related to surgeries on a monthly basis; training imparted to health professionals at the district and state levels on a quarterly basis; infrastructure-related data on manpower, equipment, cleanliness, and building; and the availability of medical services such as surgery, super-specialties services, diagnostics, paramedical and clinical services on annual basis, an IT-based solution was developed in 1993. Data were received from the states through email and placed in the database, post which monitoring reports were generated through the HMIS application. Later, with the introduction of web-based technology, the HMIS portal was redeveloped. The portal facilitates the flow of data from the facility level to the subdistrict, district, state, and national levels using web-based interfaces. The portal provides periodic reports on the status of the health services performance and the human resources and infrastructure facilities available.

5.3. Mother and Child Tracking System (MCTS)/Reproductive and Child Health (RCH)—Journey of Electronic Health Record Creation for Pregnant Women and Children

One of the prime focuses of the NHM is to reduce the infant mortality rate (IMR), maternal mortality rate (MMR) and to ensure quality services to pregnant women and children across the country. Reducing maternal and child mortality is among the most important goals of the National Health Mission [10]. The Government of India has made significant strategic investments to achieve these goals. There are two dimensions to healthcare: (1) interventions at various stages of the life cycle and (2) places where the care is provided. These together constitute the 'continuum of care'.

The NIC developed the MCTS for the MoHFW in December 2010. This software captures the date on which service is provided to pregnant women and children. About 80 data points are being captured in the MCTS.

For early detection of pregnancy and for monitoring family planning services to eligible couples (EC), the MCTS was extended and transformed into a new system known as RCH in 2014. This system comprehensively covered information about every eligible couple, pregnant woman, and child being captured and being monitored at all levels including SCs and health facilities at the district, state, and national levels. The information captured about ECs includes methods being used for family planning whereas information captured about services being provided to pregnant women includes antenatal care services, delivery services, and postnatal care services. Information related to immunization is captured for children up to 5 years of age.

The RCH application, 'an augmented version of [the] MCTS', is designed for early identification and tracking of the individual beneficiary throughout the reproductive life cycle. The RCH portal has also been integrated with

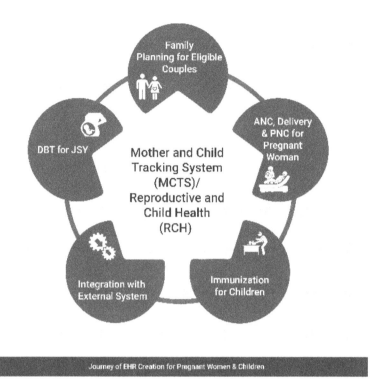

FIGURE 3.3
Key Features of the MCTS/RCH.

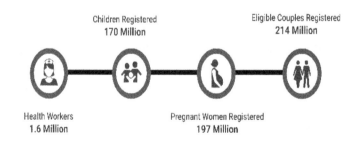

FIGURE 3.4
Major Statistics of the RCH.

several health IT applications for a variety of citizen services and planning and decision-making by the government.

The RCH played a vital role in key decision-making and monitoring the implementation of various health schemes in the country. Using the RCH, high-risk pregnant women are being identified to track their health condition, and assistance is provided during the delivery phase. This has improved the healthcare service delivery for expecting mothers and children in the country.

For the latest dashboard, visit the MCTS website [11].

5.4. CGHS

The CGHS provides comprehensive healthcare facilities for central government employees, pensioners, and their dependents residing in the CGHS-covered cities. It was started in New Delhi in 1954 and is now operational in more than 26 cities across the country. The medical facilities are provided through wellness centers (previously referred to as CGHS dispensaries)/polyclinics under the allopathic, Ayurveda, yoga, Unani, Siddha and homeopathic systems of medicines. The IT system of the CGHS has been developed with 22 modules, such as registration, doctor module, pharmacy, chemist, beneficiary, dashboard, procurement, prevention health checkup and the like. These modules have been implemented in all CGHS wellness centers. The CGHS IT system [12] has facilitated easy access to healthcare services from wellness centers and non-health services while staying at home. It has also helped the CGHS directorate in effectively monitoring the scheme.

5.5. Tuberculosis (TB) Patients Tracking System (NIKSHAY)

The MoHFW launched the revised National Tuberculosis Control Programme (RNTCP), incorporating the components of the internationally recommended Directly Observed Treatment Strategy (DOTS) Strategy for control of TB in India in 1992. It was initiated to ensure access to quality diagnosis and care for all TB patients. Several notable activities were implemented under this program in 2012 to improve its overall efficacy.

To monitor individual TB patients, NIKSHAY [13], a case-based, web-based application software was developed in 2012. Tuberculosis units register the TB patients, and a unique number is generated for future correspondence. The registration of TB patients includes personal details, DOT provider details, history of anti-TB treatment, pretreatment lab test details, and disease classification. The application facilitates a role-based search facility based on TB registration ID and through navigation. Profiles of state TB officers (STOs), district TB officers (DTOs), and Tuberculosis Unit officers and officials are also being maintained. NIKSHAY has been integrated with the PFMS to facilitate direct benefits–based payments to TB patients based on the scheme criteria. NIKSHAY is helping the MoHFW in close monitoring of every TB patient to achieve the objective of eradication of tuberculosis from India by 2025.

5.6. Non-Communicable Disease Screening and Tracking System (NCD-STS)

To prevent and control major NCDs, the National Programme for Prevention and Control of Cancer, Diabetes, Cardiovascular Diseases and Stroke (NPCDCS) was launched in 2010 with a focus on strengthening the infrastructure, human resource development, health promotion, early diagnosis, management, and referral activities. In order to monitor the NPCDCS program, the NCD-STS IT application [14] has been made operational for auxiliary nurse midwives, accredited social health activists, and medical officers. Data analytics and monitoring have been a part of this intervention, which is providing advanced insights into the overall program. The NCD-STS application has helped the central and states government in monitoring the NPCDCS effectively. It has also helped functionaries at the field level in monitoring the beneficiary's health data.

5.7. e-Hospital—Simplifying Healthcare Service Delivery

The e-Hospital suite of applications (viz. the e-Hospital HMIS, the ORS—Patient Portal and e-Blood Bank) was developed by the NIC to facilitate support the functioning of the hospitals and improve the delivery of healthcare services to the citizens across the country. The e-Hospital application has been built using open-source technology and standards with the objective of providing improved healthcare service delivery to the patients with reduced turnaround and wait times for patients at the hospitals, further ensuring effective hospital administration, efficient utilization of resources at the hospitals, better planning, and overall management.

To accelerate the process of e-Hospital implementation in the hospitals, a cloud-based version of e-Hospital was developed in 2015 and offered as a SaaS to hospitals to fast-track their digitization journey.

In September 2015, under the Digital India Program of the Government of India, the e-Hospital application was made available to government hospitals on the cloud. The e-Hospital application became the cloud-based HMIS for the digitization of internal workflows and processes of hospitals, thereby becoming a one-stop solution that helps connect patients, hospitals, and doctors on a single digital platform.

5.7.1. e-Hospital HMIS

e-Hospital is generic enough to provide a workflow-based solution for the internal functioning of different categories of hospitals. The major modules

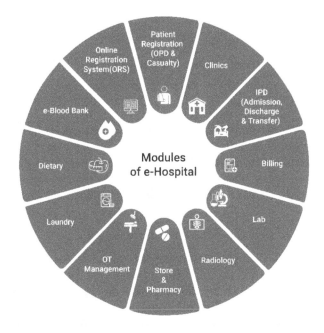

FIGURE 3.5
Major Modules of the e-Hospital Application.

of e-Hospital (mentioned in Figure 3.5) are patient registration (OPD and casualty), IPD (admission, discharge, and transfer), billing, lab information system, radiology information system, clinic, dietary, laundry, store and pharmacy and Occupational therapy (OT) management, along with the ORS and e-BloodBank.

Currently, the e-Hospital application has been implemented by more than 300-plus hospitals across the country [15] and is reporting live transactions daily [16].

5.7.2. Online Registration System (ORS)

The ORS [17] is an online patient portal for citizens to book an online appointment for visiting the hospital. The ORS is a system that links various hospitals across the country for booking online appointments and providing various patient-centric services such as viewing the lab reports, checking the bloodstock status and making online payments. The ORS also facilitates the Aadhaar based online registration and appointment system, whereby a counter-based OPD registration and appointment system through the HMIS has been digitized. To know more about ORS implementation status, refer to the ORS Dashboard [18].

5.7.3. e-BloodBank

The e-BloodBank application facilitates the implementation of a complete blood bank management system for internal workflows and processes of the blood banks. The available modules of the e-BloodBank application are blood bag preparation, component registration, aphaeresis and requisition, cross-match details, blood issue details, discard bag, patient blood grouping, blood transfer, donor registration, and checkup. To know the latest status of the e-BloodBank implementation, refer to the eBloodBank Dashboard [19].

5.7.4. Implementation Challenges and Achievements

One of the primary challenges while implementing e-Hospital was to roll out the application in every individual hospital as per the specific require-ments of a hospital. Another challenge was the digitization of lab investiga-tion reports of the patients directly from the lab analyzers in the hospitals, to ensure an error-free and effective entry of results of the lab investigation of the patients. The NIC developed a solution and integrated e-Hospital appli-cation with the lab analyzers in various hospitals.

Interoperability was also one of the biggest challenges for smooth imple-mentation and integration of e-Hospital with other health systems. E-Hospital has been integrated with a number of external systems such as e-Sushrut and MeraAsptaal, among others. Recently, e-Hospital has been integrated with Health ID of the NDHM, and this has been implemented in three hospitals in Chandigarh for health data sharing using a consent framework.

5.8. The National Health Portal

The National Health Portal was launched in November 2014 with the objec-tive of providing quality health-related content to the public in multiple lan-guages. Health tips on various subjects are provided to the public through the National Health Portal. With the popularity of the portal, it has been extended to the umbrella of other health applications such as MeraAspataal, eRaktkosh, Pradhan Mantri Surakshit Matritva Abhiyan, and Directory Services [20].

---

6. Conclusion

India has a population of 1.3 billion and providing healthcare services to a huge population without the intervention of digital technologies is a challenging task. In order to deliver healthcare services to all in an effective manner, IT enablement of all the services needs to be done in an integrated manner so that the exchange of health data becomes a reality. The NDHM is a step in this direction. In order to achieve the objective of universal health coverage, standards-based health digital systems, which are interoperable, open, and secure and maintain the privacy of health-related personal information, are the need of the current time. In the upcoming times, India will establish registries at an appropriate level to create a single source of truth for clinical establishments, healthcare professionals, health workers, drugs, and pharmacies—national portability in the provision of health services. Health professionals will employ clinical decision support systems for better and accurate decision-making. The use of AI, blockchain, and data analytics in the public and private sectors will help improve patient services as well as healthcare delivery services. Personal medical devices and their integration with health applications and personal health records will facilitate predictive and preventive healthcare for the citizens of the country.

References

[1] Ministry of Ayurveda, "Yoga and Naturopathy, Unani, Siddha and Homoeopathy (AYUSH)," [Online]. Available: https://ayush.gov.in/.

[2] Ministry of Health & Family Welfare, "National Health Mission," [Online]. Available: https://nhm.gov.in [Accessed 20 March 2020].

[3] National Health Authority, "Pradhan Mantri Jan Arogya Yojana (PM-JAY)," [Online]. Available: https://pmjay.gov.in/about/pmjay.

[4] Ayushman Bharat—Pradhan Mantri Jan Aarogya Yojana [PM-JAY], "Health Assurance/Insurance for Poor," [Online]. Available: https://pmjay.gov.in.

[5] Ministry of Health & Family Welfare, "National Health Policy," 2017. [Online]. Available: www.nhp.gov.in/nhpfiles/national_health_policy_2017.pdf.

[6] "Universal Immunization Programme (UIP)," [Online]. Available: www.nhp.gov.in/universal-immunisation-programme_pg."

[7] Ministry of Health & Family Welfare, "National Digital Health Blueprint," [Online]. Available: https://main.mohfw.gov.in/sites/default/files/Final Report—Lite Version.pdf.

[8] Ministry of Health & Family Welfare, "National Digital Health Mission, India," [Online]. Available: https://ndhm.gov.in.

[9] "Pulse Polio Programme (PPP)," [Online]. Available: www.nhp.gov.in/pulse-polio-programme_pg.

[10] Ministry of Health & Family Welfare, "Objectives of National Health Mission," [Online]. Available: https://nhm.gov.in/index1.php?lang=1&level=1&sublinkid=794&lid=168.

[11] Ministry of Health & Family Welfare, "Reproductive & Child Health Dashboard," [Online]. Available: https://rchrpt.nhm.gov.in/RCHRPT/Dashboard/PortalDashboard.aspx.

[12] Ministry of Health & Family Welfare, "Central Government Health Scheme (CGHS)," [Online]. Available: https://cghs.gov.in.

[13] N.I.K.S.H.A.Y., "TB Patients Monitoring System," [Online]. Available: https://nikshay.in.

[14] "Non-Communicable Disease Screening & Tracking System," [Online]. Available: https://ncd.nhp.gov.in.

[15] Ministry of Health & Family Welfare, "e-Hospital Dashboards," [Online]. Available: https://dashboard.ehospital.gov.in/.

[16] National Informatics Centre, "e-Hospital Live Dashboard." [Online]. Available: https://dashboard.ehospital.gov.in/ehospitaldashboard/dashboardcons.jsp?url=0.

[17] Ministry of Health & Family Welfare, "Online Registration System—Patient Portal," [Online]. Available: https://ors.gov.in.

[18] Ministry of Health & Family Welfare, "Online Registration Information System (ORS) Dashboard," [Online]. Available: https://ors.gov.in/copp/dashboard.jsp?ln=0.

[19] National Informatics Centre, "e-Blood Bank Dashboard," [Online]. Available: https://ors.gov.in/ebloodbankportal/dashboard/portal/dashboard_details.jsp.

[20] "National Health Portal, India," [Online]. Available: https://nhp.gov.in.

4

Digital Transformation of Rural Governance and Service Delivery

Deepak Chandra Misra, Madhuri Sharma, Prashant Kumar Mittal,
Rama Hariharan, Seemantinee Sengupta, Manie Khaneja,
and Rajiv Goel

1. Introduction

The SDGs have envisaged development targets for India with sustainability as a key component and an emphasis on poverty alleviation, social inclusion, institutions, and governance. World over, 'rural areas' share some common attributes, with a majority of the rural population dependent on agriculture and allied labor-intensive activities. The importance of rural development has been enhanced by the increasing urbanization in most countries, which has boosted the demand for food, goods, and services in urban as well as rural areas.

With a majority of India's population residing in rural areas, achieving Antyodaya is an onerous task. Rural development implies both the economic betterment of people as well as greater social transformation. The increased participation of people in decentralized planning and implementation of rural development programs, the integration of rural areas with neighboring urban areas, the need to harmonize modern technologies with traditional and indigenous knowledge, better enforcement of land reforms, and greater access to credit are envisaged for the rural population.

As per India's Census 2001, 71.47 percent of the population lived in rural areas. Subsequently, Census 2011 indicated that about 72 percent of the country's population (i.e., more than 830 million people) resides in rural areas. The vision [1] of the DoRD is to transform lives and livelihoods through proactive socioeconomic inclusion, integration, and empowerment of rural India. The department aims at creating sustainable and inclusive growth in rural India through a multipronged strategy for eradication of poverty and deprivation by increasing livelihood opportunities, providing a social safety net, and developing infrastructure for growth. Some of the SDGs toward which the efforts of the department are directed are depicted in Figure 4.1.

The typical facets of rural development are housing, physical connectivity, social inclusion, livelihood, and availability of basic services. ICT has a critical role to play in the effective monitoring and implementation of these various facets by ushering into a new era of transparency, accountability, efficiency, traceability, just-in-time (JIT) payments, and good governance. In March 1986, for the first time in the country, IT was introduced in governance at the district level, in 10 pilot districts, by the DoRD through CRISP, wherein the hardware was provided under a government program. The objectives of CRISP were to facilitate data processing with initiatives like the Integrated Rural Development Programme, the Development of Women and Children in Rural Areas, Training of Rural Youth for Self-Employment, Indira Awaas Yojana (IAY), the National Rural Employment Programme, and the Rural Landless Employment Guarantee Programme, at the district level, that is, in the offices of the DRDA. Subsequently, the project was expanded to cover all the districts, and other emerging programs such as Jawahar Rozgar Yojana (JRY), among others, were included in MS-DoS-based compiled (Clipper-based) application software developed by the NIC, as part of the project. Similarly, the digitization of land records started in 1988 was another pioneering IT initiative.

These ICT initiatives were focused on data processing and report generation for internal use by the concerned agencies, that is, DRDA or the Tehsil office in the case of land records. The NIC facilitated the launch of the NSAP in 1995 and Swarna Jayanti Gram Swarojgar Yojana in 1999 by preparing a web-enabled system for these schemes. Over a period, the ICT capacity at the grassroot level for these programs improved significantly through community resource persons (CRPs), Gram Rojgar Sahayak (GRS), Gram Awaas Sahayaks, members of self-help groups, and the like.

These web-enabled systems were developed centrally after consultations with states and are customizable to meet state specificities or have been integrated with their corresponding state-specific application. The continuous incorporation of new features and the increasing size of the beneficiary-

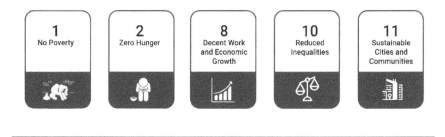

FIGURE 4.1
High-Impact SDGs (1, 2, 8, 10 & 11).

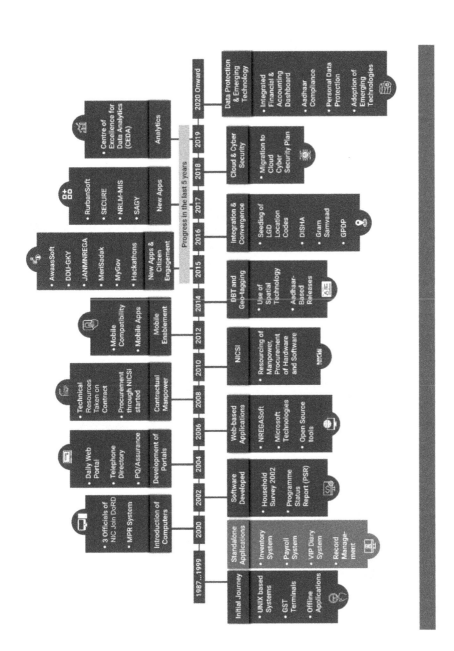

FIGURE 4.2
Evolution of ICT in Programs of the DoRD.

centric datasets necessitates the need for rapid deployment of new versions that are integrated with real-time systems of financial institutions.

With the NIC's technical capabilities, ICT support was extended to the various programs of the DoRD at the state, district, and subdistrict levels, even reaching up to the gram panchayat level. The NIC-DoRD developed an offline software using MS Access for the Household Survey 2002, whereby each block downloaded the software, entered the data offline, and collated and sent it to the DoRD by CD/email. The location master data used for the BPL Household Survey 2002 was later used in 2006 as the base directory in NREGASoft to select households. The software for the SECC 2011 was subsequently developed by the NIC as a web-based application (that also supported offline data entry) that was configurable on tablets and mobiles. The same SECC 2011 database has been considered to determine the eligibility of beneficiaries under several welfare programs of the government that seek to provide housing for all (PMAY-G), rural connectivity (PMAY-G), skilling of rural youth (DDU-GKY), health for all (Ayushman Bharat), electricity connection to every household (Saubhagya), and clean cooking gas for all homes (Ujjwala), among others.

Keeping pace with technology, the approach toward handling/storing data has also undergone a radical change. From the initial physical record-keeping days to the local storage-based electronic mode and then to the centralized data centers, now most of the databases have been migrated toward the cloud.

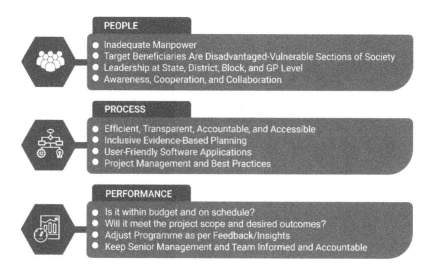

FIGURE 4.3
3P Framework for the Rural ICT System.

The use of ICT in all government programs over the last two decades has also created a tremendous amount of data, including transaction data. These data are now being processed through various analytical tools not only to gain insights and identify hidden patterns in the data of the DoRD but also to forecast the likely outcome and make informed decisions. The rural ICT system is depicted in the 3P framework in Figure 4.3.

2. Institutional Structure

Every state has a DoRD to coordinate all activities under 'rural development'. There are 670 district panchayats [2], 9,116 block panchayats, 269,312 gram panchayats/village-level committees [3], and more than 660,000 villages in the country. The DoRD coordinates with all State Rural Development Departments and District Rural Development Agencies (DRDA) and has two autonomous organizations under it, namely, the National Institute of Rural Development and Panchayati Raj (NIRD&PR) [4] and the National Rural Infrastructure Development Agency (NRIDA) [5]. NIRD&PR is a premier national institute and Centre of Excellence in rural development and Panchayati Raj that builds capacities of rural development functionaries, elected representatives of Panchayati Raj Institutions (PRIs), bankers, nongovernmental organizations (NGOs), and other stakeholders through interrelated activities of training, research, and consultancy. The NRIDA extends technical and management support to the rural roads and housing programs of the Government of India through advice on technical specifications, project appraisal, the appointment of part-time quality control monitors, the management of monitoring systems, and monitoring of progress under the PMGSY. An organizational chart depicting the relationship among the DoRD, the State Rural Development Departments, PRIs, and autonomous organizations is depicted in Figure 4.4.

The DoRD is mandated to implement several social welfare schemes on the *Antyodaya* principle—a convergence framework for measurable effective outcomes on parameters that transform lives and livelihood. Following are some of the flagship programs being implemented by DoRD:

1. MGNREGA for providing guaranteed wage employment to rural households on demand
2. PMAY-G for providing housing to all poor households under 'Housing for All'
3. NRLM for livelihood, self-employment, and skill development
4. NSAP to provide social assistance to the poor, marginalized, and vulnerable

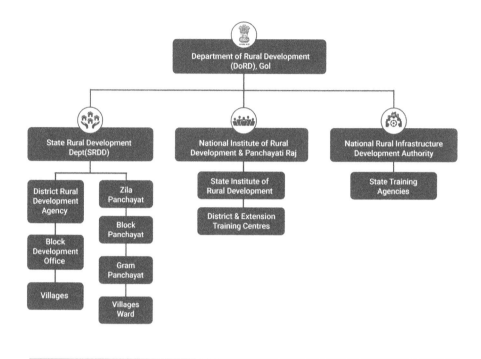

FIGURE 4.4
Institutional Structure of Rural Development.

5. PMGSY for construction of quality roads in rural areas
6. RURBAN for cluster-based development in rural areas to provide urban-like amenities
7. SAGY for an integrated development of panchayats through convergence

The **National Wasteland Development Board (NWDB)** was set up in 1985 under the Ministry of Environment and Forests with the principal aim of bringing wastelands in the country into productive use through a massive program of afforestation and tree plantations.

In July 1992, the NWDB was reconstituted and placed in the newly created Department of Wasteland Development under the Ministry of Rural Development. Subsequently, the Department of Wasteland Development was renamed as Department of Land Resources vide Gazette Notification dated 09–04–1999.

The **Department of Land Resources (DoLR)** in India ensures sustainable improvement in productivity and livelihood/income potential of land, to the rainfed cultivated areas and culturable wastelands. The department aims to develop an appropriate integrated land information management system, which will inter alia improve real-time information on land, optimize the use of land resources, and assist in policy/planning. The DoLR has instituted effective agrarian reforms, including an efficient land use policy and a transparent Land Records Management System with the aim of building an Integrated Land Information Management System. This system of integrated land information management will ultimately yield security of tenancy to citizens, reduced land disputes, a simplified procedure for transfer of property title, fraudulent free landed properties transactions, and the like. The DoLR has also launched the Integrated Watershed Development Programme to enhance the productivity of land and dependent people which was supported by the NIC through a nationwide single software and recently it has become part of Pradhan Mantri Krishi Sichai Yojna.

The 73rd/74th amendment heralded a new era as the panchayats were accorded full constitutional status in 1992, envisioning the devolution of funds, functions, and functionaries to make them effective in the local development process. The division of powers and functioning of the government is a three-tier level, that is, the union government, the state government, and the local self-governments (panchayat at the village levels and municipalities and municipal corporations in towns and large cities). This further facilitated grassroot government systems in terms of the availability of panchayat secretaries who contributed to data streamlining and data entry in a variety of e-governance systems. Initially, access to the ICT systems witnessed challenges as the rural population was not upskilled for adopting digital solutions; however, this risk was mitigated with the proliferation of assisted services provided by the GRS of CSCs/telecenters at the local level.

In 1988, the **Department of Land Records** launched the Computerization of Land Records (CLR) project with a focus on data entry of Record of Rights (RoR). The required technical and software support was provided by the NIC through NIC state/district centers through state-specific software as Land Record Acts are specific to the states.

The department led the following key initiatives over a period that brought a significant improvement in the overall management of land records in India:

- In 2008, the revamped version of CLR, National Land Record Modernization Programme was launched to modernize the management of land records, minimize the scope of property disputes, enhance transparency, and eventually moving toward guaranteed, conclusive titles to immovable properties in the country. This led to the revamping of existing software, by the NIC, by adding features such as web-enabled, service-centricity, mutation online, online interoperation with property/document registration software, and the like.

- To facilitate the management of survey data (i.e., cadastral maps), an online open-source-based common generic software BhuNaksha was made available to states, which is interoperable with the land record software. Similarly, the Unique Land Parcel Identification Number system has a 14-digit alphanumeric unique ID for each land parcel based on geo-coordinates of vertices of the parcel.

- In 2015, the program was further revamped to Digital India Land Record Modernization Programme (DILRMP), ensuring increased utilization of ICT for service delivery. In 2016, the DoLR launched an ambitious project, under the DILRMP, to have a common and configurable open-source-based software to manage the scope of activities under document and property registration. This led to the development of the National Generic Document Registration System (NGDRS) by the NIC, which enables 'anywhere access' to data to the citizens and enforcement and regulatory agencies. The NGRDS has also enabled the citizens to calculate property valuation and apply online for document submission.

The Ministry of Panchayati Raj, which looks into all matters relating to the Panchayati Raj and PRIs, was established in 2004. The ministry aims at empowerment, enablement, and accountability of PRIs to ensure inclusive development with social justice and the efficient delivery of services. In 2005–06, the MoPR released the Backward Region Grant Fund (BRGF), which was an untied fund allocated to the gram panchayats so that they can use this fund for development activities in their areas. To ensure that the funds are used efficiently, the NIC developed a generic national planning software called PlanPlus [6] to manage the planning and implementation of the BRGF. To aid the planning software, an accounting software called the PRIASoft [7] was also developed for managing the accounting activities of PRIs. A generic National Panchayat Portal (NPP) [8] was launched whereby each gram panchayats, block panchayats, and zila parishad could have its dynamic website without engaging any programmer. Customizable functionalities like changing the layout, theme, colors, language, content, and so on were provided by just using a wizard. More than 100 thousand gram panchayats are using the NPP now.

These technology-enabled initiatives acted as precursors for the creation of a complete Panchayat Enterprise Suite (PES), which was launched in 2012 under the ePanchayat Mission Mode Project. The key components of the PES are ServicePlus [9], Asset Director, and the Progress Implementation/Reporting System [10]. Furthermore, in April 2020, a revamped version of some of these products and services was launched under the eGram Swaraj Programme.

The **Department of Drinking Water and Sanitation** was earlier a part of the Ministry of Rural Development, which was later accorded the status of a separate ministry named the Ministry of Drinking Water and Sanitation in 2011. Furthermore, in 2019, the Government of India established a new ministry called The **Ministry of Jal Shakti** by merging the Ministry of Water Resources, River Development, and Ganga Rejuvenation and the Ministry of Drinking Water and Sanitation. The Ministry of Jal Shakti's vision is to ensure optimal sustainable development, the maintenance of quality, and the efficient use of water resources to match the growing demands on this precious natural resource of the country.

The Department of Drinking Water and Sanitation focuses on providing drinking water to rural households and leads the SBM (Gramin) in India. Jal Jeevan Mission (JJM) is envisioned to provide safe and adequate drinking water through individual household tap connections by 2024 to all households in rural India. The program will also implement water source sustainability measures as mandatory elements, such as recharge and reuse through greywater management, water conservation, and rainwater harvesting. The JJM is based on a community approach to water and will include extensive information, education, and communication as a key component of the mission. JJM looks to create a Jan Andolan for water, thereby making it everyone's priority.

3. Global Scenario and Trends

The changing demographics and ever-evolving technologies are continuously providing new opportunities and exploring new challenges in the delivery of government programs. The participation of women and youth in the social sector is also on the rise. Digital technologies are increasingly being used globally for tackling social issues and convergence through multiagency collaboration is the need of the hour to improve social outcomes. The concept of 'digital identities' has enabled governments to reimagine the service delivery ecosystem. For the empowerment of vulnerable sections, citizens need to be provided multiple modes of access, besides improving their awareness levels. The adoption of digital technologies is also generating tremendous amounts of data and raising several concerns on data security and privacy. Stringent government regulations are gradually being prescribed across countries to safekeep 'personal data' and penalize any misuse thereof. For instance, in many countries, the *static* beneficiary databases are giving way to a dynamic 'social registry' to capture the continually evolving deprivation status of individuals and households, for more targeted and evidence-based service delivery and monitoring mechanism [11]. Governments are also becoming more confident and amenable toward hosting their data in the cloud. Forensic science has now enabled us to determine cybercrimes and malpractices more reliably. Similarly, data and analytics-driven personalized and proactive service deliveries are gradually becoming the norm in some countries that are pioneering the use of technology in governance. Intelligent 'bots' bolstered by machine learning are providing 24/7 support to citizens in their native language. The use of blockchain technology as a decentralized verifier of truth is also being tested in many areas of governance.

4. Case Studies

4.1. Pradhan Mantri Awaas Yojana (Gramin)—Housing for All

The IAY, which started in 1996 aims to provide houses to all deprived households in the country. As per SECC 2011, India had an estimated shortage of 30 million houses [12]. In the IAY, there was limited monitoring of the selection of beneficiaries, the quality of construction was questionable due to a lack of technical supervision and the mechanism for monitoring and convergence was not robust. There was no basis for the identification of beneficiaries.

In 2016, after the scheme was restructured as PMAY-G, the entire workflow of the scheme was e-enabled by AwaasSoft and SECC database was used to determine the beneficiaries in a bottom-up approach. PFMS is used for DBT, whereby FTOs are generated online in AwaasSoft, and after

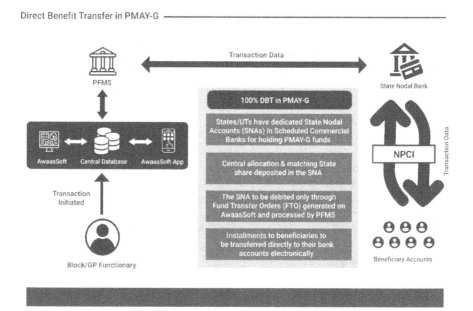

FIGURE 4.5
Direct Benefit Scheme under PMAY-G.

authentication by two ground-level authorities (using digital signatures), the FTOs are then sent through the PFMS to the corresponding state nodal bank, where the funds are credited directly to the bank account of beneficiaries. Figure 4.5 describes the workflow of Direct Benefit scheme under PMAY-G.

For effective monitoring, a mobile app (AwaasApp) was developed to capture the existing dwelling where a beneficiary lived, the proposed site of the construction of a new house, and timestamped and geotagged images at different phases of construction (foundation, plinth, lintel, roof cast, toilet) till completion. Each subsequent installment alert gets triggered when physical completion of the house to the specified level is reported in AwaasApp, which also enables online verification of house construction status. GIS-based planning and monitoring have also been enabled by leveraging the NIC's Bharat Maps services. Forecasting techniques are being used to recommend the most suitable typologies for houses in different regions of the country. Training modules on mason training are also disseminated to beneficiaries through digital means. The integration of AwaasSoft with the management information systems (MISs) of several other programs of the government is also undertaken.

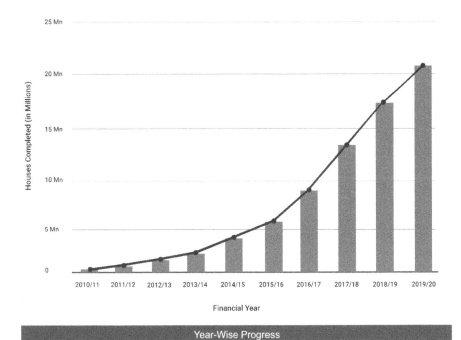

FIGURE 4.6
Year-Wise Progress of Houses Completed under PMAY.

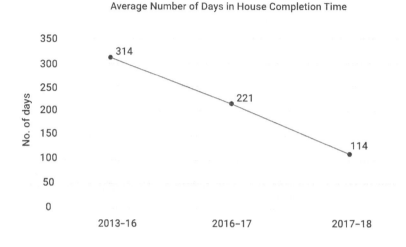

FIGURE 4.7
Reduction in Average House Completion Time.

The streamlining of the beneficiary selection process has enabled end-to-end traceability of funds and hence brought in greater transparency, awareness, and accountability. The integration with PFMS/banks and Aadhaar has enabled validation and authentication. The near-real-time evidence-based monitoring mechanism has enhanced accessibility, improved trust in the system, and enabled social audit in the system. An independent third-party study by the National Institute of Public Finance and Policy (NIPFP) had concluded that the average house completion time has reduced from 314 days in 2015–16 to 114 in 2017–18.

The integration with external databases has enabled convergence with other programs like SBM for individual household toilets, MGNREGA for 90/95 days of unskilled wage employment, and PM Ujjwala Yojana for subsidies on Liquefied Petroleum Gas (LPG) connection.

4.2. Mahatma Gandhi National Rural Employment Guarantee Scheme (MGNREGS)

Under the MGNREGS, which guarantees 100 days of wage employment every year to rural households, the central government is mandated to meet the cost of the wages for unskilled manual work and up to three-fourths of the material cost of the scheme including the payment of wages to the skilled and semi-skilled workers and the administrative expenses as decided by the central

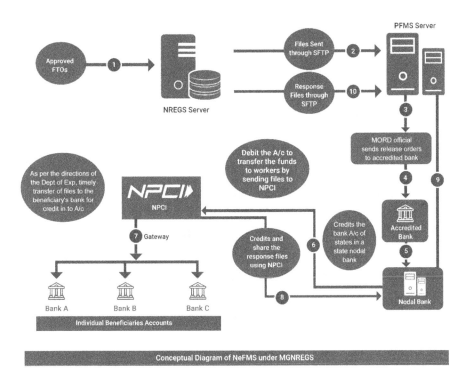

National Electronics Fund Management System (NEFMS)

Conceptual Diagram of NeFMS under MGNREGS

FIGURE 4.8
Conceptual Diagram of the NeFMS under the MGNREGS.

government. The state governments must meet the cost of the unemployment allowance and one-fourth of the material cost. Altogether, about 96 percent of the total cost of implementation is being met by the central government. MNREGS is the largest employment guarantee program in the world [13].

Although the National Rural Employment Guarantee Act (NREGA) was passed in 2005, the scheme experienced challenges related to lesser transparency in the process, and the payment of wages was either not being done or was being done after prolonged delays. This was often exacerbating the crisis in rural areas, where there is a lot of dependency on these wages for the sustenance of rural folks.

Today, almost the entire workflow of the program has been automated, namely, from registration of job cards, the capturing of work demand, an electronic muster roll, work management, the generation of wage lists and material lists, and FTO generation. The financial monitoring of MGNREGA through NeFMS module of NREGASoft is nearly 100 percent. The seeding of Aadhaar in bank accounts and integration with the NPCI and the Aadhaar Payment Bridge (APB) have also enabled 100 percent DBT through the NeFMS.

All assets under the programs are now geotagged and time-stamped and space technology is also being used for a pilot of spatial planning under the NREGA in select blocks, on the Indian Space Research Organization (ISRO)'s Bhuvan platform. Using analytics and GIS, it is now possible to better identify areas that need focus under the programs.

The engagement of citizens has also been enabled through the JANMNREGA app, which captures feedback and suggestions from citizens. The estimation of work has become more scientific and standardized through the adoption of SECURE (Software for Estimate Calculation Using Rural rates for Employment). The performance of the states is monitored based on the data updated in NREGASoft.

The effective use of technology under the program has significantly helped plug leakages in MGNREGS, besides also strengthening the monitoring framework. It has also enabled account validation, job-card verification, minimal parking of funds, and JIT release of funds by the government. This has enabled end-to-end traceability of funds, thereby enhancing transparency in the system. The elimination of ghost accounts has saved millions of rupees of the exchequer. The scheme has been extremely effective in securing the livelihood of rural households by ensuring the timely release of wages to the beneficiaries. Most of the payments are now being credited to the beneficiary's accounts within 15 days of being approved. The transparency and accountability in the public record system have also enhanced significantly, and this has further strengthened the system of social audit to hold local government leaders even more accountable to the community. The impact is clearly visible as shown in Figure 4.9 from year 2014 to 2020.

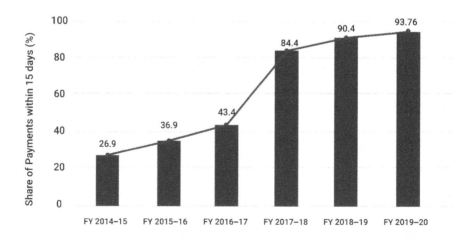

FIGURE 4.9
Impact of DBT on Timely Payment of Wages under MGNREGS.

4.3. Deen Dayal Upadhyay Grameen Kaushal Yojana (DDU-GKY)

As part of the 'Skill India' campaign, DDU-GKY started as an offshoot of DAY-NRLM in 2014 to adopt a more focused approach toward skill upgradation and upliftment of rural youth between the ages of 15 and 35 from poor families who are provided quality training free of cost. It covers all areas in the life cycle of skilling—mobilization, registration, training, assessment, placement, and monitoring the progress of candidates [14]. In order to boost awareness, motivation, demand, and accessibility, the Kaushal Panjee (Skills Register) portal was developed as a citizen-centric single-window solution to enable mobilization and registration of candidates for Rural Self Employment Training Institutes (RSETIs) and DDU-GKY through various means like project implementing agencies, trainers, employers, self-help group members, gram panchayat functionaries, block officials, CSCs, door-to-door mobilizers, and even directly by the candidate. Candidates can also choose from a list of available skilling courses, based on their choice of sector and trade, from a training institute of choice.

The integration of Kaushal Panjee with the SECC 2011 database has also enabled identification and verification of genuine candidates that has enabled the state government to plan and target their mobilization efforts in a bottom-up manner basis the socioeconomic profile of households. The Kaushal Pragati portal is now being used by States for reporting the progress of candidates and Project Implementation Agencies (PIAs) under DDU-GKY. The portal is also integrated with the Skill India portal for the timely assessment of candidates by the Sector Skill Councils. The Aadhaar Based Attendance System (ABAS) has also enabled real-time reporting and monitoring. Efforts are now underway toward e-Kaushal—an initiative to integrate the entire skilling ecosystem of the MoRD. The program has been successful in providing sustainable livelihood to them through employment generation and impact of the program can be seen with the statistics available in Figure 4.10.

FIGURE 4.10
Impact of DDU-GKY.

4.4. DAY-NRLM

To maintain a repository of the CBOs, a comprehensive directory with details of 5.93 million Self Help Groups (SHGs) with 65 million registered members, 240,000 VOs, 275,000 CRPs (Sakhis), and 17,000 CLFs is now captured online to recognize these CBOs and enable their access to credit. The Aadhaar-seeding of 33 million SHG members in this database has also enabled deduplication to prevent any misuse of funds in the system. A robust fund flow module has been developed to enable traceability of funds up to the CBO level. The details of financial activities that mostly happen at the CLF and VO level are shared by banks on the NRLM portal and DBT Bharat portal. The seeding of LGD location codes has enabled sharing of information with any level of granularity across other e-governance systems. The progress under the program is also being pushed on the DISHA platform, Gram Samvaad, Gram Panchayat Development Plan (GPDP), besides several Chief Minister/District Magistrate dashboards to strengthen governance and monitoring at the state, district, and panchayat levels. The data from five states having state-specific applications for NRLM (Bihar, Jharkhand, Andhra Pradesh, Telangana, and Rajasthan) is being ported to the national NRLM portal. All these initiatives have provided a huge thrust to financial and social inclusion and provided a strong reliable foundation for architecting poverty alleviation programs with targeted delivery of benefits to the vulnerable sections of society. Integration with other state-level systems and external systems has enabled convergence and provided a unified reporting and monitoring mechanism. Loans of more than INR 1,180 billion by 6.7 million groups (including repeated loans to some SHGs) have been accessed by SHGs with a relatively low NPA, besides many of the SHG members getting access to pension and insurance. The sharing of data by banks has also enabled the provision of interest subvention benefits to the deserving candidates to boost micro-enterprises. An independent study by the IRMA on DAY-NRLM in 2017 had also acknowledged the gradual increase in enterprises at the village level, per capita monthly income, and productive livestock assets. The program has resulted in a large growth in livelihood assets of households and has increased their participation in Gram Sabhas and other community institutions, thereby strengthening grassroots-level democracy.

4.5. ServicePlus: A Configurable Service Delivery Platform

The Government of India and its organizations face challenges at the governance level due to a lack of ICT infrastructure, nonstandard and/or undocumented processes, and the like. Many technical challenges often make the rollout of e-services difficult. For instance, for each service to be automated, one complete software system was built that was both costly and time-consuming. Furthermore, even if attempts were made to build separate software solutions, there was invariably a gap between the information service and the actual service. Many services also required information from other services and sharing of information was hindered by the differences in the standards adopted by the two software. Thus, the citizens were not able to get the advantage of integrated service delivery.

The Ministry of Panchayati Raj, Government of India, in consultation with the NIC, developed a configurable, metadata-based software solution framework for e-enabling panchayat-level services. ServicePlus was conceptualized to address these technical challenges so that any level of government could rapidly e-enable their services.

ServicePlus [9] is a metadata-based e-service delivery platform that is built on a low-code/no-code architecture. ServicePlus provides a platform whereby service definition can be tailored to suit the requirement of any service owner. Dynamic form designers are being used for generating application forms as well as official forms. The configurable workflow allows the department to route the application to various stakeholders as per the service needs. Custom-made output certificates and acknowledgments can be designed using the output designer. ServicePlus is built-in with various modules such as the ServicePlus—Report Module to generate MIS reports using JSON Data, ServicePlus—analytics which provide a detailed analysis of the data—and so on.

The success of ServicePlus can be gauged by the fact that it takes as little as 30 minutes to configure and launch a service rapidly. Though developed as part of ePanchayat, the capability of ServicePlus to rapidly roll out eServices has persuaded various states to adopt ServicePlus as a software solution under the eDistrict MMP (Mission Mode Project) and to e-enable services identified under the State Service Delivery Act as well. As of date, more than 1,950 services are being offered through ServicePlus by over 31 states in India. ServicePlus was also accorded with the Winner Award (under the category of ICT Applications: benefits in all aspects of life) at the World Summit on Information Society [15].

4.6. SBM—Gramin

The health and hygiene of the rural population is entirely dependent on the availability of potable drinking water, proper sanitation, and a pollution-free environment. Improper disposal of human excreta (open defecation) and other poor hygiene conditions were the major causes for the health issues among the rural population. India has the second-largest rural population, which has many deprivations. Having access to a toilet facility was one of them. It was in this context that the SBM—Gramin (SBM-G; Clean India Mission—Rural) [16], was launched by the prime minister of India on 2 October 2014. Sanitation coverage in rural India, which was less than 40 percent in 2014, has now reached 100 percent.

The main aim of SBM-G was to achieve an 'open-defecation-free' (ODF) India. This was achieved by the construction of individual household toilets and motivation to the rural communities to change their age-old practices of open defecation and adopt safe sustainable sanitation practices. Rural households in 600,000 villages across the country were identified for financial assistance to construct household toilets under SBM-G [17].

The challenge of covering the size of the population and the interstate variations was complex. Apart from the management and leadership required for implementing such a humongous program, an innovative ICT solution to monitor and evaluate the progress of the program needed to be put in place. The ICT solution for SBM-G included four major components: the SBM-G web portal (nodal portal for all critical information), SBM-G Core (a web-based application providing critical monitoring information about the progress of the scheme in terms of coverage of households, construction of community sanitary complexes, etc.), mSBM Mobile App (to monitor progress and to conduct verification audit of actual implementation at the grassroots level) [18], and the Swachh App for citizens as well as officials (provides sanitation coverage status at the village level, along with the name of beneficiaries).

The use of modern-day social media, online platforms, and collaboration systems were also enabled for reaching out to the masses and getting valuable feedback on the ground conditions. These platforms also helped in engaging the rural citizens and gradually building a 'Jan-Andolan' for achieving the goals of the mission. The unique feature of the SBM-G digital platform was the interface between the program managers and the field-level workers and its capability to manage the activities of motivators and volunteers at the village level.

The central data repository of the SBM-G includes up-to-date information on various parameters and acts as a single source of information, through which all the functionaries of different tiers of the government, as well as other stakeholders like NGOs and civic bodies, can monitor the progress of implementation, including financial management and transfer of funds to individual beneficiaries.

With 170 million target beneficiaries and a very large area to cover, ensuring timely implementation and real-time monitoring was a big challenge. The NIC played the critical role of technology partner in supporting this mammoth mission. The innovative use of ICT in implementing and monitoring the program was one of the critical success factors of SBM-G in India.

5. Impact Delivered

Several interventions have been undertaken by the DoRD to ensure the transfer of the right benefits to the right beneficiary and at the right time. A brief description of impact of various programs undertaken by DoRD has been mentioned in Figure 4.11. This has helped tremendously in increasing

Coverage & Transaction Processing Capabilities
KEY PROGRAM COVERAGES

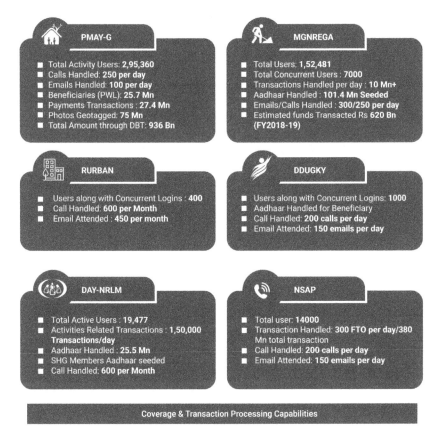

FIGURE 4.11
Coverage and Transaction-Processing Capabilities of Various Programs.

productivity, improving the quality, efficacy of program implementation, promoting transparency, and accountability. Real-time accurate data enables timely intervention and corrective decision-making for all programs of the department. The continuous adoption and enhancement of technology in the programs of DoRD have significantly transformed the governance and implementation of these programs over time. Empowered by internet technologies, help desks, and Project Management Units (PMUs) have been able to take in user feedback and further improve efficiency in the management and implementation of welfare and economic development programs of the DoRD.

Over the past five years, a lot of work has been done toward enabling convergence across schemes of the DoRD. The adoption of LGD as a common location code across all IT systems has been instrumental in realizing integrated dashboards like DISHA, which enables unified monitoring and planning at all levels of government. The state-wise progress under various schemes of the DoRD is also being pushed through APIs to DARPAN [19]—a solution being used by many states. The count of all transactions under different schemes of the DoRD is also reflected in the eTAAL [20] portal of MeitY. The statistics of transaction processing capabilities of DoRD's ICT Ecosystem mentioned in Figure 4.12 indicates the volume and impact delivered toward citizen empowerment.

Between 2014 and 2019, DBT was fully enabled in MGNREGA, PMAY-G, NSAP, and NRLM. Release of payments under schemes like MGNREGA is now happening directly to the beneficiary accounts, with total transparency. All payment requests in schemes' MISs are made through FTOs and routed through the PFMS. This has also enabled end-to-end traceability of funds with the JIT release of funds to beneficiaries, vendors, pensioners, and employees. It has the potential to reduce India's fiscal deficit by

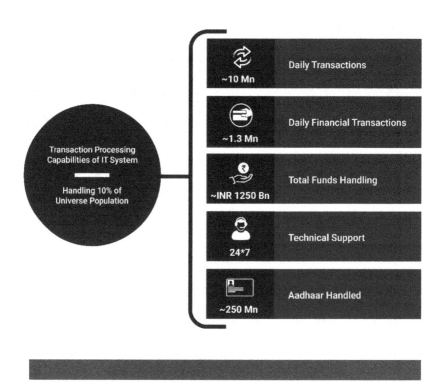

FIGURE 4.12
Transaction-Processing Capabilities of DoRD's ICT Ecosystem.

more than INR 1,500 billion [21], besides producing data-driven insights and transparency.

Until 2014, the internal workings of the DoRD were done on physical files. However, since 2015, the entire workings of the DoRD have also been e-enabled, with e-Office being used for almost every purpose. The department is now also moving toward e-enabling the receipt and appraisal of state plans and empowering the Office of Internal Audit by strengthening controls in the program management. The states will also soon be able to submit their annual financial proposals to the ministry online and will get instant feedback on the compliance of the proposal with the scheme guidelines.

The rollout of a citizen-centric Gram Samvaad mobile app in 2017 further empowered the citizens to know the quantum of funds made available to the panchayats under eight flagship schemes of the Government of India—MGNREGA, PMAY-G, PMGSY, DAY-NRLM, NSAP, DDUGKY, NRuM, and 14th Finance Commission. This has significantly strengthened governance, monitoring, and transparency at all levels of government. Efforts are also underway toward integrating the planning process of all the DoRD schemes under the GPDP through the integration of all scheme MISs with PlanPlus. Significant progress has already been achieved under DISHA to enable effective development coordination of almost all the programs of government, whether it is for infrastructure development or social and human resource development.

6. Key Challenges

Constraints of manpower, infrastructure, and capacity have always impeded the implementation of welfare programs at the last mile in rural areas. The relatively slow pace of implementation of the ambitious pan-India fiber network 'Bharat Net' (which aims to connect all the nearly 250,000 rural local bodies/gram panchayats) has been another challenge that the welfare programs have faced. Retaining experienced resources in rural areas is also a continuous challenge. Collecting rural data at the point of source remains a challenge for all programs, which creates a lot of duplication and inconsistency in data. This has also resulted in the mushrooming of multiple systems for similar activities across the country. Many of these applications are built on different technologies by different service providers; hence, for evidence-based monitoring and decision-making, complete and reliable data need to be captured. This has impeded the speedier and better targeting of the vulnerable sections of society in rural India. The need for low-cost sustainable solutions contextualized for local conditions requires continuous innovation in the application of technology to serve these developmental and social goals.

7. Conclusion and a Way Forward

As technology has permeated deep into our lives, the role of ICT has also been transformational in the design, delivery, and monitoring of any social welfare program. This has brought a significant change in the targeting and implementation of welfare schemes at the local level, particularly in rural areas. Rural development is an ongoing journey that is an important focus area for governments all over the world, guided by the SDGs. It is essential for greater socioeconomic development and for enhancing rural productivity, besides strengthening community institutions and addressing multiple dimensions of poverty. The NIC-DoRD has been pivotal in the adoption of technology in various programs of the DoRD and has helped the ministry keep pace with technology. The designs, technologies, and approaches toward the deployment of applications, maintenance of databases, provisioning of security, and the like continue to evolve as per the need of the hour. However, the evolution of technologies and their continuous adoption for improving governance, convergence, and service delivery will continue to be an ongoing journey, with each incoming wave of new technologies, further empowering the citizens and supporting the program administrators in monitoring governance and service delivery. The next decade of data-driven governance will likely see the adoption of enterprise architecture, AI, big data, and predictive analytics in most areas as the quality of data gradually improves and takes decision-making and policy-making to a new level.

To take the *Samvaad* with citizens to the next level, the current one-way flow of information from government to citizens is now being overhauled to enable a two-way flow of information between citizens and government; that is, while the government can right now convey information on various schemes to citizens through a common platform (Gram Samvaad), efforts are also being undertaken to enable the citizens to reach government through the same platform. The platform will now be leveraged to support the social audit of all programs, and citizens will also be able to submit feedback for programs through Gram Samvaad. The use of big data analytics to identify trends and predict scenarios will also be an integral part of the program governance.

For better planning under various programs, the potential of space technology also needs to be harnessed. While the geotagging of assets is now being done under almost every program, the next phase in the adoption of space technology would be the use of GIS tools to strengthen planning and monitoring. Improving the quality of data will be critical to bringing trust in such a system. This will also give a fillip to convergent and integrated planning at the local level. Spatial analytics would also bring tremendous insights for policymakers and decision-makers in implementing various social welfare programs more efficiently.

Given that the DoRD undertakes programs for millions of unskilled and semi-skilled persons, it is natural that the beneficiaries of these programs will need to be linked with several other skilling programs under Skill India to provide them a secure livelihood. The transition of select MGNREGA wage laborers into DDU-GKY is one such example. To enable convergence between programs at various levels, standard location codes have now been adopted (or mapped) across all applications of the DoRD. This will enable the horizontal convergence of the programs and will enable unified monitoring of these programs at all levels of governance that will result in optimal utilization of resources. The DISHA program, for instance, will help break silos across government departments and will enable dynamic data from multiple ministries to come together in one place, bringing in greater accountability and transparency in governance and service delivery. With the continuous evolution of technology and the advent of emerging technologies, better solutions will emerge for a more targeted, trusted, and efficient delivery of programs, and the NIC-DoRD is committed to embracing these newer technologies and harness them for the benefit of rural India.

References

[1] Ministry of Rural Development, "Transforming Lives and Livelihood Through Proactive Socio-Economic Inclusion, Integration and Empowerment of Rural India," November 2019. [Online]. Available; https://rural.nic.in/sites/default/files/Vision_Document_2019_2024.pdf.

[2] Ministry of Panchayati Raj, "Local Government Directory," [Online]. Available: https://lgdirectory.gov.in/ [Accessed 10 November 2020].

[3] Ministry of Rural Development, "The Mahatma Gandhi National Rural Employment Guarantee Act 2005," [Online]. Available: http://nrega.nic.in.

[4] Ministry of Panchayati Raj, "National Institute of Rural Development & Panchayati Raj," [Online]. Available: http://nirdpr.org.in/.

[5] Ministry of Rural Development, "National Rural Infrastructure Development Agency," [Online]. Available: http://14.143.90.243/nrida/dgs-message.

[6] Ministry of Panchayati Raj, "Panchayat Enterprise Suite," [Online]. Available: https://panchayatonline.gov.in.

[7] Ministry of Panchayati Raj, "eGramSwaraj: Simplified Work Based Accounting Application for Panchayati Raj," [Online]. Available: https://accountingonline.gov.in.

[8] Ministry of Panchayati Raj, "National Panchayat Portal-Govt. of India," [Online]. Available: https://panchayatportals.gov.in.

[9] Ministry of Panchayati Raj, "ServicePlus: Metadate based Integrated eService Delivery Framework," [Online]. Available: https://serviceOnline.gov.in.

[10] Ministry of Panchayati Raj, "eGramSwaraj: Simplified Work Based Accounting Application for Panchayati Raj," [Online]. Available: https://Reportingonline.gov.in.

[11] The World Bank, "Social Registries for Social Assistance and Beyond: A Guidance Note & Assessment Tool," 20 November 2017. [Online]. Available: www.worldbank.org/en/topic/socialprotection/publication/social-regis tries-for-social-assistance-and-beyond-a-guidance-note-and-assessment-tool [Accessed 7 November 2020].

[12] Ministry of Rural Development, "Pradhan Mantri Awaas Yojana-Gramin," [Online]. Available: https://pmayg.nic.in/ [Accessed 7 November 2020].

[13] Ministry of Rural Development, [Online]. Available: https://rural.nic.in/ [Accessed 7 November 2020].

[14] Ministry of Rural Development, "Deen Dayal Upadhyaya Grameen Kaushalya Yojana," [Online]. Available: http://ddugky.gov.in/ [Accessed 7 November 2020].

[15] World Summit on the Information Society (WSIS, ITU), "Champion Award: Category 8 — AL C7. ICT Applications: Benefits in All Aspects of Life—E-business," [Online]. Available: www.itu.int/net4/wsis/stocktaking/Prizes/2021/Champions?jts=A98IJP&idx=11&page=8#start.

[16] Ministry of Jal Shakti, Department of Drinking Water and Sanitation, "Swachh Bharat Mission Gramin," [Online]. Available: https://sbm.gov.in/sbmReport/home.aspx.

[17] Seemantinee Sengupta, Deepak Chandra Misra, Marut Chaudhury and Om Prakash, "Role of Technology in Success of Rural Sanitation Revolution in India," *ICEGOV*, April 2019. [Online]. Available: https://dl.acm.org/doi/10.1145/3326365.3326367.

[18] Ministry of Jal Shakti, Department of Drinking Water and Sanitation, "mSBM," [Online]. Available: http://sbm.gov.in/msbm/Public/Home.aspx.

[19] Ministry of Electronics and Information Technology, "DARPAN-Dashboard for Analytical Review of Projects Across Nation," [Online]. Available: https://dmdashboard.nic.in.

[20] National Informatics Centre, "eTAAL -Electronic Transaction Aggregation & Analysis Layer," [Online]. Available: https://etaal.gov.in/.

[21] "India's Public Finance Architecture is the Real Culprit in Gorakhpur and Bhagalpur," *Livemint*, 25 August 2017. [Online]. Available: www.livemint.com/Opinion/I6UMVabJwiukGs7rB5bmSM/Indias-public-finance-architecture-is-the-real-culprit-in-G.html [Accessed 10 March 2020].

5

Transforming the Indian Education System through IT-Enabled Services

Rajender Sethi, Yogesh Kumar Singh,
Saba Akhtar, and Mohd. Anwar Khan

1. Introduction

ICT-enabled solutions have been remodeling the conventional learning and teaching methodologies by the introduction of solutions such as open knowledge resources, certification, digital learning courses, digital career services, mobile learning, and so on. This chapter highlights digital interventions introduced in the public, as well as the private, education system and their impact on all beneficiaries.

The quality of education and the literacy rate play a vital role in evolving factors that pave the way for overall economic development. Indian education system aims to introduce a uniform education standard across the country while introducing national heritage and culture to students. With the digital revolution, learning has stepped out of the four-walled classrooms.

One of the factors set to impact the Indian economy in the next decade is the ability to exploit the 'demographic dividend' of having a large share of the population of working age. This dividend will only be earned with a well-educated workforce, which, in turn, requires a strong education system. Education technology can address such issues by facilitating better information exchange, faculty training, and inspiring students [1].

The National Education Policy (NEP) aims to universalize preprimary education by 2025 and provide foundational literacy/numeracy for all by 2025 [2]. It proposes new curricular and pedagogical structure, with 5 + 3 + 3 + 4 design (Foundational Stage + Preparatory Stage + Middle Stage + Secondary Stage) covering children in the age group 3 to 18 years. It aims to develop technical and entrepreneurial skills in students through vocational education in school and the higher education system. Figure 5.1 highlights the key principles of National Education Policy in India.

One thing that has remained constant throughout the transformational journey of the Indian education system since the Vedic period is the importance of education for personal development and upskilling. In the Indian

DOI: 10.1201/9781003111351-5

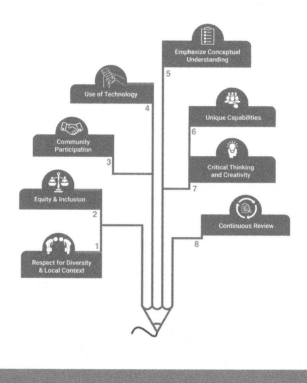

FIGURE 5.1
Key Principles of NEP 2020.

constitution, the right to education has been listed as a fundamental right as it plays a pivotal role in weaving a homogeneous socioeconomic fabric for the nation. India has 600 million people younger than 25, which is almost half of the total population [3].

The roots of Indian institutionalized teaching lie in the Vedic Gurukul system. The modern Indian education system has been developed over the years by incorporating structural and administrative changes required to develop a curriculum that can complement international standards of education.

2. Educational Setup in India

The education sector in India consists of government-operated, privately owned educational institutions and allied education products and services providers [4]. A strenuous education network is required to harness the potential of human capital from a significant young population in India. Various schemes launched by the government are directed toward providing enhanced universal access to elementary education for all groups of society. The Ministry of Education is responsible for planned development, including expanding access and improving the quality of educational institutions throughout the country [5].

The Department of School Education and Literacy focuses on the 'universalization of education' and harmonizing the school education system across different levels of the federated system including the center, the states, and districts. It is responsible for the preparation of strategic plans with a broader goal of improving school effectiveness measured in terms of equal opportunities for schooling and learning outcomes.

The Department of Higher Education is responsible for the overall development of the higher education sector, in terms of both policy and planning [6]. Under a planned development process, the department looks after the expansion of access and qualitative improvement in higher education using a digital transformational road map, through world-class universities, colleges, and stand-alone institutions. Figure 5.2 illustrates the institutional structure of the education sector in India.

Apex organizations and regulatory bodies have been given statutory authority for the enforcement of common standards across the sector. To regulate education standards, various bodies/organizations have been set up depending on specialization, for example, National Institute of Educational Planning and Administration (NIEPA), a deemed university for planning and administration, NCERT/National Council for teacher education NIOS for school education; UGC for higher education, 'All India Council for Technical Education' for technical education, National Medical Council (NMC)/Dental Council of India (DCI)/Pharmacy Council of India (PCI) for medical/dental/pharmacy, and many other councils like the Council of Architecture (COA) for Architecture.

Central Board of Secondary Education (CBSE), Indian Certificate of Secondary Education (ICSE), and state education boards outline the curriculum at the international, national, and state levels for secondary and senior secondary school students. Few schools are also affiliated with international boards such as International Baccalaureate Organization (IBO) and Cambridge International Examinations (CIE) Boards also conduct examinations, set education standards, and promote innovations in teaching-learning methodologies by devising student-friendly paradigms.

The National Testing Agency (NTA) has been set up as a specialized agency to conduct entrance examinations for admission/fellowship in higher educational institutions to assess the competence of candidates for admissions and recruitment. The National Board of Examinations (NBE) has been set up primarily for admissions to medical colleges and conducting examinations.

Universities and stand-alone institutions such as IITs, NITs, and IIMs have been established to play an important role as leaders in teaching and learning, in education, research, and technology. Universities provide professional training for high-level jobs, as well as the education necessary for holistic

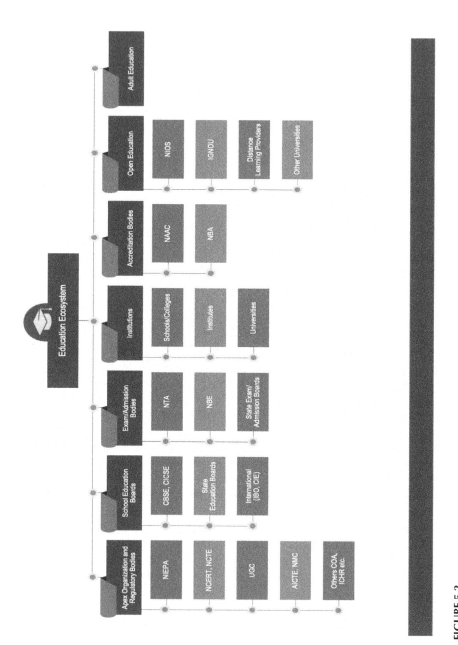

FIGURE 5.2
Institutional Structure of the Education Sector.

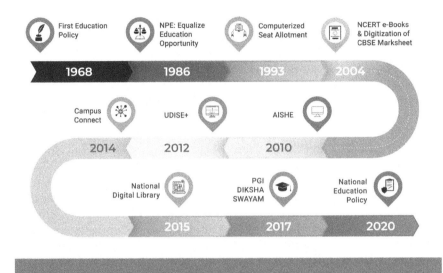

FIGURE 5.3
Digital Interventions and Timelines for Education System.

development. A nationwide network of schools and colleges offers students balanced learning opportunities in the five aspects of development, that is, moral, intellectual, physical, social, and aesthetic, thereby nurturing them to become responsible citizens. Accreditation bodies like National Assessment and Accreditation Council (NAAC) and National Board of Accreditation have been given the mandate to make quality assurance an integral part of the functioning of educational institutions. Figure 5.3 highlights the digital interventions and timelines of education system in India.

Resource centers for open and distance learning (ODL) like Indira Gandhi National Open University, National Institute of Open Schooling (NIOS), and School of Open Learning, University of Delhi (DU) are modern frontiers of knowledge and promote its dissemination through sustainable ODL systems. Adult education aims at extending educational options to those adults who have missed the opportunity and have crossed the age of formal education but now feel a need for learning of any type, including literacy, basic education, skill development (vocational education), and equivalency.

3. Global Trends Shaping Education

Globally, educational institutions have embarked on a digital journey moving from early stages of digital enablement through digital optimization to digital transformation. Gartner CIO's 2020 agenda survey identifies higher education as the industry that is most susceptible to disruptions by digital technologies [7]. Gartner has identified five trends for K–12 education, including skills-based curriculum, AI, adaptive learning, e-Sports, and immersive technologies, to create a holistic learning experience [8].

Blended learning (bLearning) supported by digital technology and competency-based medical education (CBME) are transforming professional education in the 21st century [9]. Numerous cases suggest the benefits of the bLearning modality and the possibilities it offers to boost the development of skills in different disciplines. The University of Central Florida (UCF) took on a mission to break the 'iron triangle' of access, cost, and quality by going on a journey from analog to digital [10]. UCF then reached a state of true digital transformation, introducing fully digitally dependent adaptive learning while providing affordable quality higher education to students regardless of time, preference, or other considerations. It has been observed from the interaction with students of the Gulf region that they have challenges with the online method of knowledge delivery in higher education [11]. Methods of learning and cognition are made much easier with the help of lecture broadcasting, delivering both recorded lectures and live, webcasting guest lectures, course topic demonstration videos, and so on.

Higher broadband in Malaysia is also an enabler of social transformation— one of which is education especially among secondary school students [12]. The Kingdom of Saudi Arabia has made a significant investment in deploying technology to develop infrastructure and resources for special education [13]. Various success criteria such as professional experience and technology skills of special educators, administrative support, assistive hardware/software issues, pedagogical issues, and teaching style are the key influencing factors of the implementation process.

4. School Education

The technological transformation of the schooling system started with the publication of online results followed by e-books, online classes, virtual classrooms, and digitization of academic records. As shown in Figure 5.4, there have been significant transformation in School Education in India.

4.1. Program Management and Schemes

Samagra Shiksha envisages one comprehensive strategic plan for the development of school education at all levels [14]. The scheme envisages 'school' as a continuum from preschool, primary, upper primary, secondary, to senior secondary levels. The vision of this scheme is to establish inclusive and equitable quality education from preschool to the senior secondary stage in

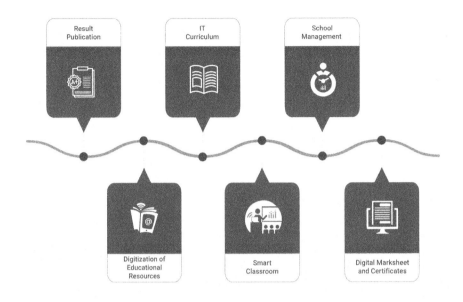

FIGURE 5.4
Transformation in School Education.

accordance with the SDG for education. The Right of Children to Free and Compulsory Education Act, or Right to Education Act, makes education a fundamental right for every child between the ages of 6 and 14 and specifies minimum norms in elementary schools.

Sarva Shiksha Abhiyan is a flagship program for the achievement of the universalization of elementary education in a time-bound manner. It seeks to open new schools in those habitations that do not have schooling facilities and strengthen existing school infrastructure through the provision of additional classrooms, toilets, drinking water, maintenance, and school improvement grants. Various student assistance programs like the Mid-Day Meal scheme, the free supply of school uniforms and textbooks, regular health checkups, and more are provided under the provision of compulsory primary education.

The Mid-Day Meals Automated Reporting and Management System has been developed to improve real-time monitoring of data [15]. Real-time reporting of midday meal data of schools to the block, district, and state levels to ensure the availability of this information for official analysis and for effective remedial actions.

Under the PM eVidya program, students and teachers will get multimodal access to digital education. The National Digital Literacy Mission, DISHA, and PM Gramin Digital Saksharta Abhiyan are empowering the citizens by training them to operate computers and digital devices.

4.2. School Management

School management is defined as the process of planning, organizing, and managing the activities of a school utilizing human and material resources to effectively and efficiently accomplish the functioning of teaching and administrative activities.

4.2.1. School Registry

Registries play an important role in the systematic data collection and monitoring for improving the quality of education. Registries act as a single point of reference for the broad set of stakeholders in the education community and play an important role in school affiliation and management. All India School Education Survey was conducted periodically by NCERT to collect, compile, and disseminate information on the country's overall progress in the area of school education. This was followed up by the Unified District Information on School Education (UDISE) for maintaining school information, like infrastructure, teachers/staff, classes, facilities, and so on, and identifying each school with a unique UDISE code.

The UDISE+ [16] is one of the largest management information systems in school education. It has drastically improved the quality and credibility of the data provided by the schools. UDISE data is the base data for allocation of Annual Work Plan and Budget of states/union territories.

4.2.2. School Management and Planning Software

School management and planning software offers an integrated solution with a built-in reporting and analysis tool for the complete automation of schools by undertaking administrative tasks such as attendance, examination, communication, payroll, admission, inventory, transfers, library, and the like.

BanglarShiksha ('education' in Bengal) portal is a one-stop place for all information related to the entire school education ecosystem of the state. Various benefits such as scholarships, textbooks, bicycles, school bags, shoes, and so on are being given to students.

ShalaDarpan is an integrated school management portal for Rajasthan, where 'live student data' are compiled to improve the accessibility of data, promote standardization, and enable data usage to improve efficiency, create transparency and enhance accountability in the system.

4.3. Teacher Management

Various examinations have been introduced at the national and state levels for the implementation of standards and benchmarking of teacher quality in the recruitment process. Score/ranks generated from these examinations act as one of the essential qualifications for a person to be eligible for appointment as a teacher. These examinations are a marked deviation from the conventional recruitment process wherein the candidates were shortlisted from employment exchanges on a seniority basis followed by pen-and-paper-based examination and/or interview.

CBSE conducts an OMR sheet-based Central Teacher Eligibility Test using the examination management system for eligible candidates for recruitment as a teacher. Similar examinations like Uttarakhand Teacher Eligibility Test (UTET) are conducted for teacher recruitment for teachers in Uttarakhand.

4.3.1. Learning and Assessment

A robust system of adaptive assessment has been implemented at all levels in the education sector in order to help teachers regularly evaluate their progress and identify specific topics on the learning ladder continuum and thus draft individualized learning plans for themselves. Present-day faculty have been equipped with digital course repositories like DIKSHA and handheld devices to undertake courses and topic references as and when required in classroom studies.

DIKSHA has been launched to support the digital infrastructure for knowledge sharing in the form of an open-source digital platform to support teachers and learners leverage technology for improved teaching and learning outcomes. The application helps to create training content, profile, in-class resources, assessment aids, news, announcement, and connect with the teacher community at large.

4.3.2. Transfers and Posting

Online modules have been developed to monitor the deployment of teachers across schools at the state and national levels. The system monitors the faculty requirement at an institution level based on the total number of students and subjects included in the curriculum. A transparent process has been implemented wherein the transfer process is executed as per government norms, eligibility, and choice of posting.

4.4. Student Management

Student management involves information systems to maintain a centralized database accessible to the trusted beneficiaries. The system allows storage, management, and distribution of information to facilitate direct benefit transfer, performance tracking, communication updates, and regulatory compliance.

4.4.1. Academic Results

The first wave of the digital revolution in the education sector was in the form of result publication. Earlier, the results were consolidated manually and stored in printed form and were published in gazette notification and communicated through the newspaper. Under an initiative led by the CBSE, secondary school results were published online and soon gained popularity among other departments and institutions in the country.

The Results Gateway [17] has been established indicating previous and current results to be announced. Within an hour, the results are disseminated to all stakeholders. The cost of result publication and publishing time was significantly reduced as compared to print practices.

4.4.2. eTextbooks

In 2004, a tsunami struck the coastal areas of the country leading to an acute shortage of books in these areas. NCERT came up with the solution by creating and uploading e-copies of all the books, which ensured instantaneous delivery of educational resources to students.

It has also led to a decline in carbon footprint by reducing the hewing of trees for manufacturing paper. In the National Repository of Open Educational Resources, more than 10,732 files are uploaded. Some of the e-content have been translated and are now available in 29 languages [18].

4.4.3. Information Communication Technology in Curriculum

With the introduction of e-books, computer science was introduced as one of the subjects in the senior secondary curriculum. The students were introduced to programming techniques using C++, Pascal, and other tools. Virtual vocational training, virtual labs, and skill development courses have been incorporated as part of the school curriculum. Multimodal access to education material is provided to students through web portals, mobile apps, TV channels, radio, podcasts, and the like with a coherent user experience.

4.4.4. Smart Classroom

The next wave of technology adoption was in the form of smart classrooms moving from blackboard to digital board [19]. Smart classrooms are digital learning spaces that provide opportunities for teaching and learning by integrating technology solutions, such as PCs, software, firmware, feedback, internet connectivity, machine learning, AI and data analytics, and digital boards. For visually and hearing-impaired students, study material has been developed in Digitally Accessible Information System and in sign language.

Speech–to–sign language conversion software has been developed by the NIC in Chhattisgarh for converting the classroom sessions into sign language for specially abled students. The system uses artificial intelligence to analyze the audio and video in recorded sessions and converts them into relevant sign language.

4.4.5. Digital Marksheets and Certificates

Another major transformation that is currently underway is the digitization of academic marksheets and certificates. Originally, the marksheets/certificates were printed, signed in ink, and dispatched to students through schools, resulting in manual errors, postal delays, and high paper consumption with no inbuilt mechanism for verification. The online availability of documents and their verification have simplified the process. Education and technical boards have been onboarded on DigiLocker to provide marksheets and certificates to students [20].

5. Higher Education

This department covers the gamut of higher education services, including examinations and counseling and acting as a medium of transition between school and higher education.

5.1. Entrance Examination

Examination management services started with the introduction of the qualifying examination for admissions to central institutes such as IIT and regional institutes such as the NIT. Examination management services have evolved over the years by incorporating IT technologies like responsive web applications and facial recognition technology to provide a streamlined process of examinations to users. Figure 5.5 showcases the transformation of examination system in India.

5.1.1. Registration System

Earlier, every institute conducted its own examination, and the reservation was based on social category and domicile. Forms were made available through the existing network of banks, post offices, and colleges. Forms had to be filled in and sent to the regional offices by post. Examinations were conducted in offline mode with a subjective question paper. Examination bodies had to invest a lot of time, money, and manpower in printing, test center management, faculty management, and communications.

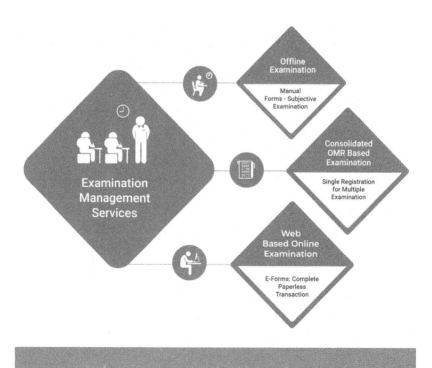

FIGURE 5.5
Examination System Transformation.

Previously, students had to fill multiple forms and cope up with the dispro-portionate supply of forms with respect to demand. There was a considerable expenditure on travel and registration fees. To reduce the financial burden and time efforts for the candidates', common examinations were adopted for admission to central institutes. The IIT JEE was inducted for admission to IITs while the All India Engineering Entrance Examination for NITs. Gradually, ranks generated through these examinations became benchmarks for the selection of a candidate and were adopted by other public and private institutions as well. Around the same time, scanning technologies and image processing introduced OMR, which was widely used for the examination process for assessing candidate-marked data.

With the introduction of the common examination, students could contest for seats in multiple colleges through a single form, which led to reduced physical reporting. The introduction of OMR sheets reduced the manpower and time effort required for examination bodies to assess the applications. Examination management services provide end-to-end technical services for conducting various examinations by assisting premier organizing bodies and other institutions.

5.1.2. E-Forms: Complete Paperless Transaction

The application mode using offline forms was marred with postal delays and cases of mismanagement arising due to manual intervention at multiple stages. An immense amount of paperwork and time was spent printing and collecting the forms. The proliferation of broadband networks across the country and increasing affordability of desktop PCs laid the foundation for web-based forms providing the convenience of 24/7 form filling. A nation-wide network of digital examination centers and computer labs have been created providing state-of-the-art infrastructure facilities for conducting online examinations.

Automated systems strengthened the transparency and authenticity of the selection process. Email and short message service integration for triggered updates ensures the uniform dissemination of information to all candidates. The service has been designed in a dynamic and user-friendly interface for a simple form completion process. The real-time monitoring of key param-eters is carried out, and every process performed by the user is tracked and recorded for maintaining an audit log.

5.1.3. Payments

Postal orders and demand drafts were the initial mode of payment. The candidate had to visit the issuing post office/bank and get a demand draft/postal order issued in the name of the examination body. The system gener-ated three copies of the challan that were issued to the candidate, who had to visit a nearby partner bank to make the payment and get the challan copies signed and stamped. The examination body's copy of the challan was sent by post along with the application forms.

With the advent of banking technologies including Bharat UPI, payment wallets, internet banking, and the like, external payment gateways offered by leading banks were integrated with the application. Candidates are not required to visit a bank/post office to complete the application process and receive instant information about the payment success/failure.

5.1.4. Examinations

Subjective examinations were conducted in pen-and-paper mode, with the candidate responding to the questions in short or long answers.

An objective-type examination was introduced whereby multiple choices were given for each question. The candidate had to mark the bubbles for correct answers in the OMR sheet. The OMR sheets were scanned to create a database of recorded responses for the candidate and subsequent marking.

Examinations are being conducted online using desktop/web-based applications. Exam proctoring is conducted using audio/video analytics to impose curbs on malpractices during the examination. The NTA is entrusted to improve the equity and quality in education by administering research-based valid, reliable, efficient, transparent, fair, and international level assessments. Some of the major examinations are NEET, CMAT, GPAT, JEE, NCHM, IIFT, and UGC-NET, among others.

5.2. Counseling and Admission

Counseling and admission services have transformed manifold since their inception in the form of manual OCR forms. Currently, the process has been decentralized using digital technologies, providing the facility to apply from anywhere anytime.

5.2.1. Institute and Course Selection through OCR Forms

Brochures were printed by counseling boards with detachable OCR forms. Students had to fill in the forms as per the instructions and forms were sent to regional offices set up by counseling boards via post. The postal order was the integrated mode of payment. With the introduction of the brochure booklet, information required for participating in the counseling process was made available to applicants in a single document.

5.2.2. Centralized On-Campus Counseling

To have centralized control and impart greater knowledge regarding seat matrix and reservation policies, the entire process of counseling was shifted to reporting centers equipped with internet connectivity. Students had to report to these centers to register and lock the preferred choices in the presence of a curating official. The demand draft was the integrated mode of payment.

Due to the centralized counseling process, counseling board could administer greater control over the counseling process and candidate management. The allocation of seats was done as per merit, reservation policies, and preferences of institutions and branches exercised by the candidates. The NIC provided the requisite infrastructure and network connectivity at reporting centers. In 1993, the computerized allotment of seats was conducted for Bachelor of Medicine and Bachelor of Surgery (MBBS)/Bachelor of Dental Surgery (BDS) courses with teletext display of seat allotment status on multiple television monitors.

5.2.3. Distributed Off-Campus Counseling

Setting up a regional center required high infrastructure cost and internet connectivity. Failure of the network at one center stalled the entire process. To address all these concerns, some of the activities related to candidate registration and application submission were shifted to a distributed off-campus mode wherein candidates had to register online and visit the reporting centers for choice filling and locking.

The counseling and admission services developed by the NIC are used by central/state counseling boards for admission to premier institutions such as IITs, NITs, IIITs, and central-/state-funded universities/institutions in India. Various domains are covered, including engineering (degree, diploma, and ITI), medical, architecture, pharmacy, agriculture, hotel management, and so on, catering to candidates from 8th/10th standard up to postgraduate [21].

5.2.4. e-Counseling and Admission Services

Earlier, physical reporting was mandatory for participating in the seat allotment while modes of payment were limited to demand draft and bank-generated challan. The entire counseling process was shifted online and made available to the user as a service suite. All the steps involved in the process are rolled out in the form of sub-modules. The process starts with candidate registration and fee payment. The seat matrix for the current academic year

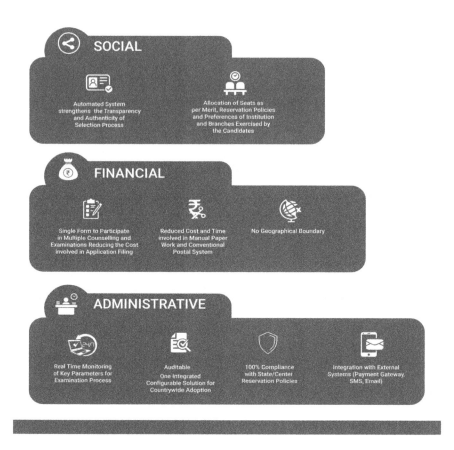

FIGURE 5.6
Impact of e-Counseling Services.

and reservation policy are updated by participating institutes. Seat allotment is done in multiple rounds, with provisions for seats up to gradation and seat locking [22]. A mock counseling round is carried out to provide the probable institute and course to the candidate. Figure 5.6 explains the social, financial, and administrative impact of e-Counseling services.

5.3. Scholarships

Different scholarship schemes are being offered at the central and state levels to provide financial support to students from weaker economic and social backgrounds. Students had to fill multiple forms and assess the eligibility criteria of different schemes. The introduction of a scholarship management system has led to a centralized and transparent system with faster disposal of scholarships along with unique beneficiary identification.

The National Scholarships Portal is a one-stop solution through which various services starting from student application, processing, sanction, and disbursal of various scholarships to the students are enabled.

5.4. College/University Management

5.4.1 Institute Registry

Institute registries play a crucial role in making data-backed policy decisions and research for the development of the education sector. A centrally managed institute registry is being provided as a service to all stakeholders via an API. A unique identifier is provided to each college, institute, university, and other educational institution with varied semantics.

All India Survey on Higher Education (AISHE) [23] has emerged as a single source of truth for the higher education sector providing an all-inclusive spectacle of higher education in the country. Data are being collected on several parameters such as teachers, student enrollment, programs, examination results, education finance, infrastructure, and the like. Sustainable Development Pointers for the education sector, such as gross enrollment ratio, pupil–teacher ratio, and gender parity index, are calculated from the data collected through the AISHE.

5.4.2. University Administration and Information Management

The system provides a comprehensive automated system for digitizing the administrative operations such as student enrollment, affiliation, admission, fees, examination management, curriculum, academic records, and so on. Figure 5.7 represents the key components of University Management System in India.

CHANAKYA is a web-enabled, role and workflow-based solution to accomplish tasks like admission, registration, fee payment, examination form entry, result processing, transfer request generation, result publication, certificate generation, and so on. The Integrated University

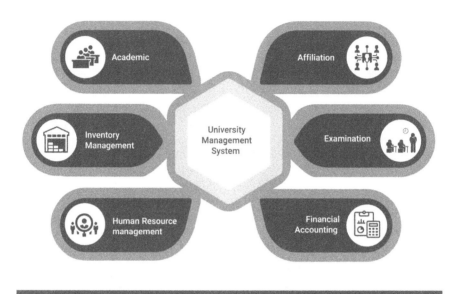

FIGURE 5.7
College/University Management System.

Suite has been implemented in the states of Kerala, Manipur, and Tamil Nadu. It provides management, faculties, staff, and students with immediate access to real-time information and is an adaptable solution serving all sizes and types of institutions.

6. Open Education

Distance learning in India for higher education was initiated in the form of correspondence courses in 1962 in response to the ever-increasing demand for higher education that could not be met by the conventional system. The Delhi University established a School of Correspondence Courses and Continuing Education in 1962. The establishment of IGNOU in New Delhi in 1985 further proved to be a significant milestone in the adoption of Distance Learning in India. It provides a central organization for guiding and coordinating the activities of all distance education institutes and state open universities in the country. The NIOS was established in November 1989 and provides several vocational and community-oriented courses as well as general and academic courses at the secondary and senior secondary level.

The study center is a part of an overall system of support for learners. Almost all the distance education institutes (DEIs) have established study centers at different places for attracting students and to offer support services. A few open universities, in addition to study centers, established regional centers for greater administrative efficiency and to serve as a liaison between the parent institution and the study centers in the respective regions. It is the sub-office of the parent institution for all practical purposes.

Many in India still live in its villages. The most significant surplus of human talent in India lies in its interior. Virtual classrooms are tools that will help educators tap this talent pool. Virtual classrooms will also help talented educators living in rural areas connect students across India and the world. The inclusion of virtual classrooms in rural areas can certainly have a tremendous impact on youth and pave the way for their success and the sustainable growth of the nation.

Massive Open Online Courses (MOOCs) provides the participants with free access and unrestricted participation to any course of their choice. Besides the conventional modes of teaching such as lectures, videos, and reading material; MOOCs also provide a platform for interactive forums. Learners' performance can be monitored easily by using the data captured during the start of courses. The flexibility of course has opened new gateways for working professionals or people with a daily obligation to aspire and complete higher degree programs.

Education tech initiatives have extended the scope of learning beyond the four-walled classrooms by providing a flexible environment and a personalized progress report. The government has created various digital learning platforms and repositories, including NPTEL [24], SWAYAM [25], ePGPathshala [26], NISHTHA, and eAcharya, among others, providing a diverse array of courses for subject matter expertise and soft skill development. Distance learning programs are also offered by various private institutions including Symbiosis Centre for Distance Learning, Sikkim Manipal University, Institute of Management Technology (IMT), and the like.

The Government of India has launched Pradhan Mantri e-Vidya, which will be a comprehensive e-learning platform integrating all efforts relating to digital and on-air education to provide multimodal access to free educational resources. Thirty-four Direct to Home (DTH) channels are devoted to telecasting high-quality educational programs on a 24/7 basis using the GSAT-15 satellite under the Swayam Prabha initiative. Course content provided by leading government agencies/bodies like NPTEL, IITs, UGC, CEC, IGNOU, NCERT, and NIOS is telecasted at multiple time slots during the day.

With the COVID-19 pandemic creating a global impact and bringing a state of lockdown, education technology platforms by leading startups have witnessed astonishing adoption and growth. Products and services developed by several Indian companies like BYJU's, Toppr, Unacademy, and Vedantu have tried to mimic the live classroom environment by introducing new features. These companies have developed interactive learning programs for the student along with courses for competitive exam preparation such as for the JEE, NEET, CAT, IAS, GRE, and GMAT.

7. Conclusion

India has been successful in developing an extensive network of educational institutions across the country. The government is determined to develop a national digital education infrastructure that could play an important role in the Government of India's vision to achieve a 5 trillion-dollar economy by 2025. Digital transformation has led to process reengineering, improving the ease of services including digital contents, results, specifically in examinations and admissions for preferred institutes using consolidated forms without any traveling hassles. The system incorporates principles of e-governance and social inclusion allowing candidates from diverse backgrounds to benefit from financial assistance offered by the central/state governments as per the eligibility.

> Education is accepted worldwide as a fundamental asset for individuals as well as societies. The digitization of the Indian education system can play an important role in increasing the affordability and quality of education. Education technology (edtech), mainly information and communication technology can devise new methods of information exchange by delivering better lessons, training teachers, and empowering students.

The curriculum is being updated to develop industry and academia connections, teaching methodologies, and career advisory services. Existing channels of accreditation and regulation need to be revamped for developing higher system resilience. Various spheres related to capacity utilization including brain drain, high dropout rate, student-to-teacher ratio, and gross enrollment pattern need to be worked on.

National directories of key identifiers for the education sector can be created for subsequent usage in all dependent applications and schemes. Various pilot programs should be initiated for the adoption of emerging technology to facilitate immersive learning, parametric assessment, and gamification of teaching practices. There is a need to personalize the teaching practices by identifying and motivating each student as per their ability.

India can be at the forefront of dynamic technological disruptions in the education sector by becoming a digital education hub in the world. Our country boasts a wide palette of prolific institutions in the higher education sector and has been striving for the internationalization of our schools by developing multidisciplinary universities. Technology will play an important role in the expansive growth of the Indian education sector.

References

[1] N. Sawaikar, "Education Technology and Indian Schools," *Forbes India*, 2019. [Online]. Available: www.forbesindia.com/article/weschool/education-technology-and-indian-schools/53149/1 [Accessed 1 April 2019].

[2] Ministry of Education, "National Education Policy (NEP)," 2020. [Online]. Available: www.education.gov.in/ [Accessed 1 December 2020].

[3] Ian Jack, "India Has 600 million Young People—and They're Set to Change Our World," *The Guardian*, 13 January 2018. [Online]. Available: www.theguardian.com/commentisfree/2018/jan/13/india-600-million-young-people-world-cities-internet [Accessed 20 March 2020].

[4] British Council, "The School Education System in India," 2019. [Online]. Available: www.britishcouncil.in/sites/default/files/school_education_system_in_india_report_2019_final_web.pdf [Accessed 1 December 2019].

[5] Ministry of Education, [Online]. Available: www.education.gov.in/ [Accessed 1 December 2020].

[6] Ministry of Education, "Department of Higher Education," 2020. [Online]. Available: www.education.gov.in/en/higher_education [Accessed 20 December 2020].

[7] Robert Yanckello, "Education Digital Transformation and Innovation Primer for 2021" *Gartner*, 12 January 2021.

[8] Kelly Calhoun Williams, "Top 5 Trends Impacting K-12 Education in 2021," *Gartner*, 1 February 2021.

[9] E. M. T. Maza, et al., "Blended Learning Supported by Digital Technology and Competency-Based Medical Education: A Case Study of the Social Medicine Course at the Universidad de los Andes, Colombia,"in *International Journal of Educational Technology in Higher Education*, vol. 13, no. 1, 2016, pp. 1–13.

[10] Jan-Martin Lowendahl, "Case Study: Digital Transformation Journey (University of Central Florida)," *Gartner*, 9 April 2020.

[11] H. U. Khan, "Possible Effect of Video Lecture Capture Technology on the Cognitive Empowerment of Higher Education Students: A Case Study of Gulf-Based University," *International Journal of Innovation and Learning*, vol. 20, no. 1, 2016, pp. 68–84.

[12] Megat Zuhairy Megat Tajuddin and Ibrahim Rohman, "The Impact of Broadband Penetration on the Student Performance in Primary and Secondary School in Malaysia," Proceedings of the 11th International Conference on Theory and Practice of Electronic Governance (ICEGOV'18). Association for Computing Machinery, New York, NY, 2018, pp. 111–117. https://doi.org/10.1145/3209415.3209490.

[13] M. Fakrudeen, M. H. Miraz and P. Excell, "Success Criteria for Implementing Technology in Special Education: A Case Study," arXiv preprint arXiv:1708.09404, 2017.

[14] Ministry of Education, "Mid-Day Meal Scheme," 2020. [Online]. Available: http://mdm.nic.in/ [Accessed 20 December 2020].

[15] Ministry of Electronics & IT, "DigiLocker," 2020. [Online]. Available: https://digilocker.gov.in/ [Accessed 20 December 2020].

[16] Department of School Education, "Unified District Information System for Education," 2019. [Online]. Available: https://udiseplus.gov.in [Accessed 1 December 2020].

[17] Ministry of Education, "National Repository of Open Educational Resources," 2020. [Online]. Available: https://nroer.gov.in/ [Accessed 19 October 2020].

[18] Minisrty of Education, "HRD Minister Launches Operation Digital Board," 20 February 2019. [Online]. Available: https://mhrd.gov.in/sites/upload_files/mhrd/files/PR_ODB.pdf [Accessed 20 March 2020].

[19] National Informatics Centre, "e-Counseling Services," 2019. [Online]. Available: https://ecounseling.nic.in [Accessed 1 February 2020].

[20] Ministry of Education, "Joint Seat Allocation Authority," 2019. [Online]. Available: https://josaa.nic.in [Accessed 1 January 2020].

[21] Department of Higher Education, "All India Survey on Higher Education," 2019. [Online]. Available: http://aishe.gov.in [Accessed 1 December 2020].

[22] Ministry of Education, "National Programme on Technology Enhanced Learning," 2020. [Online]. Available: https://nptel.ac.in [Accessed 20 December 2020].

[23] Ministry of Education, "Swayam," 2020. [Online]. Available: https://swayam.gov.in/ [Accessed 20 December 2020].

[24] Ministry of Education, "ePG-Pathshala," 2020. [Online]. Available: http://epgp.inflibnet.ac.in/ [Accessed 20 December 2020].

[25] eCounseling Division, "Gateway to Exam Results in India," [Online]. Available: https://results.gov.in.

[26] Department of School Education, "Samagra Shiksha," 2020. [Online]. Available: http://samagrashiksha.in/ [Accessed 20 December 2020].

6

The Changing Landscape of Government Budget and Treasury Operations with IT as Key Driver

Nagesh Shastri, Dipankar Sengupta, and Pradeep Kumar Garg

1. Introduction

Finance is the fulcrum for the development of the economy of any country. Initiatives for the development in various areas by the government are largely dependent on the availability of finance to fund the various schemes and programs in the social, as well as the economic, sector. Keeping the fiscal deficit in check by reducing the gap between the expenditure incurred and revenue earned is the basic tenet to prudent fiscal management, which, in turn, can lead to a buoyant economy. It is a complex exercise and involves proper planning of expenditure by various ministries, departments, and implementation of policies to mobilize the revenue from various sources, be it direct taxes related to individuals and corporates or indirect taxes such as customs, excise, service tax, and so on.

Given the complexity and multidimensional facets of sound financial management, it is imperative that digitalization has a critical role to play in public finance management involving functions such as budget preparation, management of borrowings, and expenditure. Although the services to be provided are more in the ambit of government-to-government (G2G) services, services to other stakeholders such as employees—both serving and pensioners—vendors, and others also play an important role.

The central government, as well as the state governments, recognizing the far-reaching impact of digitalization, have devoted efforts in this direction in the late 1980s. The concerted efforts made by various agencies have altered the digitalization landscape in the finance domain significantly in the last four decades. Fueled by advancements in ICT and business process reengineering, the current applications in the sector have increasingly become the backbone of public financial management in the country. These cover the entire gamut of functions ranging from budget estimation, preparation, distribution, preparation of bills, treasury operations, expenditure monitoring,

DOI: 10.1201/9781003111351-6

and non-tax revenue to the integration with external stakeholders such as banks, payment gateways, the NPCI for DBT payments, the Reserve Bank of India, implementing agencies, and others.

The gradual metamorphosis is due to the enthusiastic participation of various stakeholders such as banks, line departments, and ministries. Dependency on these systems has also brought new challenges such as providing a business continuity plan, countering rising cyber threats, and others. While the current applications have served the functional requirements of the stakeholders in the domain, efforts are also underway to transform these applications using emerging technologies such as blockchain, AI, and so on and make these applications ready to cater to the next level of governance.

2. Institutional Structure

The Controller General of Accounts (CGA) in the Department of Expenditure of the Ministry of Finance manages the financial resources including budget and treasury operations in different ministries.

The principal chief controller of accounts (Pr. CCA), the chief controller of accounts (CCA), or the controller of accounts (CA) heads the accounts and internal audit wing in each ministry with the secretary of the ministry designated as the chief accounting authority. The Pr. CCAs/CCAs/CAs delegate their duties and responsibilities through the Principal Accounts Office (Pr. AO) at the ministry's headquarters and many Pay and Accounts offices (PAOs) at the field level. At present, there is a network of more than 650 PAOs with about 9,000 personnel spread across 78 locations in the country.

The organization accounts for all revenues collected through the extensive use of a banking system, right from its initial deposit with an authorized bank to its final credit to the government account. Regular detailed reconciliation of transactions is undertaken on a daily, monthly, and annual basis between the banking system and the accounting units. An important related function of the organization is to prepare the estimates of the annual receipts in all civil ministries. The organization also performs the payment function of the civil ministries of the government. The receipts and payments travel through an elaborate banking channel involving about 28,000 bank branches (besides pension work) consisting of majorly public-sector banks and some select private-sector banks. These banks provide service as agents of the central bank, that is, the Reserve Bank of India, which is the banker to the Government of India. Figure 6.1 illustrates the Financial Management Ecosystem of the Government of India.

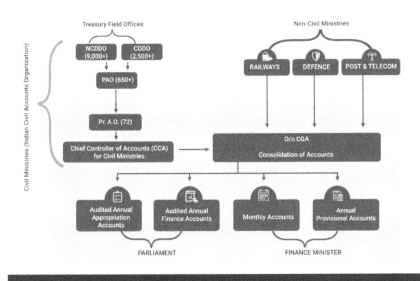

FIGURE 6.1
The Government of India Financial Management Ecosystem.

3. Global Scenario and Trends

Sound public financial management plays a key role in spurring the growth of the economy of any country. The trigger for reforms in public financial management in different countries is due to various factors [1], such as the need to enhance transparency and accountability of the governments, fiscal crises, political changes, changes in priorities of the government, and so on. However, these reforms are time-consuming, do not follow any fixed template, and have largely succeeded when customized to cater to local requirements following a prioritized agenda.

Implementations of the IFMIS world over include both commercial off-the-shelf products, such as Oracle Financials, Free Balance, SAP, and EPICOR, and several bespoke developments [2]. While the cost, as well as time in commercial off-the-shelf implementation, is high and fraught with risks, it also poses challenge vis-à-vis the agility to align with changing business rules and priorities of the government. Therefore, bespoke development plays an important role in the implementation of the IFMIS because of the flexibility it offers. Capacity building is another important factor in the implementation of the IFMIS that can make or mar the transition.

For the IFMIS to demonstrate an optimal performance, an iterative approach could be more prudent, particularly in the case of developing countries. An iterative approach with limited scope, providing for the assessment of outcomes at every stage of development seems to be best suited for a domain as complex as finance. This has also been borne out by various studies.

SIAFI, the IFMIS of Brazil, provides a central system for monitoring all accounts payable of the central government and regularly reports amounts carried over fiscal years. All accounting transactions are recorded in the SIAFI and it has strong inbuilt controls which play an important role in ensuring that expenditure commitments are only undertaken within the limits established by the budget and financial programming decrees. Accounting transactions in the SIAFI are updated in real time, enabling the reconciliation of government accounting records with its accounts daily. The Budget Division in the Ministry of Finance also uses SIAFI, thereby making it possible to generate a budget execution report with the desired level of details at any point in time.

Organizations such as the World Bank, the Asian Development Bank, the International Monetary Fund, and others have played an important role by aiding various countries in the development of the IFMIS and creating a knowledge repository for sharing experiences and best practices. The World Bank had suggested a global data set in 2017 [3] to present the trends in modernization and integration of PFMSs and online services (e-services) in 198 economies worldwide. Another World Bank study report released in 2011 is a comprehensive document that illustrates 25 years of World Bank experience—what works and what doesn't [4]. However, each country needs to adopt a model that suits it best.

Since 1984, the World Bank has financed 87 Financial Management Information System (FMIS) projects in 51 countries [4]. The findings of this study include 55 closed and 32 active Treasury/FMIS (T/F) projects. The Latin America and Caribbean region of the World Bank stands out with the largest number of completed (25) and active projects (4). The Africa region follows with 13 completed and 12 active projects. Most of these completed projects are comprehensive FMIS solutions (32) or an expansion of similar systems (13). The performance ratings indicate that the majority of 55 completed projects were 'satisfactory' along most dimensions of performance (67 percent of the outcome, 87 percent of sustainability, 56 percent of development impact, 61 percent of bank performance, and 59 percent of borrower performance ratings were satisfactory or above).

---

4. Case Studies

4.1. Computerization of the Union Budget

The Computerization of Union Budget commenced in 1985 in the Ministry of Finance. Early efforts were limited to capturing the data in individual spreadsheets in respect of each ministry/department, performing basic computations to generate the Statement of Budget Estimates, and formatting these through desktop publishing software in Budget Press. With the experience gained, native capabilities of spreadsheets were harnessed to automate the compilation of other consolidated budget documents.

In the earlier years, the NIC's country-wide computer communication network based on C-200 VSATs was used to transmit the budget documents. To overcome the challenge of low bandwidth prevalent in those days, these were split into smaller documents. Beginning in 1997, the budget documents were disseminated to a large cross section of people.

The webcast of the live Budget Speech commenced in 2005 using a streaming server. All previous budget documents starting from the first budget for 1947–1948 were digitized and hosted on the website [5]. To demystify new initiatives of the government to the common person using innovative infographics, a separate micro-website was developed as part of the main website during 2015.

During 2009–2010, a major initiative was taken to migrate the budget preparation process from spreadsheets to a relational database. A wide variety of test cases across the demands and the formatting of the outputs to match the functionalities of desktop publishing software, presented unique challenges. An intranet application for ministries/departments was developed with both online and offline spreadsheet-based data entry modules. The role-based application enabled data entry of estimates and notes in English as well as Hindi from various sections in the Budget Division. This also facilitated the generation of voluminous documents in PDF format such as the Statement of Budget Estimates and Demands for Grants, which could be used by Budget Press directly for printing, without using desktop publishing software.

During 2016–2017 and 2017–2018, major changes happened in the budget process, including the rationalization of schemes—both in the central sector and centrally sponsored—the elimination of plan and non-plan categorization of the expenditure, the presentation of the Statement of Budget Estimates with the breakup of capital and revenue expenditure, and the merger of Railway Budget with the Union Budget. These changes necessitated a major overhaul of the application which was redeveloped on a web-enabled platform using a Relational Database Management System (RDBMS), enabling data entry directly from ministries/departments and the generation of reports. The challenges related to formatting and incorporation of notes were addressed by using OpenXML and comprised generating the outputs in XML format and storing the results in the database before exporting the data to predefined Word template and later converting to PDF to provide it to the Budget Press.

Other critical components of the budget process including setting up of budget calendar, preparation of briefs from ministries/departments for revised estimate meetings, automatic alerts to Integrated Financial Units

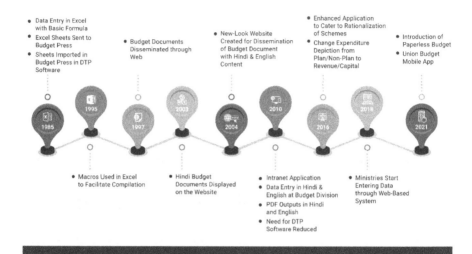

FIGURE 6.2
Journey of Union Budget Computerization.

for timely submission of data, and Budget Division to monitor the status of submission of data by different ministries/departments through a dashboard, Supplementary Budget, Medium Term Economy Framework, and Detailed Demands for Grants were also developed over a period. Detailed Demands for Grants now also incorporate mapping of an individual head of account or line item to a scheme in the Statement of Budget Estimate, which facilitates summarizing the expenditure figures by schemes and sharing of data with the PFMS. Union Budget Mobile app enabled the presentation of a paperless budget for the financial year 2021–2022, a major step during the post-COVID era. Today, IT is facilitating the entire spectrum of activities involved in budget preparation. Figure 6.2 showcases the journey of computerization of the Union Budget in India over a period of 35 years.

4.2. Central Government Accounting and Expenditure Management

Around the same time, when the computerization of the Union Budget commenced, efforts were afloat toward the computerization of another important area of government finance, that is, accounting and expenditure management. The journey commenced with the development of applications to capture the details contained in payment vouchers that included expenditures incurred under various budget heads by the ministries/departments.

The first-generation applications included IMPROVE and CONTACT. In 1985, IMPROVE was developed in dBase III initially and was subsequently distributed to various PAOs for decentralized capturing of voucher-level data. CONTACT was developed in 1989 to compile the monthly accounts for the Office of Controller General of Accounts by aggregating the data obtained through IMPROVE application implemented in various PAOs, thus providing the status of expenditure in the central government.

During 1999–2000, the client server–based application PAO-2000 was developed to computerize the functions at PAOs. The application was built on a client server architecture with servers and client systems at PAO offices across the country. It incorporated the budget estimates of the respective PAO at the beginning of each financial year and allowed the presentation and passing of bills at three levels of PAO, namely, dealing hand, Assistant Audit Officer (AAO), and PAO. The data obtained from various PAOs were used to consolidate and present monthly accounts for the central government. Several IT systems were developed and deployed to support the core business needs over the years.

Three major applications were developed to support three-tier accounting operations and internal audit in civil ministries: (1) Comp-DDO automation system in 2003 for DDOs, (2) COMPACT (developed in 2001) for payment processing and accounting in PAOs, and (3) e-Lekha was developed in 2009 for the daily consolidation of accounting information at the central level by the CGA. In parallel to these core IT applications, several other information systems have been deployed to support additional needs and consolidate information about the revenues (tax and customs), pensions, payroll payments, market and state loans, public debt, and procurement activities. Since 2011, three web-based applications were introduced: (1) the CPSMS to monitor the utilization of funds transferred under the Centrally Sponsored Scheme and to obtain a reliable financial MIS, (2) GePG (developed in 2011) for e-payments in civil ministries, and (3) the management of budget documents (e-DDG/ Detailed Demand for Grants).

4.3. PFMS

The PFMS in its previous existence as CPSMS of the Planning Commission was initially started as a scheme in 2008–2009 as a pilot in four states: Madhya Pradesh, Bihar, Punjab, and Mizoram for four flagship schemes: MGNREGS, NRHM, Sarva Shiksha Abhiyan (SSA), and PMGSY [6]. The modules of Agency Registration, Sanction Generation, and Bank Integration were designed and developed to track the fund devolved from the central government by registering bank account details of implementing agencies and obtaining their bank account balances through an interface with various banks.

The expansion of the CPSMS for tracking all fund releases from the Government of India was announced by the Hon'ble Finance Minister in his budget speech for 2012–2013 [7], based on the recommendations of the high-level Expert Committee on Efficient Management of Public

Expenditure headed by Dr. C. Rangarajan [8]. The Detailed Project Report was then prepared by the CPSMS project cell and got approved by the Second Expenditure Finance Committee/Union Cabinet in December 2013 for a nationwide rollout of CPSMS for all schemes and was rechristened as the PFMS [9].

To fulfill the mandate given by the Union Cabinet, a few more functionalities/ modules were designed and developed in PFMS, namely, expenditure management and fund utilization through the Expenditure Advance Transfer (EAT) module, the accounting module for registered agencies, the State Treasury Interface, the DBT module, the utilization certificate management and monitoring module, enhancements in Bank Interface module, India Post integration for DBT payments, external application systems integration for DBT payments, and others. The application was developed using the latest technology stack and soon became a mission-critical application in the Government of India. The Ministry of Finance, through an Office Memorandum issued on 2 December 2014 [10], set the course for further enhancement of the PFMS functionality to achieve consolidation of various systems being operated by O/o CGA to establish a single source of truth for all the financial information for the Government of India. Figure 6.3 showcases the Public Financial Management System in India involving various organizations and stakeholders.

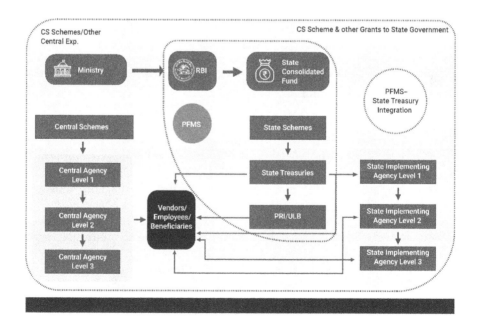

FIGURE 6.3
The PFMS Ecosystem.

4.3.1 Bank Integration

The unique PFMS-CBS interface with more than 500-plus banks, namely, all public-sector banks (21), private-sector banks (20), regional rural banks (60) and cooperative banks, has positioned the PFMS as an ideal e-payment platform for payment to individual beneficiaries of the social sector programs, thereby eliminating the existing intervening layers. This enabled immediate validation of bank accounts, prompt electronic credit to the beneficiary's bank account, and reconciled bank expenditure statements to the program-implementing agencies. As the bank accounts of implementing agencies are registered on the portal, the PFMS extracts the actual balances in these bank accounts at the end of the day through CBS and populates the report on 'Level-wise Bank Balances'. The system is also capable of further aggregating the balance of unutilized funds at each level, namely, panchayat/block/district/state.

4.4. DBT: e-Payment to Individual Beneficiaries

When the Government of India announced DBT under selected schemes in selected districts of the country with effect from 1 January 2013 [11], the PFMS was the only system geared up to take on the daunting challenge of transferring subsidies directly to the beneficiaries eliminating the existing intervening layers and pilferage, through its large network of banks. This enabled the PFMS to emerge as a game changer in the transfer of funds to the public.

The payment of wages directly into the bank/post office account of beneficiaries was successfully piloted in Nalanda district of Bihar under the MGNREGA scheme in 2012, which paved the way for DBT by the government with effect from 1 January 2013. The erstwhile Planning Commission issued detailed guidelines on 12 April 2013 [12] regarding the use of CPSMS by ministries/departments/implementing agencies for DBT. Furthermore, the use of the PFMS has been made mandatory for payment, accounting, and reporting under DBT, with effect from 1 April 2015. The PFMS has been used to transfer amounts due to the beneficiaries directly to their bank accounts or Aadhaar linked bank accounts under 28 identified schemes initially. Since then, the number of DBT beneficiaries in the PFMS is close to 248 million, with DBT payments of almost INR 3,350 billion made using PFMS under central/state schemes since 2013–2014.

PFMS now processes more than 4 million electronic DBTs per day to the bank accounts of beneficiaries. The beneficiary list can be prepared on the beneficiary management module for the respective scheme on PFMS or can be imported from existing external applications of the ministries/departments integrated with the PFMS for seamless processing of payments. These payments can be processed at different levels, namely, ministry/department, state government departments, or the program-implementing agencies as per scheme guidelines.

PFMS has emerged as the game changer as far as DBT payments are concerned. A recent case in point is the DBT under the government's flagship scheme PM-KISAN. The Hon'ble Prime Minister disbursed more than INR 120 billion directly into the bank accounts of a total number of 64.7 million farmers under the flagship PM-KISAN scheme at a public meeting in Tumkur, Karnataka, on 2 January 2020. This was the third and last installment of INR 2,000 for the period from December 2019 to March 2020. The PFMS achieved record delivery of the benefit to more than 60 million beneficiaries right on schedule. Figure 6.4 represents the growth in number of DBT transactions and the amount disbursed through DBT in the last five years in India.

4.5. Non-Tax Receipt Portal (NTRP)—Bharatkosh

Non-tax revenue constitutes about 13.5 percent of the total revenue receipts of the central government and comprises interests, dividends, profits, and other receipts to the government by way of the fee collected for various examinations, Right to Information, auction of obsolete assets, guest house/holiday home charges, spectrum charges, purchase of forms/magazines, donations to the Swachh Bharat Kosh, and so on, with the remaining collected through direct and indirect taxes. In earlier days, the collection was carried out by the concerned ministries/departments manually, and therefore, it was difficult to ascertain the status of non-tax revenue collected.

The NTRP Portal, renamed 'Bharatkosh', was inaugurated on 15 February 2016 by the Hon'ble Finance Minister [13]. It is an end-to-end solution

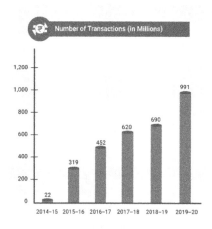
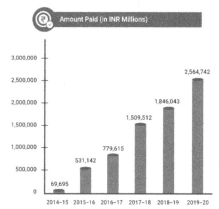

FIGURE 6.4
Growth of DBT Transactions during the Last 5 Years.

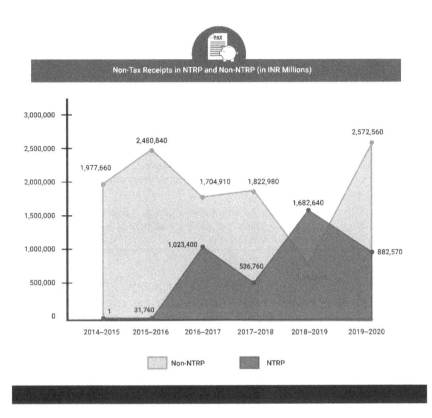

FIGURE 6.5
NTRP Growth—Last 5 Years.

for e-receipts right from deposit to accounting thus acting as a major enabler for digital receipts. It uses the modality of the Payment Gateway Aggregator. The depositors have access to various channels for making deposit/payment, namely, internet banking (individual/corporate), debit, and credit cards based on the integration available from respective resources. The depositor can also use National Electronics Fund Transfer (NEFT)/Real Time Gross Settlement (RTGS) mode for depositing the challan. The challan/deposit slip gets generated, and the amount can be remitted to the designated bank by intra-bank transfer or using NEFT/RTGS using the format generated by the non-receipt portal system. Figure 6.5 depicts the growth of NTRP in the last five years.

4.6. Employee Benefits Payment Initiatives

COMPDDO, the client server–based application for DDOs paved the way for the web-based application—Employee Information System, a personnel information and payroll system for payment processes of the drawing

TABLE 6.1
PFMS—HR Management Modules

EIS (Employee Information System)	Regular salary, supplementary bills, subsistence allowance for suspended employees, DA arrears, arrears for other allowances, deductions, Pay Bill Register (PBR), employee personal claims like honoraria, tuition fee reimbursement, leave encashment, salary arrears, overtime allowance, etc.
Centralized GPF Module	Advance/withdrawal, GPF bill generation, schedule verification, manual adjustments (missing debit/credit, capturing advance/subscription for deputation employees), financial year-end operations, final settlements, employee nominee details and transfer, MIS reports
Centralized Pension Module	Superannuation, voluntary retirement, family pension, generation and transmission of digitally signed PPO (e-PPO), SMS alerts to pensioner, MIS reports

and disbursing officers under ministries/departments of the Government of India. The Employee Information System is fully integrated with the PFMS system with a single sign-on, for disbursement of payments and post-payment updation. It is implemented for more than 6,000 DDOs of 62 ministries/departments and covers more than 0.34 million (340,000) employees for their salary payments, GPF, and income tax deductions, as well as schedules for license fee recovery and the like.

Table 6.1 shows the HR management modules along with their core functionalities.

Thus, the present Employee Information System covers all the payroll-related functionalities and caters to the diverse requirements of various DDOs and timely payments to employees.

4.7. Pension Accounting

While the applications for computerization of the Union Budget and government accounting and expenditure management largely cater to G2G services, an area in which automation went beyond G2G services was the payment of pension to superannuating central government civil employees and redressal of their grievances. Pensioners compose an important segment of the government, and the disbursement of pension in a timely manner, as well as the settlement of other dues at the time of superannuation, is a critical activity. The use of IT in this sector has substantially helped in achieving these objectives.

The CPAO was established on 1 January 1990 with the primary objective of simplifying the accounting procedure and reducing the number of agencies for pension payment thereby speeding up authorization, revision, and transfer of pension through authorized banks. It is administering the 'Scheme for Payment of Pensions to Central Government Civil Pensioners by Authorized Banks (both Public Sector and some Private sector Banks)'. The coverage of the scheme extends to all pensioners of the central government employed in civil ministries/departments (other than railways, posts, and defense), the National Capital Territory of Delhi, Union territory administrations without legislatures, retired judges of the High Courts and the Supreme Court, and All India service officers. This scheme also covers the payment of pension to former members of parliament and the payment of pension and other amenities to the former presidents/vice presidents of India.

One of the mandates of CPAO [14] was to create a database of pensioners facilitating timely payment of pension to the pensioners. Initially, the Pension authorization system was developed which subsequently evolved into PARAS—a workflow-based backbone system of CPAO that remained at the center of activity for CPAO. In the initial stages, CPAO was working in isolation as far as computerization was concerned as inward documents were received as paper documents and outward documents were printed and sent to stakeholders (banks).

From 2009 onward, the CPAO was opened to the public and other stakeholders with the launch of a revamped dynamic website, which provided an interface to various stakeholders, namely, banks, ministries/departments, PAOs, and, most important, pensioners. At present, more than 1.246 million pensioners are provided pension-related services by the CPAO through more than 70,700 paying bank branches all over the country.

5. Impact Delivered

5.1. Union Budget

The computerization of the Union Budget has brought about a significant change in the way budget processing was carried out in previous years and led progressively to a less-paper budget and then to a completely paperless budget for the financial year 2021–2022. Now ministries/departments can directly enter or upload the data and generate reports related to their demands. The capturing of master information with respect to the ministry/department name, demand name, development head name, major head code description, and so on has enabled uniformity across various documents. This has enabled the officers/staff to avoid repetitive tasks and thus improved their overall efficiency.

As the outputs are generated directly in PDF format (English, Hindi, and diglot versions for documents), the need to reprocess the same through desktop publishing software and rechecking are now eliminated. This has resulted in saving valuable time and reducing the use of consumables such as paper and printer toner without compromising on accuracy, freeing the operators from doing routine and repetitive tasks. Coupled with a paperless budget, disseminated through the website, as well as a mobile app, shortly after the completion of the budget speech of the Hon'ble Finance Minister in Parliament, it has resulted in substantial savings to the government.

5.2. Accounting and Expenditure Management and the PFMS

The introduction of computers for financial accounting functions has greatly improved the quality of service rendered. The macro-level contributions can be summarized under the following categories:

Reporting and Public Disclosure—It is greatly enhanced by achieving full compliance of the statutory requirement of laying the audited annual accounts in Parliament, the release of provisional accounts within two months of the closing of the financial year, meeting the Fiscal Responsibility and Budget Management Act requirements by satisfying fiscal deficit and other reporting requirements, timely reporting of monthly revenue and expenditure data to enable better cash management and government borrowings, and effective tracking of scheme funds.

Revenue Collection and Accounting Services—It has ensured that the entire revenue deposited by payees into the collecting banks reaches the government account and is credited within the shortest possible time/prescribed time limits.

Payment Function–Related—It has facilitated effective exchequer control through IT systems, the reduction in the payment process, the cost of payment processing through an electronic process, the reduction of manual work and paper documents, and increased employee/pensioner satisfaction through streamlining of GPF management, prompt salary, and pension payments.

Accounting-Related Services—It has achieved a 100 percent record of timely and accurate accounts consolidation and reports generation which is fully compliant with the International Monetary Fund's Special Data Dissemination Standard (SDDS)-enabled management of common grants, authorization, and suspense balances.

Creation of a Skilled Workforce and Capacity Built—Another major benefit accrued while implementing IT systems is the creation of a highly skilled workforce with the right skills and adequate capacities.

5.3. DBT

Direct credit to the beneficiary account with DBT payments has resulted in eliminating delay, as well as pilferage, and brought efficiency, effectiveness, transparency, and accountability into the government system. It has led to accurate targeting of beneficiaries and, therefore, enhanced confidence of citizens in government welfare schemes. It has also ensured that that money is transferred to a validated account, thereby reducing the risk of misdirected payments and curbing leakages and duplication.

5.4. NTRP—Bharatkosh

Major benefits brought about by its implementation include bank neutral remittance, faster remittance to government accounts, transactional transparency, complete and real-time accounting, better cash management, and the like. By eliminating the hassle of visiting banks for the issue of drafts, and later to government offices to deposit the instrument for availing services and providing the convenience of 24/7 usage, it has greatly helped the citizens.

6. Conclusion and a Way Forward

The existing applications in the finance domain have evolved over a period and continue to serve the requirements of the various stakeholders. However, there are mounting challenges, particularly around the exponential growth in the number of transactions, an increasing number of DBT schemes, the need for business continuity plans, data-sharing requirements with other systems, rising cyber-security threats and frauds, and the subsequent need to constantly innovate to mitigate these threats, long procurement cycles for critical infrastructure components, and the like. The ever-evolving technology-powered systems have led to heightened expectations vis-à-vis service delivery that is further aggravated by the attrition rate of skilled resources.

The analysis of business requirements in India suggests that an integrated government financial management system is needed that shall include budget preparation and approval; budget execution, accounting, and fiscal reporting; cash management; debt management; revenue administration; and audit support, macroeconomic forecasting, and personnel management. The 'Integrated Government Financial Management System' shall have suitable interfaces with the other entities and applications, for example, National Security Deposit Ltd, the Reserve Bank of India, banks, EIS, the PFMS, and the PARAS for seamless information exchange.

The data captured over the years in respect of budget, expenditure, borrowings, and so on can be made available in the public domain using open APIs for use by economists, researchers, and start-ups, among others, to develop interesting use cases. The open data on expenditure coupled with outcomes in welfare programs can help in assessing the success of these programs and identification of factors that can further improve the service delivery.

Although the current systems have stood the test of time and coped well with the rising number of transactions, these can substantially benefit by leveraging emerging technologies such as blockchain, AI, and others. The use of blockchain technology for the distribution of benefits and reconciliation of payments can significantly alter the DBT landscape. The use of data analytics and AI will help in the better management of funds. By using historical data of receipts and expenditure, the future receipts and expenditure can be forecast and hence can formulate the best policies (automated) of fund management. AI algorithms can analyze large, complex data sets faster and more efficiently than humans, thereby helping the government make quick decisions. A text-based or voice-based chatbot for citizens can help address all queries about government schemes and benefits instead of people having to visit government offices or CSCs.

References

[1] Wencai Zhang, "Global Trends in Public Financial Management," 1 March 2016. [Online]. Available: www.adb.org/news/speeches/global-trends-public-financial-management.

[2] Stephen Peterson, "Automating Public Financial Management in Developing Countries," 2006, John F. Kennedy School of Government Working Paper No. RWP06–043. [Online]. Available: http://ssrn.com/abstract=902386 and http://dx.doi.org/10.2139/ssrn.902386.

[3] Demirgüç-Kunt Asli, et al., *The Global Findex Database 2017: Measuring Financial Inclusion and the Fintech Revolution*, Washington, DC: World Bank, 2018. [Online]. Available: https://openknowledge.worldbank.org/handle/10986/29510.

[4] C. Dener, J. A. Watkins and W. L. Dorotinsky, *Financial Management Information Systems—A World Bank Study*, Washington, DC: World Bank, 2011. [Online]. Available: http://documents.worldbank.org/curated/en/485641468139212120/pdf/61640-REVISED-PUBLIC-WB-Study-FMIS-ENGLISH.pdf.

[5] Ministry of Finance, "Union Budget," [Online]. Available: www.indiabudget.gov.in/.

[6] Controller General of Accounts, "Central Plan Scheme Monitoring System (CPSMS)," February 2012. [Online]. Available: https://pfms.nic.in/Static/Notifications/cpsms-pamphletfor%20Competition-Feb%202012.pdf.

[7] Ministry of Finance, "Budget Speech of Finance Minister," March 2012. [Online]. Available: www.indiabudget.gov.in/budget2012-2013/ub2012-13/bs/bs.pdf.

[8] "Report of the High-Level Expert Committee on Efficient Management of Public Expenditure," [Online]. Available: https://niti.gov.in/planningcommission.gov.in/docs/reports/genrep/rep_hle.pdf.

[9] Controller General of Accounts, "National Roll-out of Public Financial Management (PFMS) Earlier Known as Central Plan Scheme Monitoring System (CPSMS)," 16 January 2014. [Online]. Available: www.cga.nic.in/writereaddata/CPSMSPlanCom16012014.pdf.

[10] Controller General of Accounts, "Digitalisation and Reconciliation in Government Accounts and Integration of PFMS with Various Standalone Systems of Receipts and Payments," December 2014. [Online]. Available: http://cga.nic.in//writereaddata/file/DigitizationandreconPFMSwithstandaloneSystems 02ndDec2014.pdf.

[11] Controller General of Accounts, "Public Financial Management System," [Online]. Available: https://pfms.nic.in.

[12] Planning Commission, "Direct Benefits Transfer: Use of Central Plan Scheme Monitoring System (CPSMS) By Ministries/Departments/Implementing Agencies," April 2013. [Online]. Available: https://niti.gov.in/planningcommission.gov.in/docs/sectors/dbt/om_4.pdf.

[13] Controller General of Accounts, "Inauguration of Not-Tax Revenue Portal by Hon'ble Finance Minister," February 2016. [Online]. Available: http://cga.nic.in/writereaddata/file/Inauguration%20of%20Non%20Tax%20Receipt%20Portal%20NTRP/NTRPPressRelease15022016.pdf.

[14] Ministry of Finance, "Central Pension Accounting Office," [Online]. Available: https://cpao.nic.in.

7

A Transformational, Effective, and Smart Public Distribution System

An Innovative Journey

G. Mayil Muthu Kumaran, Gautam Ghosh, and BVC Rao

> We will frame a new rule and abide by it forever; we will set ablaze the entire universe if a single human is left in hunger.
> —Subramanian Bharati

1. Introduction

The PDS is India's major food subsidy scheme and the world's largest distribution network of its kind. It reaches out to households and provides food grains at subsidized rates. The PDS emerged in the 'rationing' method adopted by the British during the Second World War (1939–45) and was maintained during the period of planned economic growth initiated in 1951 as a core component of social policy.

The PDS is a subsidy program that has evolved aftermath of critical nationwide food shortages of the 1960s before the Green Revolution. The Green Revolution in India refers to a period in India when agriculture was converted into an industrial system due to the adoption of modern methods and technology, such as the use of high-yielding variety seeds, tractors, irrigation facilities, pesticides, and fertilizers. It aims to provide essential commodities at subsidized prices [1]. The PDS is one of its kind in the world with the motive of 'Food for All'.

Maintaining price stability, increasing healthcare services for the needy (by ensuring access to basic foods at reasonable prices for the vulnerable population), rationing in circumstances of scarcity, and maintaining private trading under regulation were the initial goals of the PDS. Over the years, the PDS has managed to supply deprived sections of the population with food grains and other essential items at subsidized prices as a conscious social policy.

Until 1997, the PDS provided food subsidies to all beneficiaries without targeting. While the service has served millions of the nation's poor, it has been

DOI: 10.1201/9781003111351-7

highly criticized for its inability to represent the entire population BPL, urban bias, insignificant distribution, and a lack of transparency and accountability. It was observed that 40 to 50 percent of the population benefits from the distribution system, of which many are not deprived, indicating that a large portion of the PDS benefits is accrued to the people who don't require it, which led to no positive effect on the nutritional value of the targeted population. Due to this, it was thought that a structural change that could not be postponed was to target the PDS to the poor [2].

2. Food Security in India

India produces more than 285 million tonnes of food grains annually, which is enough to feed its population of 1.3 billion. India has experienced remarkable economic growth in recent years and is one of the fastest-growing economies in the world. However, poverty and food insecurity are still areas of concern despite many strides. The PDS of India plays an important role in reducing food insecurity by acting as a safety net by distributing necessities at a subsidized rate. Whereas the PDS forms a cornerstone of government food and nutrition policy, India continues to be home to an outsized population of hungry and starving individuals [3]. The TPDS emphasizes the implementation and identification of the poor for proper arrangement and delivery of food grains. The implementation of the TPDS was rife with problems, including errors in identifying beneficiaries, diversion of food commodities, leakage of subsidies, and a lack of monitoring and accountability as well as issues related to viability and therefore poorly functioning FPSs. These issues severely impacted the effectiveness of TPDS.

Food security plays a pivotal role in boosting the agricultural sector, controlling food prices, economic growth, and job creation, leading to poverty reduction, trade opportunities, increased global security and stability, and an improved health and healthcare sector.

With its introduction, the PDS obtained 75 percent coverage of the rural population and nearly half of the urban population, thereby providing monetary and nutritional assistance to pregnant and lactating women, combined with various welfare schemes. The NFSA marked a significant landmark in the grant of legal status to the Indian food safety network in compliance with the basic right to good health and nutritious food. The NFSA tackles the problems experienced by the TPDS by enforcing more stakeholder responsibility while ensuring increased transparency in its functioning [3].

With the NFSA, the TPDS expanded its scope and financial implication. The NFSA covers 800 million people via 0.5 million (538,000) FPSs and is undoubtedly one of the largest food security net programs in the world.

India's global food security index scores have improved since 2013, although it is still ranked at 72nd position out of 113 countries in 2019.

To achieve an efficient system of the PDS, the NIC as the technology partner of the Ministry of Consumer Affairs Food and Public Distribution brought automation to the PDS system, which included procurement of food grains, digitization of ration cards database, automation of supply chain, automation of FPS and transparency portal for social audit.

2.1 Institutional Structure

The TPDS is a centrally sponsored program that is financed by the Government of India and jointly implemented by the central and state governments. The central government is responsible for providing food grain (procuring, storing, and transporting) and determining the minimum number of beneficiaries and benefits (amount and price of grain to be distributed). States bear the responsibility of transporting food grains from these storage godowns to each FPS (ration shop), where the beneficiary buys the food grains at nominal prices, fixed by the government. Many states further subsidize the price of food grains before selling them to beneficiaries.

The FCI is the nodal agency at the center that is responsible for transporting food grains to the state godowns. Specifically, FCI is responsible for (1) procuring grains at the MSP from farmers, (2) maintaining operational and buffer stocks of grains to ensure food security, (3) allocating grains to states, (4) distributing and transporting grains to the state depots, and (5) selling the grains to states at the central issue price to be eventually passed on to the beneficiaries [4].

The FCI is also issuing food grains to various welfare schemes of the Government of India like Mid-Day-Meal, Integrated Child Development Services, and Annapurna, along with the TPDS and the NFSA.

In the last few years, TPDS has undergone several reforms, leveraging technology to improve overall efficiency. Biometric transactions have enabled the realization of progressive and pro-poor initiatives, including 'One Nation, One Ration Card', currently assuming a central role in about 30 states/union territories and with the potential to benefit 80-plus million migrant laborers.

2.2 Evolution of the PDS in India

The traditional manner in which the food security system began to take shape has evolved from problems that originated due to famines and droughts that cause extreme shortage situations and the subsequent steps taken by the government to support the victims. Thus, the measures were 'only providing a temporary relief to the affected population'. This kind of effort was taken up for the first time in 1939 under the British government when the Second World War began. The government was thinking of supplying food grains to the poor of some chosen cities, facing extreme conditions of scarcity, as well

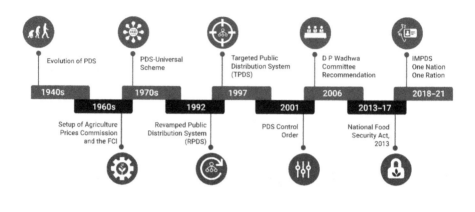

FIGURE 7.1
PDS Timeline.

as a situation in which the private sector failed to provide affordable commodities to the poor. This delivery scheme was expanded to several more cities and towns later in 1943, after the great Bengal Famine. A model of food security system has been developed over extended periods of economic stress and disruption, such as wars and famines. It initially dealt solely with the management of scarce food sources and gradually made it appropriate to implement a more coordinated and institutionalized approach, including steps to suspend normal market and trade operations. Figure 7.1 depicts the evolution of the PDS from its inception till now.

3. PDS—Global Trends

Even in the 21st century, access to and distribution of food so that people do not have to die from hunger continues to remain elusive, making food security one of the major global challenges. The Food and Agriculture Organization, World Food Programme, and other organizations of the United Nations and the World Food Convention are providing food in emergencies and helping save many lives. Some country-specific programs have been successful in providing food to their people and reducing poverty. Across the world, there are several technology interventions and strategies which intend to support livelihoods and improve access to food and generate income. Globally, various federal nutrition assistance programs have been launched to benefit low-income individuals and families.

CASE STUDY: FOOD SECURITY IN SRI LANKA

Sri Lanka's shift from a universal food ration scheme to a food stamp scheme and then to a cash transfer program was driven by various factors, including the continuation of the universal and generous food rationing during World War II. As early as 1940, the food ration system was adopted by the Government of Sri Lanka to assure the availability of a minimum quantity of food to households. Such a system is still used though with some modifications. Food subsidies and food stamps contributed much to improved food security in the country. The Janasaviya, Mid-Day Meal, and the Food Stamp programs were among those that offered such interventions. However, when the Samurdhi Program was introduced, these three programs were discontinued. In 1995, the new poverty alleviation program—Samurdhi—followed the principles of poverty alleviation and social mobilization, with three key components: a welfare (grant) component, a credit-and-savings scheme, and a community-based program [5].

CASE STUDY: FOOD SECURITY—BURKINA FASO

Achieving food security has been Burkina Faso's key priority. In the aftermath of the drought which hit the Sahel region from the late 1960s to the mid-1970s, the country's susceptibility to weather conditions was completely manifested. Several policy steps have been taken to resolve the crisis related to food poverty, including macro policies (public finance restructuring), soil management and water harvesting policies, new land settlements, household income-generation policies, and transfers [6].

The USAID is reducing food insecurity through a combination of emergency humanitarian and development assistance. FTF (Feed the Future) and FFP (Food for Peace) programs comprise the core elements of the food security program in Burkina Faso. RISE (Resilience in the Sahel-Enhanced) uses a multisectoral approach to address the diverse and structural causes of chronic vulnerability by increasing sustainable livelihoods and improving health and nutrition. The FFP Development Food Assistance Program aims to improve the diversification of household food production and income generation; reduce chronic malnutrition among children younger than 5, as well as pregnant and lactating women; and empower women through increased school enrollment and attendance of girls [7].

In Burkina Faso, the Moderate Acute Malnutrition Out (MAM'Out) program, a seasonal, unconditional cash transfer program instituted in Tapoa Province in the eastern region, improved diet quality for children in the intervention group but did not affect child-stunting or child-wasting levels.

4. PDS in India

The Indian PDS is a food security system that distributes subsidized food to poor people in the country. Presently, under the PDS, commodities, namely, wheat, rice, sugar, and kerosene, are being allocated to the states/ UTs for distribution. Apart from this, states/UTs distribute additional items of mass consumption through the FPSs such as pulses, edible oils, iodized salt, spices, and the like. The PDS is directing the 'Right to Food' in India.

The PDS in its endeavor to reach and serve the people of the country was launched to ensure food and nutritional security. The scheme had a focus to bring stabilization in the prices of food making it available to the poor at affordable prices. With the maintenance of the buffer stock of food grains in the warehouse, food remains available even during the period of scarcity, less agricultural food production, natural calamities, and so on. The system of MSP and procurement has contributed to the increase in overall food grain production. Figure 7.2 depicts the ICT transformation in the PDS from procurement storage to the ONOR.

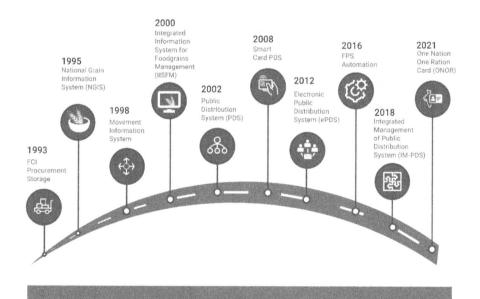

FIGURE 7.2
ICT Transformation in PDS.

5. ICT Intervention in the PDS

The PDS encompasses the procurement of food grains and their delivery to the intended beneficiaries. The TPDS works in a multilevel mechanism in which accountability is divided between the center and the states. The system faces challenges related to multiple ration cards being issued to one person, a lack of authentic identification for users, a faulty system of record keeping, the diversion of PDS food grains to market, a lack of monitoring system to track the trucks in transit, and a lack of real-time monitoring of inventory and centralized record keeping.

ICT provides a comprehensive solution to these challenges by focusing on automating the allocation process at all stages of the PDS supply chain. A perfect monitoring system is covering the transactions and transport at all levels starting from an FCI-controlled central store for FPSs. The key objective of automation was to make the food grains available to FPSs through the godowns at a right time in the right quantity. Figure 7.3 depicts the distribution system from procurement to last-mile delivery with their stakeholders and other departments.

5.1. Procurement

Food grains provided to beneficiaries under TPDS are procured from farmers at MSP. The MSP is the price at which the FCI specifically buys the product

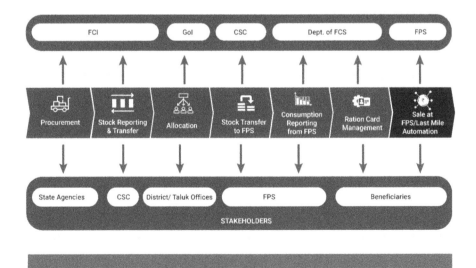

FIGURE 7.3
The PDS Workflow.

from farmers, which is usually higher and better than the offer in the market. This is meant to provide market support and incentivize production for farmers. To bring transparency into the procurement system and to reduce the issue of procurement, an NFPP, was developed. It fetches the procurement-related data of wheat, paddy, and coarse grain from the online procurement system of the states to enable online compilation of procurement data for the country as a whole in the NFPP on a real-time basis and to generate analytical reports based on this information.

The portal aims at providing the details of farmers registered, quantity procured, farmers benefited, MSP payments made, paddy stock in mills, paddy stock in storage, and grain stocks (wheat/rice/coarse) in depots—both the central pool and the decentralized procurement stock (DCP stock). The portal effectively captures and includes detailed information using the web services and refines the data to produce and display relevant information [8].

5.2. Digitization of Ration Cards

A ration card is issued by the Food and Supplies Department of a State to the beneficiary (resident of the state) for purchasing essential commodities under the PDS from the FPSs. Paper-based (preprinted booklets) ration cards were used to avail food grains. The record of family members, their entitlement, and their monthly transactions were maintained manually, which was prone to human errors and tampering.

The existing Ration Card Management System (ERCMS) was created to capture demographic data of existing ration cards beneficiaries. To complete the demographic data capture and verification, the existing databases were made available to the registrars (e.g., state governments BPL or NREGA databases) and the enrolment workflow used to import data into ERCMS.

As of date, in all 36 states/UTs, 235.8 million ration cards covering nearly 800 million beneficiaries have been digitized. The seeding of Aadhaar is completed with almost 209.3 million ration cards and nearly 700 million beneficiaries [9].

5.3. Electronic Public Distribution System (ePDS)

After the digitization of ration cards, the ePDS system was developed using MDDS (Meta Data and Data Standards). It is a workflow-based ration card management application that includes ration card issuance, modification, surrender, document storage, the printing of ration cards, and online status tracking of new ration cards or modification requests.

The application provides a wide variety of reports depicting insight into the ration card beneficiary database. These reports allow the user to drill down at various levels and an option to print the data for either category (pending request, completed request, etc.). It also provides a role-based dashboard view to the application users displaying the pending request along with the nature of the request, thereby reducing the efforts in terms of searching the pending request.

The system focuses on the reconciliation of data whereby all transactions can be reconciled to get the allocation of commodities and their lifting by actual beneficiaries through the ePDS system. The ePDS is further integrated with the Aadhaar database for de-duplication and the removal of fake and bogus ration cards across the country [10]. Census recording takes place in India once in 10 years, thus, updating the ration card constantly is a major activity in the system, which leads to the correct identification of beneficiaries and a reduction in inclusion/exclusion errors.

5.4. Allocation and Supply Chain Solution (Aadhaar-Enabled)

Earlier, the allocation of food grains to states was done on a demand basis, but the system witnessed issues like inaccurate identification of beneficiaries, shop owners creating a large number of bogus cards or ghost cards (cards for nonexistent people) to sell food grains in the open market, and leakage and diversion of food grains during transporting. It was realized that if the total food grains allocated to a state can be compared with the actual disbursement to beneficiaries, then pilferage can be prevented. To prevent this diversion, a supply chain solution was developed, which maintains the operational and buffer stocks of grains to ensure food security, allocating grains to states, distributing and transporting grains to the state depots/godowns, and selling the grains to states at the central issue price to be eventually passed on to the beneficiaries as a last-mile solution. Figure 7.4 depicts the supply chain solution process flow in the states and central governments. However, this system was fraught with many difficulties such as inefficiency, deterioration of food grains, unsatisfactory quality of commodities, malpractices in weights and measures, mismatch of demand and supply, long waiting times, FPS owners' behavioral aspects, and poor service delivery.

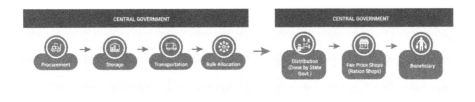

FIGURE 7.4
Supply Chain Solution in the PDS: Process Flow.

Under the End-to-End Computerization Integrated Supply Chain Solution of PDS, every aspect of the system has been computerized with complete traceability and tracking. Minimum entry is ensured, and the system is integrated with banks to facilitate digital payments.

The system has undergone significant innovation as the automation of the procurement process has been done. The government allotments for multiple welfare schemes have been automated in supply chain management. This has also been coupled with an Aadhaar-based authentication for increased accountability at the godowns as well as the FPSs. The godowns and FPSs are now geo-fenced, and electronic stock maintenance is done. Finally, the transport vehicles are fitted with GPS equipment to ensure effective vehicle monitoring.

5.5. FPS Automation—Leveraging a Transparent Digital Transaction System

Earlier, FPS sales were manual in nature, which led to a lot of diversions as it is not possible to probe whether actual sales happened at the FPS or not. The solution is to ensure the fair last-mile delivery of essential commodities. To keep the records of transactions at FPS to know how much ration is lifted last month to ensure the last mile delivery FPS automation comes into play. The goal of the FPS automation is to use the ICT tools and management practices to make PDS more efficient, effective, and transparent and to bring about increased accountability in the system. This is achieved by making the delivery and management system transparent, addressing the current challenges of the PDS.

At present, out of the total 0.5 million (545,869) FPSs in the country, about 81.8 percent, that is, 0.4 million (446,726) FPSs have been automated [9].

The FPS automation allows the issuance of rations to genuine and eligible cardholders on a real-time basis, thereby improving service delivery. It also monitors the movement of PDS stocks to FPS and is improving the digital inclusiveness in rural areas.

5.5.1. POS Terminal and Smart Card in the PDS

In India, e-ration PDS has become a revolutionary solution in the PDS using smart card and Global System for Mobile Communications (GSM) technology, which is very useful for efficient, precise, and automatic distribution of ration. The primary purpose of the planned scheme was to replace manual labor with ration atomization to increase the transparency in the PDS.

The traditional ration card for the PDS has been replaced by smart cards comprising all the details of the cardholder, such as family details, card form, and validity, among others. The consumer information is stored in a microcontroller supplied by the government. With smart card readers or POS machines, the consumer needs to scan the smart card, and then the microcontroller scans the beneficiary card and check their details and entitlement. After successful verification, the beneficiary enters the type of entitlement and its quantity using a keypad post, and the material is automatically dispatched without manual interpretation. After delivering the proper material to the beneficiary, the microcontroller sends the information to the beneficiary as well as PDS authorities through GSM technology.

Smart cards, under the TPDS, were tested in the Kangra district of Himachal Pradesh, Ernakulum in Kerala, and Vidisha in Madhya Pradesh. This was further extended to Haryana, Chandigarh, and Puducherry in 2008. The system was successfully run in Puducherry for three years and more.

The application can function online as well as offline depending on the availability of connectivity the devices on which the FPS Sales app has been installed. It is challenging to implement a fully online FPS automation model in those regions where connectivity is unreliable. To mitigate this challenge, another model for FPS automation has been envisaged whereby the FPS gets occasional connectivity and gets connected with the PDS server as and when connectivity is established but still should be able to perform sale transactions using a POS or mobile tablet [11]. Figure 7.5 depicts the process flow of FPS automation.

5.5.2. ePoS Transactions (Annavitran Portal)

The Annavitran Portal [12] captures and displays electronic transactions made through ePoS devices, from distribution of subsidized food grains to beneficiaries. This portal also shows a national-level picture of Aadhaar authentication of beneficiaries as well as the allocated and distributed quantities of food grains up to the district level.

Procurement, storage, and transportation are part of an all-inclusive spectrum of supply chain management solutions in the context of India's PDS, thereby ensuring the distribution of scheduled commodities to the targeted citizens through a network of institutions comprising FCI warehouses and the FPS.

The problem of food availability for migrants is a major concern as they travel due to work; however, their ration card remains valid in their home state only. So, to curb this problem, the portability of ration cards was tested and then implemented whereby beneficiaries can avail their entitlements of food grains from anywhere in the country from any FPS shops.

5.6. Nationwide Portability—IM-PDS

To sustain the reforms brought in by the scheme on 'End to End Computerization of Targeted Public Distribution System (TPDS) Operations', the department has launched a new scheme, namely, the Integrated Management of the Public Distribution System (IM-PDS), for implementation

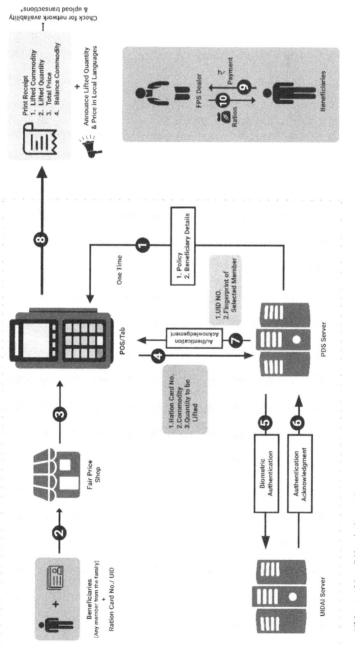

FIGURE 7.5
FPS Automation.

during 2018–19 and 2019–20. The main objective of the scheme is to introduce nationwide portability of ration card holders under the NFSA, 2013, to avail their food grains from any FPS of their choice in the country without the need of obtaining a new ration card. This is facilitated by integrating the existing PDS systems/portals of states/union territories with the central systems/portals under the central repository of all NFSA ration cards/beneficiaries, thereby enabling the One Nation One Ration Card (ONORC) system [13].

The application is ensuring a national-level Aadhaar-based deduplication by identifying duplicate ration cards. The process of identification is done by capturing all the national-level records under the central repository and running the de-duplication utility. This is a continuous process of cleaning and removing duplicates and ensuring that only eligible beneficiaries are applicable for national portability.

Once the duplicates are identified, the report is shared with the state officials for verification of the identity, and accordingly, the fake and bogus cards are removed from the system. The system is using advanced data analytics to bring about continuous improvements in PDS operations.

5.7. ONORC

The implementation of the ONORC is to provide an option to all eligible ration card holders/beneficiaries covered under the NFSA to access their entitlements from anywhere in the country. Under this plan, the distribution of highly subsidized food grains is enabled through nationwide portability of ration cards through the implementation of IT-driven system by installation of ePoS devices at FPSs, the seeding of Aadhaar number of beneficiaries with their ration cards, and operationalization of biometrically authenticated ePoS transactions in the state/UTs.

This system has enabled migrant workers and their family members to access PDS benefits from any FPS in the country. This scheme will reduce the practice of black-marketing at the PDS shops. Currently, the PDS shop owner sells these food grains in the market in the absence of the actual beneficiaries. It will reduce the incidence of hunger death in the country which will further improve India's ranking in the Global Hunger Index ranking.

6. Impact Delivered

The PDS helps in ensuring the food and nutritional security of the nation. The buffer stock of food grains is maintained in the warehouse so that the flow of food remains active even during the period of less agricultural food production. In the PDS, the redistribution of grains is done by supplying food from surplus regions of the country to deficient regions. The system of MSP and procurement in the PDS has contributed to the overall increase in food grain production.

During the COVID-19 pandemic, as per various government instructions, free food grains were provided to daily wager, laborers, and migrants. Various states provided e-coupons to people having no ration card to get free rations. During the pandemic, the universal PDS proved to be helpful to everyone in need.

The PDS impacts the various aspects, as it brings transparency in the governance system as the integrated system removes redundancies and increases collaboration. It increases the convenience for the citizens with anytime, anywhere capabilities, online payments, and online processes. On the economic front, it brings more revenue to the government, provides employment to the people for running the various process, systems around the project, and a reduced scope for pilferage and malpractices.

The end-to-end computerization and reforms in the TPDS led to achievements like end-to-end tracking, which means through real-time POS device transactions and demand base allocation, it has become easier for the system to be monitored remotely. This is also helping in the rationalization of monthly allocations to each shop as now regular data is available on the monthly allocation and consumption patterns at the FPS, thus paving the way for more efficient implementation. From procurement to the lifting of entitlement by beneficiaries can now be easily monitored or tracked. It brings awareness to the beneficiary as at the beginning of the project, it was noted that beneficiary awareness levels about their entitlements and the TPDS were very low. Through campaigns organized for the project, awareness on issues, including TPDS entitlements, has increased manifold among the beneficiaries.

7. Conclusion and Way Forward

The PDS is a significant contributor to the economic, social, and technological journey of a country. Digital platforms have enabled a whole new level of experience by eliminating the issues of interoperability. The technology revolution has been a catalyst in enhancing the reach of government services to citizens. The existing TPDS system has a tremendous scope of improvement with new emerging technologies in multiple avenues leading to improved user-friendly, efficient, accessible, and transparent systems.

Now, the focus should also be on providing PaaS so that it can benefit the citizens of India at all levels, namely, individuals, organizations, and the government. The ration card as a service, that is, cash or kind by choice of beneficiaries, is one such offering. With this, the process of scanning and submitting the copy of the ration card for various online services offered by the central and state government will be eliminated. Applications that are environmentally and user-friendly must be implemented to enhance the efficiency on the government side by benefiting citizens with a smooth and convenient system that enhances the level and ambit of integration with all stakeholders toward providing more holistic services.

References

[1] R. Radhakrishna and K. Subbarao, "India's Public Distribution System—A National and International Perspective," World Bank Discussion Paper No 380,1997. [Online]. Available: http://documents1.worldbank.org/curated/en/820471468750260965/pdf/multi-page.pdf.

[2] Department of Food and Public Distribution, "Evaluation Study of Targeted Public Distribution System in Selected States," 2015. [Online]. Available: https://dfpd.gov.in/1sGbO2W68mUlunCgKmpnLF5WHm/TPDS-140316.pdf.

[3] Neetu Abey George and Fiona H. McKay, "The Public Distribution System and Food Security in India," 3 September 2019. [Online]. Available: www.ncbi.nlm.nih.gov/pmc/articles/PMC6747310/.

[4] Sakshi Balani, "Functioning of the Public Distribution System- An Analytical Report," *PRS Legislative Research*. [Online]. Available: www.prsindia.org/administrator/uploads/general/1388728622~~TPDS Thematic Note.pdf.

[5] Food and Agriculture Organization, United Nations, "Sri Lanka Case Study Samurdhi Programme," [Online]. Available: www.fao.org/3/Y5030E/y5030e17.htm.

[6] Food and Agriculture Organization, United Nations, "Success Stories in Food Security," [Online]. Available: www.fao.org/3/w2612e/w2612e02.htm#BM2.

[7] USAID, "Food Assistance Fact Sheet Burkina Faso," 14 April 2020. [Online]. Available: www.usaid.gov/sites/default/files/documents/1866/FFP_Fact_Sheet_Burkina_Faso.pdf.

[8] Department of Food and Public Distribution, "National Food Procurement Portal: Farmers Benefited," [Online]. Available: http://nfpp.nic.in/.

[9] Department of Food and Public Distribution, "National Food Security Portal," [Online]. Available: https://nfsa.gov.in/Default.aspx.

[10] OneWorld Foundation India, "Case Study: e PDS Portal of India," December 2012. [Online]. Available: https://dpar.mizoram.gov.in/uploads/attachments/4531f1d0dfeb0102f12a053f417bba0a/pages-174-e-pds-portal-of-india.pdf.

[11] National Informatics Centre, "Functional Requirements Specification for Fair Price Shop Automation," 2015. [Online]. Available: http://fs.delhigovt.nic.in/wps/wcm/connect/56ef9d0045dc0e8a863ee69fdec5f098/Appendix_7_FRS_for_FPS_Automation_Draft.pdf?MOD=AJPERES&lmod=423076941.

[12] Department of Food and Public Distribution, "Distribution of Foodgrains through ePoS," [Online]. Available: https://annavitran.nic.in/.

[13] Department of Food and Public Distribution, "Integrated Management of Public Distribution System (IM-PDS)," [Online]. Available: https://dfpd.gov.in/impdsforportabilityofrcs.htm.

8

eCourts Services—Transforming the Judiciary for Effective Justice Delivery

Ashish Shiradhonkar, Shyam Bihari Singh, and Manoj Kumar Mishra

1. Introduction

India is one of the largest and most populous democracies in the world. Since historic times, 'Nyaya' has been an integral part of Indian society and culture. The Constitution of India has given utmost importance to providing justice to all citizens. The preamble speaks of the resolve to secure justice for all the citizens of India, which is defined as social, economic, and political.

Over a period, the justice delivery system in India, which is largely dependent on and monitored by the courts, has set a high example of end-to-end management. Today, courts are handling a variety of disputes, ranging from individual quarrels, disagreements in family matters, deciding the successors or legal heirs of the deceased, commercial disputes involving institutions/companies, litigations involving public interest, and the like. Determining guilt or innocence of the accused, awarding compensations to the victims, and so on are also handled by the courts. Whether it is civil proceedings or criminal proceedings, courts have been instrumental in delivering justice.

Today, 39.33 million cases are pending in subordinate courts of the country (*as on July 2021*) [1]. Managing the litigation manually has become a challenging task. The use of ICT has assisted courts to enhance judicial productivity, both qualitatively and quantitatively, while making the justice delivery system accessible, cost-effective, transparent, and accountable.

eCourts, a Mission Mode Project, was conceptualized for ICT enablement of the judiciary. The National Judicial Data Grid (NJDG), is a consolidated nationwide judicial data warehouse providing a real-time update and availability of the cases. The NJDG has more than 147.61 million pending and disposed cases from 20,718 courts across the country. NJDG is the backbone of the eCourts project, which is being used to provide citizen-centric services. Citizens and stakeholders can access the case information free of cost at one's fingertips without physically visiting the courts. More important, with the digital enablement of the courts, true and reliable information has become accessible to the common man through several delivery channels.

The system has brought transparency and efficiency and, at the same time, assisted the judiciary in policymaking and decision support for better management of resources.

2. Judicial Setup in India

The legislature, the executive, and the judiciary are the three pillars of the Indian constitution. The Constitution of India delineates these three pillars. The separation is aimed at distributing the political, administrative, and judicial duties among the respective pillars. This has safeguarded the values enshrined in the Constitution of India. Judiciary is one of the important pillars of democracy. In India, there is a unified judicial system with the Supreme Court at the highest level in the country, High Courts at the highest level in the state, and subordinate courts at the districts in the country. Figure 8.1 depicts the hierarchy of courts in India.

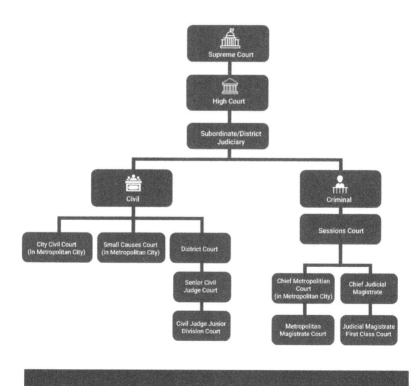

FIGURE 8.1
Hierarchy of Courts in India.

The Supreme Court of India, which is the highest court of India under the constitution, has original, appellate, and advisory jurisdiction. Its exclusive original jurisdiction extends to any dispute between the Government of India and one or more states or between the states. Besides, Article 32 of the constitution gives an extensive original jurisdiction to the Supreme Court concerning the enforcement of fundamental rights. The Supreme Court also has broad appellate jurisdiction over all the courts and tribunals in India in as much as it may, in its discretion, grant special leave to appeal under Article 136 of the constitution from any judgment, decree, determination, sentence, or order in any cause or matter passed or made by any court or tribunal in the territory of India [2].

The High Court is at the top of the hierarchy in each state. Normally there is one High Court in every state, but some High Courts have jurisdiction over one or more states and union territories. There are 25 High Courts across India. Under Article 227(1) of the Indian constitution, every High Court shall have superintendence over all courts and tribunals throughout the territories in which it exercises jurisdiction. A High Court has the power to frame the rules for the functioning of subordinate courts under its jurisdiction. High Courts also have original and appellate jurisdiction over the respective states and union territories. The High Court primarily deals with the appeals from subordinate courts in the states and writ petitions under Articles 226 and 227 of the constitution.

Subordinate courts are the trial or the first instance courts in the country. These courts are located in talukas and districts of the country and have territorial jurisdiction over respective taluka or districts. The district court exercises jurisdiction, both on the original side and the appellate side. District judges and additional district judges have jurisdiction to try civil matters whereas the sessions judges and additional sessions judges have jurisdiction to try criminal matters arising in the district. The judge dealing with both types of matters is designated as a district and sessions judge. District courts, also called the district and sessions courts, have appellate jurisdiction over all subordinate courts situated in the district on both civil and criminal matters. In the subordinate courts, the civil side is presided over by the Civil Judge Senior Division or the Civil Judge Junior Division, whereas the criminal side is presided by the chief judicial magistrate or junior magistrates first class. In India, district and sub-ordinate courts constitutes of 20,718 courts spread across 3296 court complexes (*as on July 2021*) [1].

3. Use of IT in Indian Courts—Transforming Judicial Service

IT has transformed the way justice is delivered to the citizens and is catalyzing the complex judicial processes which were difficult to manage earlier. The Supreme Court of India had introduced computerization way back in 1990.

The List of Business Information System (LOBIS) was developed and implemented by NIC primarily for scheduling of cases and generation of cause lists. Successful implementation of LOBIS software in the Supreme Court encouraged the replication of the same software in the High Courts. By 1993, many High Courts had taken the initiative to implement the LOBIS system.

Before 1993, Litigants and Advocates were required to visit Delhi or make a phone call to know the status of the case in the Supreme Court. With the introduction of COURTNIC over NICNET [3], the status of the case in the Supreme Court was made available to the litigants and advocates from the NICNET node in the High Court or the nearest district headquarters. This was the first ICT-led initiative taken by the judiciary almost three decades back to provide services to the litigants at the place of their stay.

Supreme Court of India and the NIC launched the project the Computerization of District Courts in 1997. This was the first nationwide implementation in which courts from all 430-district headquarters were selected. Adopting the system was a challenge as the procedures were differing from one state to another.

Realizing an overwhelming need for reforming the judicial sector in India by the adoption of new technologies and to devise a national policy and action plan to implement ICT in courts, in 2005, the then chief justice of India, proposed the constitution of the e-Committee, for policy formation and implementation of ICT in the courts across the country. e-Committee has enabled the Indian judiciary to prepare itself for the digital age, to adapt and apply technologies and communication tools making the justice delivery system more efficient [4].

In the current setup of the e-Committee, the Hon'ble Chief Justice of India is the patron-in-chief of the e-Committee, and the Hon'ble Supreme Court Judge is the chairman of the e-Committee [5].

In 2005, the e-Committee prepared the National Policy and Action Plan for the implementation of IT in the Indian judiciary. This was the beginning of Phase I of the computerization and modernization of courts under the aegis of the e-Committee Supreme Court of India [6].

As every High Court developed and implemented the system using different technologies, the need was felt to bring all subordinate courts in the country on a common unified platform for better monitoring, transparency, and efficient service delivery through a common platform.

For deciding on the unified platform, the e-Committee studied the contemporary implementation of application software developed and implemented by various states. After comparing different versions, CIS software, developed and implemented on a free and open-source platform in the district and subordinate courts of Maharashtra since 2003, was found suitable for replication in other courts of India. Later, CIS was designed as a single product to accommodate all such variations in terms of workflow, nomenclature, and local language. It was later renamed as the National Core Version of CIS 1.0 (NC CIS 1.0) for the country.

In Phase I of the eCourts Project, 14,249 district and subordinate courts were computerized with the installation of hardware, LAN, and deployment of NC CIS 1.0. In 2013, the Hon'ble Chief Justice of India launched the eCourts National Portal for providing services like case status, cause lists, orders, judgments, and more. The concept of the NJDG was conceived for bringing transparency to the system by enabling the citizens to track the pendency of cases in the country.

CASE STUDY 1: THE NJDG

The NJDG is a platform created to bring transparency, efficiency, and accountability to the judicial system. The NJDG provides a statistical analysis of cases on various parameters in the form of graphical dashboards. The facility to analyze the pendency of cases based on the type of case, the stage of the case, the age of the case, the reason for the delay, and so on helps in understanding the case at a micro-level. Further drill-down on any of these criteria helps in identifying and locating a particular case. By further viewing the history of the case, one can also identify the reason contributing toward pendency. Similar facilities are available in the disposal dashboard. The disposal of cases based on case type, the nature of disposal, the pendency versus disposal curve, and the time to disposition required for a particular type of case are provided. This helps in analyzing the overall pattern of disposal and time taken for disposing of cases based on several such criteria.

Citizens are curious about the pendency in the courts and expect timely resolution of their cases. Some High Courts started publishing pendency figures periodically on the website or as a part of some reports published by the High Courts. Every High Court has a separate administrative branch dealing with pendency and performance monitoring of the courts. Traditionally, returns or pendency figures are collected by High Courts from every individual court under its jurisdiction in the prescribed format. Such returns are further consolidated to arrive at state-wise pending figures. The collection of returns from the respective courts, quarterly or half-yearly, and compiling it further is a time-consuming process.

The NJDG is a game changer that has brought significant transparency to the judicial system. The information is now available publicly to the common man. Researchers and academicians have started utilizing the data for analyzing case data. Several reports are published using data collected from the NJDG.

The NJDG also serves as a decision support system to the management authorities like the Supreme Court and the High Court to monitor pendency on varied attributes for effective decision-making.

Several tools like dashboards and dynamic query builders have assisted judicial management to track pendency and disposal of cases on various criteria instantly. The creation of the NJDG has also been lauded by the World Bank as an innovation and has contributed to improving India's ranking in the ease of doing business index.

The Indian courts were early to adopt open-source technology. A Phase II policy document approved by the e-Committee mandated that all the software solutions to be implemented under the eCourts project shall use FOSSs, which also have community-driven support on the web. This is for ensuring that the support on FOSS can be managed through in-house experts and competing multiple vendors. FOSS, without any licensing/subscription charges, has resulted in savings for the exchequer.

In 2015, CIS NC 2.0 was launched for the subordinate courts of the country on the latest FOSS technology. The system provided several new features like a unique Case Number Record (CNR) and QR code to every case in the country. Apart from implementing case life-cycle workflow, additional features like the automated generation of process, templates for orders/judgments, kiosks, query builders, dashboards, and improved interfaces were provided for increasing the transparency and speed of the system.

The execution and implementation of such a project at remote taluka places were challenging tasks. The availability of technical manpower, training, adoption by the staff, management of infrastructure, and the like needed to be envisioned while planning such a nationwide implementation. The logistics for implementation by introducing automated installation and thrust on capacity building were thoroughly planned.

While developing the CIS, it was felt that greater flexibility needed to be provided to respective High Courts to fulfill their state-specific requirements. This led to the formation of a core–periphery approach where the national core of CIS was developed centrally, and the periphery was developed by the respective state. The national core version of CIS manages the entire case life cycle and the key functions of the justice delivery system, whereas the periphery part includes the state-specific functionality governed by the respective state government and High Court rules. Interfaces like judicial deposit, accounting, certified copy, various returns, and reports specially designed by the respective state High Courts fall in the periphery.

The main objective of the eCourts project was to provide efficient services to the litigants. The effective implementation of CIS pan India created a massive wealth of data. The proactive delivery of services in the form of automated short message service (SMS) and emails informing about progress of the case was initiated. The facility of displaying case status, judgments, orders, history of the case, through the services portal, and district court websites ensured free of cost services to citizens without any hassle. Figure 8.3 lists the various applications developed under the eCourts Mission Mode Project.

Leveraging the potential of smartphones and considering the penetration of technology in the country, eCourts Services App was launched. Several features, including searching the case by QR code, litigant's name, advocate bar registration number, and police station/First Information Report (FIR), among others, are available in the mobile app. The creation of a portfolio of cases in which the user is interested in future tracking is also provided.

The revolutionary idea of reporting the entire pendency and disposal of cases through the NJDG to the world has set a new benchmark in the judicial space. Facilities are provided to the judicial management to track pendency through the NJDG based on various parameters for effective decision-making.

JustIS mobile app, specially developed for judges, is assisting the judges as an electronic case management tool to manage their courts [7]. Attempts are made to curtail delays in the judicial system, like service of process, by developing mechanisms like NSTEP (National Service and Tracking of the Electronic Process). The facility to track the service and delivery of the process through a mobile app given to bailiffs is increasing the speed and transparency of the system [8].

CASE STUDY 2—VIRTUAL COURTS

Citizen services provided in the eCourts project enabled access to case information through various delivery channels. However, all these services were unidirectional, and citizens had to still visit the court even for minor processes such as payment of court fees by procuring judicial stamps from stamp vendors, and so on. The problem was addressed in the later phase of the project by providing a facility for online payment of court fees, fines, and penalties. This enabled citizens and advocates to pay the court fee or fine online without visiting the courts. For adjudication purposes, the litigant may still have to appear in person or through the advocate physically in the court. This required synchronous meetings of judges, litigants, and lawyers in the courts at the specified time. It was observed that many cases are procedural in nature and may be adjudicated online, in an asynchronous mode, avoiding synchronous meetings. Online adjudication of such cases could considerably reduce pendency and save the time and efforts of litigants in visiting the courts.

Considering these aspects, a novel concept of virtual courts has been introduced under the eCourts project. The concept is aimed at reducing footfall in the courts by eliminating the physical presence of litigants or advocates in the court. A virtual court can be managed by a judge whose jurisdiction can be extended to the entire state. Neither litigant needs to visit the court, nor does the judge need to physically preside over the court, thereby saving the precious judicial time.

Initially, traffic challans filed in the physical courts are tried by the virtual courts. e-Challan system developed by the Ministry of Road Transport and Highways is integrated with the virtual courts. e-Challans are filed electronically in the virtual court. The facility is provided for the judge to adjudicate the cases online. Assistance in the form of an automatic calculation of a fine helps the judges to adjudicate cases quickly. Once the virtual court has imposed the fine, an SMS is sent to the violator and the violator can plead guilty and pay the fine online by visiting the virtual court's portal. If the violator wishes to contest the case, a response is recorded by entering the OTP on the portal. In such eventuality, the case is transferred to a regular court for a further hearing [9]. Figure 8.2 illustrates the functioning of virtual courts system in India.

The virtual court is currently functioning in several states. More than 7.3 million cases have been adjudicated online. Violators had pleaded guilty in more than 1.47 million cases resulting in a collection of INR 1605 million as a fine. In more than 82000 cases, violators chose to contest the case by physically visiting the courts. Presently, 5.8 million cases are pending for want of action from violators (*numbers as on July 2021*). On becoming overdue, these cases will be transferred to regular courts for further proceedings. Not only it has become convenient for litigants to plead guilty online, but it also has helped in reducing the carbon footprint by obviating the visit of litigants or other stakeholders to the court using a vehicle. Enormous savings of paper is one more benefit of implementing the virtual court. The concept of virtual courts may be extended to try other types of cases fully or partially.

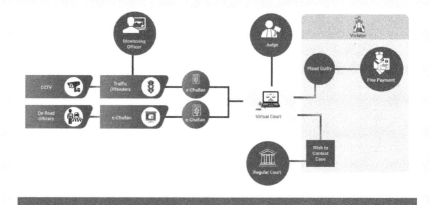

FIGURE 8.2
Virtual Courts System.

FIGURE 8.3
eCourts and Its Family of Applications.

The introduction of virtual courts in 2019, aimed at adjudicating the case online in asynchronous mode without physically meeting the client, advocate, and judge, has taken the delivery of justice to a whole new level. Currently, traffic challan cases are adjudicated through virtual courts, and this may be extended to try other types of cases fully or partially.

As IT is promoted in other departments of government and the respective applications have attained maturity, the exchange of data with these departments through publishing eCourts' APIs and consuming departments' APIs is initiated. The integration with police, land records, and treasury portals for online payments commenced.

CASE STUDY 3: E-FILING

Several papers in support of a case are submitted by the advocates or litigants in the courts. In legal terms, these papers are called pleadings, plaints, written statements, documents, and the like. Appendix A to the first schedule of Civil Procedure Code (CPC) prescribes such forms in which the pleadings are to be submitted. All such papers are submitted by physically visiting the courts and an oath is administered to the litigant submitting these documents.

Before the submission of the pleadings in the court, briefings by clients to the advocates, drafting of pleadings, signing pleadings by the clients, paying court fees, and more are performed. All these aspects are more strenuous when the client, advocate, and courts in which the case is to be filed are in geographically different areas.

In an effort to deal with such problems, the e-filing system was designed which provides several templates for easy drafting. The facility of e-signing enables the client to e-sign the document uploaded by the advocate from anywhere. The online payment of court fees is also possible by integrating the respective state treasury payment gateway with the e-filing software. On completion of all the payment of court fees, e-signing of the pleadings, recording of the oath, a case can be finally submitted in the court.

The features are designed in such a way that the entire filing of pleadings can be done in asynchronous mode without the advocate and clients meeting each other and further submission of pleadings in the courts, which may be situated at a geographically different location. e-filing is integrated with the Bar Council data. A facility is also provided for the verification of the data, and only verified advocates can file the cases online [10].

The e-filing system will save time, money, reduce the usage of paper, and traveling of various stakeholders thereby minimizing the need to physically visit the court. The e-filing system will result in an automatic digitization of case records. The electronic service of processes and the preparation of paper books for submission in appeals are much easier now.

As of today, the eCourts Project is implemented in 20718 courts across the country. The data of 147.61 million cases are available online, of which 39.33 million cases are pending and 108.28 million cases are disposed of [1]. A repository of 138.5 million interim orders and judgments is also available online. The voluminous data have ensured seamless service delivery to the litigants through various service delivery channels like websites, SMS, email, mobile app, and the like. Same data are also leveraged for showing several pending and disposed dashboards on the NJDG. Figure 8.4 highlights the transformational journey of courts in India.

4. Challenges

Mounting of arrears of cases in courts has been a cause of great concern for the litigants as well as for the State. It is a fundamental right of every citizen to

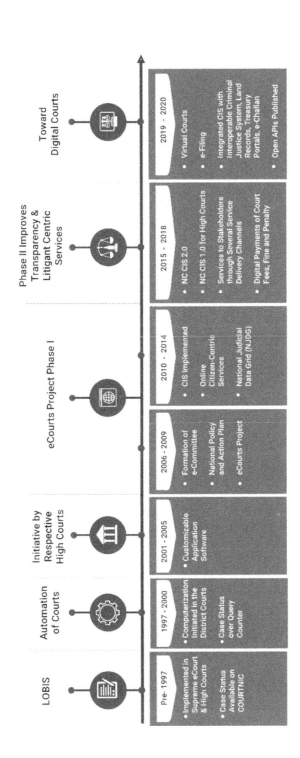

FIGURE 8.4
Transformational Journey of Courts in India.

get speedy justice. Law Commission of India in its 221st report has suggested legal changes for ensuring speedy justice [11]. Skewed judge/population ratio or judge/case ratio is also a matter of concern. In 245th report the Law Commission defined key concepts as pendency, delay, arrears, and backlog. The report also discusses on the mechanism to set timetables for cases [12].

Basis the previous delays and challenges, Supreme Court observed that at the time of filing of the plaint, the trial courts should prepare a complete schedule and fix the dates for all the stages of the suit and should strictly adhere to the said timetable as far as possible. IT enablement of the systems can assist in alerting the deviations, but setting up the timetable becomes more important and is a real challenge.

Many state treasury portals used by the High Courts and subordinate courts are yet to provide an online mechanism accepting payments. Personal ledger accounts, which are followed for accepting judicial deposits like maintenance, compensation, and so on, are not yet online in any of the state treasuries.

In the long term, it will be critical to explore the applications of emerging technologies to make relevant changes in procedures, practices, and enhancements in supportive applications in the respective domains (e.g., treasury portals, police integrations) to unleash the full potential of technology implementation in the courts.

5. Impact Delivered

The computerization of the courts has brought a paradigm shift in the functioning of the judiciary and how judicial services are delivered to stakeholders including citizens, litigants, advocates, government stakeholders, and institutions. The impact in terms of speed, transparency, and efficiency can be seen as a major achievement.

5.1. Judicial System

The judicial system is governed by procedures and practices. Courts have a traditional method of functioning. Advancements such as the mechanism of alerts, generation of reports, and dashboards are some examples that are assisting the judicial administration in performing the tasks and deal with high volumes of litigation. The bilingual feature of the CIS is assisting the subordinate courts to perform the activities in local languages. Another initiative like the NSTEP is assisting in minimizing delays in service of processes. Integration with the Interoperable Criminal Justice System (ICJS) is helping the judicial administration directly fetch the data from the source.

5.2. Service Delivery

Stakeholders like litigants, advocates, institutional litigants were unaware of the progress of the litigation and orders passed or compliance to be made in the case. All such services are now provided online through several service delivery channels, including websites, mobile apps, automated emails, SMS, and more. Information is proactively provided on the occurrence of any event in the case through SMS and emails. A common litigant, who is not aware of the judicial case number, can also search the case by several different search options like name of the litigant, CNR, QR code, and the like. Facilities like portfolio management in the mobile app are also assisting various stakeholders in easily managing multiple litigations in different courts.

6. Conclusion and Way Forward

The Indian judicial system had shown significant improvement in its functioning and service delivery by using the latest technologies and by designing and implementing innovative solutions like the NJDG and virtual courts. While the current applications have served the functional requirements of the stakeholders in the domain, efforts are also underway to transform these applications using emerging technologies, such as blockchain, AI/machine learning, and the like, and make these applications ready to cater to the next level of justice delivery.

Digitization of court records and solutions like e-filing coupled with massive data in the structured and unstructured form available in the NJDG, may be useful to leverage the advancements in AI and machine learning. Solutions ranging from assistance in judging, finding similarities, providing neutral citations to language translations are some of the examples in which the potential of AI/machine learning or deep learning may be used.

Videoconferencing, e-filing, and virtual courts combined can move toward the evolving concept of digital courts. Digital courts may provide more convenience to the advocates and litigants and will increase transparency in the system. Technology has brought radical changes in the functioning of the courts and service delivery to citizens. The judiciary is moving toward digital and online courts by providing efficient services to litigants, advocates, and judges.

References

[1] Cases are pending in Sub-ordinate Courts of the country njdg.ecourts.gov.in.
[2] History of Supreme Court of India https://main.sci.gov.in/history.

[3] Introduction of COURTNIC www.financialexpress.com/archive/the-jury-is-out-is-the-singapore-tech-model-best-for-us/57391/.

[4] Constitution of e-Committee: Policy and Action plan Document Phase I https://ecommitteesci.gov.in/document-category/policy-action-plan-documents-en/.

[5] e-Committee Organisation https://ecommitteesci.gov.in/#.

[6] eCourts Project policy document https://ecommitteesci.gov.in/document-cate gory/policy-action-plan-documents-en/.

[7] JustIS Mobile App https://ecommitteesci.gov.in/court-management-tool-justis-app/.

[8] NSTEP https://ecommitteesci.gov.in/nstep/.

[9] Virtual Courtshttps://vcourts.gov.in/virtualcourt/.

[10] e-Filing https://filing.ecourts.gov.in.

[11] Law Commission of India reports https://lawcommissionofindia.nic.in/reports/report221.pdf.

[12] Law Commission of India reports https://lawcommissionofindia.nic.in/reports/Report245.pdf.

9

Technology Led Transformation of the Election Process

Rajiv Rathi, Varindra Seth, Pradip Kumar Upadhyay,
and Pramod Sharma

1. Introduction

The first elections in independent India were held between 25 October 1951 and 21 February 1952. Since 1952, 17 general elections for the Lok Sabha and more than 350 elections for state assemblies, besides elections for presidents and vice-presidents, have been conducted. The duration taken to conduct elections themselves is a reflection of the size of the exercise and the number of people required to manage the process to bring out a fair and trustworthy outcome. Since then, elections have been held at regular intervals.

There are three levels of direct elections in India in which every registered voter is allowed to participate in the process. These are (1) general elections for the Lok Sabha, (2) general elections for the state assemblies, and (3) elections for local bodies (e.g., municipalities, zila parishads, district panchayats, panchayat samitis, gram panchayats).

Unlike other countries, conducting fair and peaceful elections in India is a gigantic task with 898 million voters. There are practical challenges in such a large organizational structure dispersed over the length and breadth of the country including difficult geographical locations where election officials reach with EVMs and forces (paramilitary and police) are deployed. This is the reason Lok Sabha and state general elections are conducted in different phases. The election commission sets up a polling station for every 1,200 voters in rural areas and every 1,400 voters in urban areas. With the growing population, polling stations are reorganized, and new polling stations are set up in every election. In 1951, there were 0.19 million (196,084) polling stations, which increased to 0.93 million (927,553) polling stations in 2014 elections and 1.36 million in 2019 elections. This increase in polling stations necessitates an enhanced deployment of resources and monitoring mechanisms during the election process. During the conduct of the Lok Sabha elections of 2019, about 13 million officials were deployed. The use of IT plays a major role in handling this challenge of countrywide resource deployment and tracking [1].

Apart from the management of elections, the use of ICT for facilitating the voter has also increased in tandem with the penetration of broadband and mobile networks. Voter services like information related to their electoral roll, polling station, candidate details have been made accessible to the common citizen by the use of ICT applications. ICT has been used for increasing transparency and the voters' trust in the electoral process. For decades, technologically advanced ways of casting a vote have been replacing the paper ballot, but technological interventions in the voting process have not been adopted by many countries [2] [3]. Keeping in view the technological risks, the International Foundation for Electoral Systems (IFES) [4] has published a report in October 2018 on cybersecurity strategies for election management bodies (EMBs) to strengthen their technology and procedures to resist vulnerabilities [4].

The NIC [5] is the pioneer in introducing IT in the election process in India. In 1991, during the Tamil Nadu state assembly elections, the first IT infrastructure was developed for the transmission of election results directly from the field using the NIC satellite network (NICNET) and further processing it using the mainframe computer manufactured by NEC Corporation (Japan) for faster delivery of trends and results. With the ever-increasing use of technology in elections and state-of-the-art ICT infrastructure established by the NIC, the role of the NIC in making the entire event a success has become paramount.

2. Institutional Structure for Election Management

The Election Commission of India is a constitutional body established on 25 January 1950 under Article 324 of the Constitution of India. The Election Commission of India conducts elections for the offices of president and vice-president of India, both Houses of Parliament (the Lok Sabha and the Rajya Sabha), state legislative assemblies, and state legislative councils. Registered voters are allowed to participate only in general elections for the Lok Sabha and state assemblies conducted by the commission. However, elections for the Rajya Sabha, legislative councils, the posts of president and vice-president of India are indirect forms of elections and may not require large-scale management systems [6].

For local body elections, there are state election commissions that are independent of the Election Commission of India and work as per the legislation of the state assemblies. For the third tier of governance in both rural and urban areas (local bodies) the 73rd and 74th constitutional amendments were brought for setting up of a State Election Commission (SEC) for conducting these elections. Registered voters also participate in elections conducted by the SEC of the state for local bodies such as district panchayats, intermediate panchayats, and village panchayats in rural areas and municipal corporations, municipal councils, and town/nagar panchayats in urban areas.

The election process in India is governed by the Representation of People Act—1950, which describes the procedure to be followed for conducting free and fair elections.	*The Election Commission of India (ECI) is responsible for all elections to* • *Both houses of the parliament* • *The legislative Bodies of the States and the Union Territories* • *To the offices of the President and the Vice-President of India*	*For 3rd tier of governance in both rural and urban areas [local bodies], through the 73rd and 74th constitutional amendments, there are State Election Commissions who are independent of Election Commission of India and work as per the legislations of the state assemblies.*

As shown in Figure 9.1, election authorities work for the management of elections up to the booth level.

A booth-level officer (BLO) is the first touchpoint for a citizen for election-related services, with its jurisdiction restricted to one polling station or about 1,200 to 1,400 voters. There are about 1 million BLOs to cater to approximately 1.36 million polling stations in India. For every 10 BLOs, there is a supervisor. There are more than 100,000 booth supervisors in the country.

For each assembly constituency, there is an electoral registration officer (ERO) supported by an assistant electoral registration officer (AERO). There are more than 7,000 EROs/AEROs in the country. The ERO/AERO report to the district election officer (DEO). There is no dedicated DEO appointed, but the Election Commission in consultation with the state government designates state government officials as the DEO. There are more than 700 DEOs as of now. The chief electoral officer (CEO) is not part of the state government but an independent entity under the superintendence of the ECI.

With such a large organizational structure spanning across the country, an effective mesh of communication, IT, and mobile technologies is required for fulfilling the requirements of real-time communication between the various hierarchical layers, real-time monitoring, and decision-making. In Indian elections, the potential of all these technologies has been effectively tapped as and when they have proliferated in the market and industry. The new tools and technologies have enabled the commission to bring in more efficiency and accountability in the conduct of free and fair elections [7]. Many applications used by election authorities are designed in collaboration with the NIC's state and district centers for election-related activities. District centers of the NIC become the hubs of election management activities during pre-poll, in-poll, and post-poll periods [8].

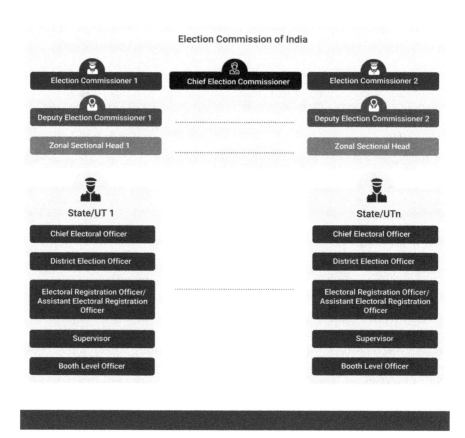

FIGURE 9.1
Management of Elections Up to the Booth Level.

3. Election Technology Trends Worldwide

Many countries use ICT to try to improve their election process. According to research data of electoral management bodies from 72 countries, there are considerable differences in the number and kinds of technologies, but most countries use some form of election technology for carrying out election-related activities. The use of technology for actual voting in the election process (voting computers or internet voting) is relatively rare. Most countries use technology to support the tabulation process (60 percent), voting registration process (54 percent), and voting machines (14 percent) [9].

The majority of the world's EMBs use hand-counted paper ballots despite the availability of technologies. Before the 2016 American presidential election, the Atlantic Council released a report covering the benefits and challenges of voting technology systems. The way technology has disrupted business, civil society, and daily behavior, the use of these technologies is significant in accelerating the election management also [10].

New voting technologies in the electoral process are playing important roles in improving overall efficiency. There is a growing interest in open public data for predicting the voting pattern. Research by Timnit Gebru at Stanford University finds that Google's Street View images may be used to identify likely voting patterns on the street from a car parked outside the house [11]. The use of new digital platforms like Facebook, Twitter, blogs, and YouTube by women candidates in Russia and Colombia in the 2018 presidential elections has altered the perception of women and their aspirations in modern societies [12].

Social Media: Today, social media is being applied for making opinions, analyzing sentiments, and running digital campaigns. It is also being used for collecting information and political advertising. With the advent of social media platforms, it has become challenging for the election-conducting bodies to keep track of each and every piece of information of voters.

Voter Registration and Verification: Maintaining an error-free voters' list, effective verification of voters, and transparent and credible conduct of the election process is the hallmark of any democracy. For smaller countries, this does not seem to be a challenge, but for countries like India that are so diverse or for Africa that has been divided based on ethnicity for a very long period—conducting free and fair elections is a big challenge. These countries have used technology to overcome such challenges. The voter registration process has transformed from a simple name list to a photo electoral roll and then to biometric voter rolls. Across Africa, for example, in Kenya, Nigeria, and Uganda, there is widespread interest in the use of technology in elections. It is gaining popularity because it increases transparency and accuracy, reduces corruption and fraud, and helps improve the voting experience [13].

Trends in Voting: Estonia became the first nation to hold legally binding general elections over the internet for municipal elections in 2005. Since 2007, Estonian parliamentary elections have been using internet voting, and Estonia has become the first country in the world to offer internet voting as an option in all elections [14] [13]. In the last European Parliament elections held in 2019, 44 percent of Estonian voters have chosen to vote using i-voting, and the cumulative time saved in the last Estonian election was estimated to be 11,000 working days [15]. In the Philippines, which is spread out across 2,000 inhabited islands, the Commission on Elections implemented an automated voting system for the 2010 elections. It selected a credible OMR system, and vote counting machines were used to avoid irregularities of the paper-based election system and precinct count optical scan machines used in 2010 and 2013. The automated voting system has contributed to peaceful elections because election results have been released very quickly [16].

4. Technology Ecosystem in Indian Elections

The ecosystem of new technological applications, such as mobile computing, cloud, cybersecurity, AI, analytics, and GIS, plays a significant role in election management activities. The ECI has used this opportunity and developed a suite of applications that provides a perfect ecosystem right from voter registration to results. One of the recent solutions for complete election management, ENCORE, was developed by the commission and implemented pan India in association with the NIC. The transformation in election systems in India is driven by the following pillars related to the management of the election process: (1) the non-election and pre-poll phase, (2) the in-poll phase: conduct of elections, and (3) the post-poll phase: counting and results dissemination. The major technology ecosystem used different phases of elections has been depicted in Figure 9.2.

4.1. Non-Election and Pre-Poll Phase

During the non-election phase, when voters register and there are no major election schedules, activities are performed such as the transformation of

FIGURE 9.2
Electoral Technology Ecosystem.

electoral rolls, customized web portals, redressal of public grievances, GIS for election management, the rationalization of polling stations, and the planning for elections and the display of results. The pre-election phase is characterized by election planning and preparation.

Electoral roll management is the largest exercise of the election commission during the non-election period. The electoral rolls are managed at an assembly constituency level at the district headquarters under the supervision of the DEO. With the setting up of district centers by the NIC in 1988, local-level computerization of electoral rolls was initiated by many districts. The systems started providing online citizen services such as online applications for service requests, tracking of application status, searching names on the electoral roll, and voter detail corrections.

In many states, these systems were initially developed by the NIC. In 2017, the ECI integrated these systems and rolled out a national-level web-based uniform citizen interface for all the voters and a centralized web-based uniform system of processing of the citizen applications for electoral roll maintenance. The system provides a dashboard view to the election officials at various levels related to monitoring service delivery, data quality, and analytics with drill-down capabilities.

In 1994–95, an EPIC in India was introduced to check the impersonation of any voter. Since 2015, EPICs are printed in a PVC color version, compliant with the ISO/IEC 7810 size standard.

A new voter is engaged using the Voter Portal, the voter helpline mobile app, SMS, or calling a toll-free number, 1950. The portal is integrated with DigiLocker facilities for uploading the necessary documents. DigiLocker ensures the 'Digital Empowerment' of citizens by providing access to authentic digital documents to citizen's digital document wallet [17].

Technology has also transformed the way differently abled voters are supported in casting their votes. Through mobile apps, disabled voters can not only register but also seek facilities such as transport from their residence or a wheelchair to improve their voting experience. Special efforts were made during the Lok Sabha elections in 2019 to ensure ICT enablement for persons with disabilities.

Pre-polling activities include ICT support for nominations, polling party formation, sector, zonal magistrate appointment, route chart preparation, and EVM randomization. This pre-election phase starts generally 6 to 12 months before the elections and extends up to the date of the announcement of elections, apart from machine movement and randomization.

4.2. In-Election Phase: Conduct of the Elections

This phase commences from the date of the announcement of elections to the date of polling. In India, conducting elections is a mammoth exercise, whereby a large number of government/semi-government officials are deployed at each polling booth across the country. A large number of vehicles are required for transporting the election machinery, and the police force is deployed for the safety and security of polling officials and the smooth conducting of elections. In 2019, during the parliament general elections, more than 13 million officials were deployed for election duty [1].

It was in 1991 that the ELECON software of NIC Nalanda District Centre (Bihar) was released for use in all districts of the country by then chief election commissioner T. N. Seshan. Apart from providing support for development and implementation of various applications as per the requirements of election authorities, NICNET services of the NIC were used extensively for messaging, videoconferencing, web hosting, and results dissemination.

Initially, all these activities were carried out manually by the district election staff. The manual process was time-consuming and prone to human error. With the setting up of the NIC's district centers and the availability of computing infrastructure, local software was developed for these poll-related activities. The district administration was able to use this locally developed software with randomization for creating teams of selected officials and allocating them to randomly selected polling stations. All this activity was done only 1 to 2 days before the actual date of election to ensure that the political parties do not know the details of the team and which team is deployed at which polling station. This was done to control election malpractices, and a similar process was followed for the police force also.

When the Election Commission decided to use EVMs in 2004, the randomization requirement was visualized for EVMs like the randomization of personnel. NIC district centers developed local software for random selection of EVMs for deployment at randomly selected polling stations. The process was required to control any possibility of EVMs being manipulated. Figure 9.3 shows major activities involved in the election process using EVM and VVPAT.

Election officials monitor several parameters during the election like voter turnout percentages, the law-and-order situation, violations of model code of conduct, or election guidelines. With the use of ICT, this monitoring has improved manifold. With a centralized, web-based system and the penetration of mobile data network, the hourly voter turnout is updated directly from each polling station using a mobile app. Historical data are analyzed for identifying sensitive polling stations, and live webcasting from these polling stations is done to perform real-time monitoring at various levels.

The Election Commission uses a well-designed communication plan enabled by a web-based software through which every official is involved

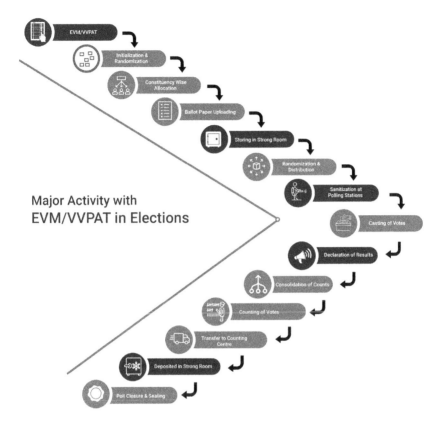

FIGURE 9.3
Major Activity with EVM/VVPAT in Elections.

in the election process and the facilities available near each polling station are mapped so that faster communication happens in the case of some emergency. All these steps have considerably reduced the occurrence of malpractices and repolling events. Using a mobile application, any citizen may report election code violations directly to election authorities for prompt disposal of violation cases. During the 2019 parliamentary general election, out of 0.142 million (142,250) complaints received, 99 percent were disposed of, and 80 percent of those were found correct. Previously only 20 to 25 percent of complaints received were found to be correct for the cases reported under the model code of conduct [7].

The ECI is also working on providing a technology solution for queue management at polling stations to facilitate citizens by informing the expected waiting time at the polling booth. This will further help voters in planning their activities on the poll day.

The 1991 Tamil Nadu assembly election was the sunrise period for the use of the NIC communication network and NEC computers in election counting. The NIC set up a satellite-based network (NICNET), and it was used for the first time for transmission of round-wise counting data directly from the counting centers. Also, mainframe computer NEC was used for compilation and processing of election results for the Doordarshan program. During the Lok Sabha elections in 2009, for the first time, Tamil Nadu did live recording and video streaming to the district electoral office for some polling stations in Chennai, Madurai, Kanyakumari, and Sivaganga districts.

A strong communication network among the various officials is required for preparations of the poll and during the polls. Videoconferencing has played a major role in saving travel time, money and making it possible to mobilize and communicate with a huge number of officials in a few days which earlier used to take gigantic efforts. The communication channel which was earlier limited to Public Switched Telephone Network phones and fax machines slowly transformed to VSAT-based videoconferencing over NICNET.

EVMS

With 898 million voters, India is the largest democracy in the world [18]. The country first conceived electronic voting in 1977, began electronic voting pilots in 1982 in the general elections in Kerala, and continually made system refinements until its countrywide adoption in 2004 [19]. India with its experience in using electronic voting has ensured knowledge exchange with other countries and assisted them by providing equipment to neighboring countries so that they can also pilot electronic voting. Bhutan successfully conducted fully electronic national elections in July 2013, during which almost half of its machines were gifted by India [10].

India has successfully implemented a homegrown electronic voting system. Since 2004, the ECI has deployed EVMs in nationwide parliamentary elections. Along with indigenously designed and developed EVMs, a credible web-based inventory management system has been deployed for tracking the inventory and movement of each EVM right from the factory to its current location from placement to destruction. To further increase voters' trust in EVMs and to increase transparency, the VVPAT was introduced in select constituencies in 2014. In the 2019 Lok Sabha elections, the use of VVPATs was made universal in all constituencies.

EVMs are manufactured by two central government undertakings: Bharat Electronics Limited and Electronics Corporation of India Limited. An EVM has two parts: a control unit, which acts as the power supply, recording, storage, and retrieval device, and a ballot unit, which is a voting panel used by voters to cast their votes. NIC district centers developed local software for the random selection of EVMs for deployment at randomly selected polling stations. Later on, a centralized system was developed to track end-to-end movement of each machine. The whole process of the randomizing ballot unit, control unit, and VVPAT is done multiple times in the presence of political parties and then is finalized using the software. After polling, the seal from the control unit is removed for counting, and the results compartment is opened by pressing the 'Result' button on the control unit [6].

4.3. Post-Poll Phase: Speedy Counting and Result Dissemination

Election vote counting and the transmission of counting data are highly distributed and time-bound exercises. During Lok Sabha elections, the counting of all the parliament constituencies is carried out simultaneously in a single day through multiple rounds over multiple counting centers, set up in each district according to the number of assembly constituencies.

Previously, for paper ballots, the counting process of the ballot boxes from each polling station used to take three to four days. National broadcaster Doordarshan started telecasting special election coverage in 1988. During those days, the information to the Doordarshan telecast center was transmitted by fax machines or communicated through public phone (Public Call Office) by field agents deployed outside the counting centers by Doordarshan. The NIC team at Doordarshan performed the compiling and analysis of the counting trends.

A significant reduction in the counting period came with the introduction of EVMs. In 1998, for elections to legislative assembly constituencies, the ECI introduced EVMs in a few constituencies on a trial basis. With the introduction of EVMs, the counting could be completed in one day. In 1995, the internet was launched in India, and in December 1996, Microsoft released Active Server Pages scripting technology for creating web applications. The first web-based system for election results was developed in Active Server Pages (ASP) for collecting the candidate information online and result counting details for Doordarshan. With a technical solution from the NIC, the results data were published on the website for real-time analysis by the anchors and also for public dissemination on Doordarshan. For faster data transmission from the fields, multiple channels like web-, SMS-, Interactive Voice Response (IVR)-based, and hybrid systems were used. To cater to the huge access load of the interested visitors during the counting day, the Content Distribution Network solution was used for the dissemination of election results.

5. Transformational Journey: Impact on Election Services

Through the 1980s and 1990s, the ECI, the NIC, and state governments have been implementing various technologies to strengthen electoral processes. A journey starting with the establishment of the ECI in 1950 through

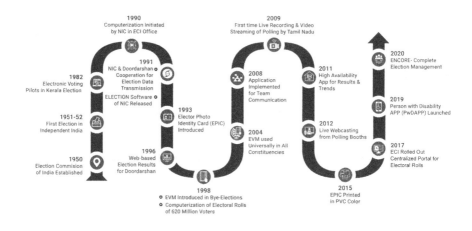

FIGURE 9.4
Evolution of Electoral Technologies in India.

TABLE 9.1
Election Process Transformation: From Voter Registration to Election Result

Key Steps	Earlier Scenario	Current Scenario
New Voter Registration	Paper forms submitted in designated offices. Later on, some states had portals.	From home or cybercafe on a single-window national voters' service portal.

Key Steps	Earlier Scenario	Current Scenario
Documents Submission, Verification, and Approval	Manual submission and verification at some places localized systems. BLO was also not there.	Online upload of documents from home or cybercafe. Integration with DigiLocker [17]. Verification by mobile app. Contact details of BLO. Online workflow system for approval.
EPIC	EPIC numbers non-uniform and not portable. EPIC started in 1993, printed in black ink on normal paper and laminated.	EPIC numbers portable across states. Colored plastic cards are issued.
Candidate Nomination and Affidavits	Paper forms submitted in designated offices. Data entry done later, leading to errors.	Online/Offline nomination. Online upload of affidavits from home or cybercafe. Verified affidavits published online for citizens' viewing.
Rally Permissions	Completely manual permission process.	Online request and approval.
Enforcing Model Code of Conduct	Most of the complaints received through multiple channels such as letters and email. Delay in inquiry; fact-finding challenging and often delayed.	Mobile app used for citizen reporting, team deployment, fact-finding, reporting and monitoring.
Voter Turnout	Voter turnout was consolidated at various levels in a cascaded manner and not hourly.	Mobile app for hourly updating the voter turnout directly from the polling booths to the central server.
Polling Party Management	Each district used its own method of preparing polling parties as per the guidelines.	Centralized state-/district-level application used. Deployment of polling officials and forces using web-based online data.
Voting	Use of paper ballots.	EVMs with VVPAT used for voting. Real-time monitoring of sensitive polling stations.
Counting Process	Paper ballots counted manually taking large time and many times resulted in recounting based on objections by candidate.	Counting of votes in EVMs is a press of a button. Multiple EVMs counted in parallel. Consolidated round-wise count uploaded online in a centralized software.
Dissemination of Results	Manual submission of affidavits by candidates in designated offices.	Real-time counting results are disseminated using the website and mobile app.

technological evolution is shown in Figure 9.4. Various technological innovations and tools have made the electoral process more efficient with a widespread reach and enhanced accountability in the conduct of free and fair elections. Table 9.1 illustrates the transformational journey for various election services with the induction of technologies.

6. Key Challenges and a Way Forward

Although the advent of technologies in elections has provided opportunities, there are associated challenges also for election authorities. Cybersecurity is one of the key concerns because the entire election process, including EVM management, is significantly dependent on IT systems. As the citizen becomes more informed about the cybersecurity vulnerabilities, the questions and doubts around the security aspects of technological solutions are pertinent. The Election Commission has to take faster decisions during the election process based on realities on the ground. These decisions are to be implemented in a time-bound manner on very short notice and may need customization in existing IT systems or the development of new IT systems. High agility is required for customizing the IT applications during an election period.

Whether it is the use of a communication network in the form of the NIC network for a speedy flow of information or management information systems for the conduct of elections or mobile app for citizen interface, India has been leading in adopting the latest ICTs in various processes related to elections. At a time when technology is influencing almost every aspect of life, data analytics and AI will be utilized in election processes at large. AI may be used more intensively to analyze the images and videos received from the public as part of citizen vigilance. Aadhaar and other identification methodologies may bring in automation in voting wherein no intermediary official may be required for voter verification and no ink marks may be required to avoid multiple voting.

It is quite feasible that soon there will be a live register of the population that may enable automatic voter registration after attaining an eligible age of voting. Research and developments are already in progress to use blockchain technology powered by Ethereum to overcome the challenges in the existing voting system [20]. Voter fraud may be prevented using blockchain-based mobile voting with tokens and smart contracts. Like the internet voting used in Estonia, India is exploring the possibility of internet voting. The possibilities are enormous, and so are the challenges. But there is no doubt that elections in the future will use technology even more.

7. Conclusion

Free and fair elections, in which each citizen can cast a vote, are the touchstone of any democracy. In India, there have been continuous systemic and technological improvements by the central and state governments and the ECI in collaboration with the NIC is working toward achieving this goal. India has been a world leader in adopting EVMs and VVPAT recently. The latest technologies, such as data analytics, GIS, GPS tracking, and mobile apps, are being effectively used in polling booths, and transparency is maintained by the ECI. The electoral rolls have become, by and large, clean, and there are negligible complaints of missing names in the voter lists. The monitoring of the polling has improved drastically.

Still, there are challenges to be overcome to ensure that every eligible voter is registered and that the election malpractice is completely curtailed. Election authorities are continuously working in that direction by adopting the latest ICTs in a significant way with fewer amendments to the laws framed by Parliament in 1950 and 1951.

References

[1] Election Commission of India, "Statistical Reports—General Elections 2019 Highlights," [Online]. Available: https://eci.gov.in/files/file/10991-2-highlights/ [Accessed 3 December 2020].

[2] M. A. Allers and P. Kooreman, "More Evidence of the Effects of Voting Technology on Election Outcomes," *Public Choice*, vol. 139, pp. 159–170. doi: 10.1007/s11127-008-9386-7.

[3] T. Aguayo and C. J. Sexton, "Florida Acts to Eliminate Touch-Screen Voting System," *New York Times*, 4 May 2007 [Online]. Available: www.nytimes.com/2007/05/04/us/politics/04vote.html [Accessed 7 December 2020].

[4] Katherine Ellena and Goran Petrov, "Cybersecurity in Elections: Developing a Holistic Exposure and Adaptation Training (HEAT) Process for Election Management Bodies," International Foundation for Electoral Systems, Arlington, VA, October 2018.

[5] "National Informatics Centre," [Online]. Available: www.nic.in [Accessed 7 December 2020].

[6] "Election Commission of India," [Online]. Available: https://eci.gov.in/about/about-eci/ [Accessed 3 December 2020].

[7] Election Commission of India, "ICT Apps Create a Perfect Ecosystem," [Online]. Available: https://eci.gov.in/divisions-of-eci/ict-apps/ [Accessed 3 December 2020].

[8] National Informatics Centre, "Elections," *Informatics- An e-Governance Newsletter of NIC*. [Online]. Available: https://informatics.nic.in/content/tag/2 [Accessed 7 December 2020].

[9] Leontine Loeber, "Use of Technology in the Election Process: Who Governs?" *Election Law Journal: Rules, Polity & Policy*, June 2020, pp. 149–161. doi: 10.1089/elj.2019.0559.

[10] Conny B. McCormack, "Report: Democracy Rebooted: The Future of Technology in Elections," *The Atlantic Council of the United States*, March 2016. [Online]. Available: https://publications.atlanticcouncil.org/election-tech/assets/report.pdf [Accesses 12 December 2020].

[11] Timnit Gebru, et al., "Using Deep Learning and Google Street View to Estimate the Demographic Makeup of Neighborhoods Across the United States," *Proceedings of the National Academy of Sciences*, 2017. doi: 10.1073/pnas.1700035114.

[12] M. R. Rojas and V. V Boguslavskaya, "The Use of New Technologies by Women in Politics in the 2018 Elections in Russia and Colombia," 2018 IEEE Communication Strategies in Digital Society Workshop (ComSDS), St, Petersburg, pp. 46–48. doi: 10.1109/COMSDS.2018.8354984.

[13] Richard W. Soudriette, "Pioneering Digital Democracy Worldwide," *International Elections Advisory Council*. [Online]. Available: www.thefutureof elections.com/#pioneering-digital-democracy-worldwide [Accessed 9 December 2020].

[14] C.E.F.Digital, "EstonianInternetVoting," [Online]. Available:https://ec.europa. eu/cefdigital/wiki/display/CEFDIGITAL/2019/07/29/Estonian+Internet+voting [Accessed 9 December 2020].

[15] e-Estonia Briefing Centre, "I-Voting," [Online]. Available: https://e-estonia. com/solutions/e-governance/i-voting/ [Accessed 10 December 2020].

[16] Smartmatic, "The Philippines 2016 General Elections: Technology," 2020. [Online]. Available: www.smartmatic.com/case-studies/article/the-philip pines-2016-general-election-technology [Accessed 12 December 2020].

[17] Digital India Corporation, "DigiLocker: Document Wallet to Empower Citizen," [Online]. Available: https://digilocker.gov.in/ [Accessed 12 December 2020].

[18] Election Commission of India, "E-Roll Data 2019," [Online]. Available: https:// eci.gov.in/files/file/9401-e-roll-data-2019/ [Accessed 12 December 2020].

[19] Election Commission of India, "History of EVM," [Online]. Available: https:// eci.gov.in/voter/history-of-evm/ [Accessed 12 December 2020].

[20] I. A. Srivastava, B. Saini, S. Phansalkar and S. Patwe, "Secure and Transparent Election System for India using Block chain Technology," Pune, India: 2018 IEEE Punecon. pp. 1–6. doi: 10.1109/PUNECON.2018.8745404.

[21] Brigalia Bam, "Future of Elections Report: Digitizing Democracy in Africa," *International Elections Advisory Council*. [Online]. Available: www.thefutureof elections.com/#digitising-democracy-in-africa [Accessed 8 December 2020].

10

Digital Transformation of the Transport Sector

Joydeep Shome, Gautam Ghosh, and Pawan Kumar Joshi

1. Introduction

In the last 100 years, all over the world, the transport sector has seen phenomenal growth due to technological innovations, the increased purchasing power of citizens, and improvements in road infrastructure. But, as with any growth sector, there arise concerns regarding standardization, safety, environmental issues, conflicting interests, and so on. Like every country, India, too, has an elaborate governance mechanism to control, regulate, and manage the transport sector. The Ministry of Road Transport and Highways (MoRTH) at the central level, the respective state transport departments at the state level, and the regional transport offices at the district/regional level are the key agencies and establishments—which are responsible for managing this sector through policy intervention, administrative control, and enforcement of rules and regulations.

In recent years, these activities have been modernized with comprehensive adoption of ICT technology and change in the business processes with the ultimate objective of (a) ensuring better governance, (b) facilitating efficient services to the citizen, and (c) bringing efficiency and transparency to the system. This chapter highlights the various ICT-led innovations and development in the Indian transport sector, where a wide range of government initiatives and schemes have improved the public transportation services in the country.

1.1. Modes of Transport

The transportation of goods and passengers is carried out by diverse modes—road, railways, air, and water. However, road transport in India is the dominant mode both in terms of share in passenger and freight carried and in terms of contribution to the national economy. Between the two main modes of surface transport, namely, road and railways, road transport carries about 90 percent of the total passenger traffic and 67 percent freight traffic

DOI: 10.1201/9781003111351-10

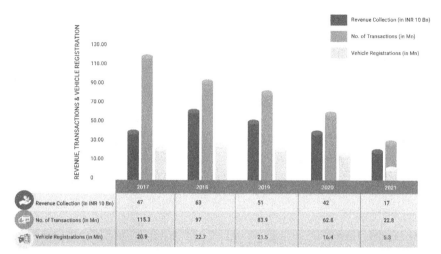

TRANSACTION: New Registration, Change of Address, Transfer of Ownership, NOC, Duplicate RC, Fitness Certificate, Hypothecation, etc.

FIGURE 10.1
Vehicle Registration over Time.

[1]. In terms of contribution to the economy, road transport contributes about 3.3 percent of gross value addition (GVA) against the total transport sector contribution of 5 percent in the GVA [2].

In the last few decades, road transport in the country has experienced an exponential rise in the number of vehicles sold, the option of automobile models and variants, issuance of driving licenses, growth in tax revenue, and so on. On the flip side, there have been challenges regarding the increasing number of accidents, level of pollution, congestion on roads, and so on. Policymakers are taking a considered approach in mitigating the negative fallouts through policy interventions like strict emission norms, compliance with traffic rules, road safety norms, promotion of clean fuel technology, and so on.

The number of registered motor vehicles has grown from a mere 0.3 million (300,000) in 1951 to 270 million in 2019. The share of two-wheelers has grown far higher than other categories—from 8.8 percent in 1951 to approximately 75 percent of total registered vehicles. For the latest information, please refer to the dashboard [3]. Figure 10.1 illustrates the revenue, transactions, and the number of vehicle registration in the last five years.

1.2. Institutional Structure

The MoRTH is the apex body under the Government of India that formulates and administers the regulatory framework related to vehicles and driving licenses, in coordination with the transport departments of various states and Union territories. The scope includes administration and regulation of operations and enforcement of compliances. The operations are primarily carried out following the Central Motor Vehicle Act and Rules (CMVA and CMVR, respectively). However, being a sector under concurrent list, state governments can also enact/notify their own acts and rules regarding taxation, permits, and some specified areas, as allowed by the Central act and rules.

Most of the regulatory operations are carried out through district-level transport offices—also called District Transport Offices (DTOs) or Regional Transport Offices (RTOs) or Motor Licensing Offices (MLOs) in different states. They operate as the registering or licensing authorities and perform activities as per the provisions of the CMVA and CMVR and respective state acts/rules. In recent years, some states have delegated part of the authority to private entities like automobile dealers, private driving test tracks, automated fitness centers, pollution control centers, and so on. Figure 10.2 represents the institutional structure of the Ministry of Road Transport and Highways in India.

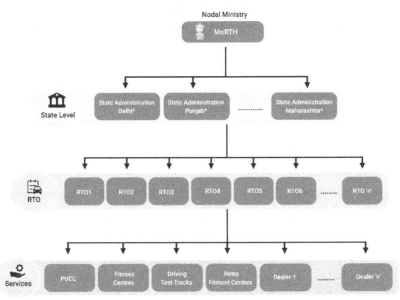

* States names used for representation purpose only

FIGURE 10.2
The MoRTH Institutional Structure.

1.3. Types of Transport

In terms of operational scope, purpose, and regulatory framework, the road transport system in India is majorly categorized into two modes—public and private transport.

Public transport comprises commercial vehicles that operate for public service—goods as well as passengers. These are owned either by private transporters or by state transport corporations. Goods transport is served by vehicles of different sizes and capacities—container trailers, trucks, mini-trucks, goods vans, and small e-carts/auto-rickshaws. Similarly, public transport (passenger) comprises buses, omnibus, vans, cabs, three-wheelers auto-rickshaws/e-rickshaws, and the like. The public transport sector is regulated through a system of permits, which provides wide variations like National Permits, Goods Permits, and others, for goods transport whereas it includes Stage Carriage, Contract Carriage, Taxi, All India Taxi, and so on for passenger transport. Depending on the permit type, a commercial vehicle can move only for a defined route or for any point-to-point trip or an all-India movement [2]. There is restricted movement across state boundaries whereas permits are defined and administered by the respective states.

Private transport comprises all types of vehicles used for personal purposes, namely, two-wheelers, cars, SUVs, tractors, and the like. Private vehicles normally do not require any permit and have mostly unrestricted movement across states. The tax liability and other requirements related to fitness, entry fees, and so on are also much relaxed compared to transport vehicles. However, such vehicles are only meant for personal use and cannot be used for any commercial purpose—like carrying goods or passengers on a chargeable basis.

2. Sector Overview

2.1. New Trends—Innovations and Initiatives

Over the last few years, innovation and willingness to change have resulted in many new functionalities and services being available to the citizens and allied stakeholders. The intention is to facilitate better services safely and sustainably. A few new trends/innovations implemented successfully are discussed in the following:

> **Integrated Vehicle Life Cycle:** similar to other countries like the United Kingdom, the entire vehicle life cycle (manufacturing, sale, registration, insurance, repair/testing/fitness, and finally to the scrapping

process) is set to be integrated [2]. It enables the comprehensive history of a vehicle to be maintained in an integrated manner.

Faceless and Cashless Services: toward an efficient and completely digital approach to delivering services have been initiated in several states to reduce the Regional Transport Office (RTO) touch points for availing of transport-related services. Business processes have been reengineered along with technical support to ensure ease of getting services.

Intelligent Traffic Management System (ITMS): to achieve traffic efficiency by minimizing traffic bottlenecks, providing advance information/alerts about traffic, local convenience, real-time driving information, seat availability, and so on, thus reducing the commuter travel time and improving safety and convenience. Additionally, intelligent transport systems offer a gamut of solutions to solve transport challenges related to public transport. Cities across the world, including some in India, are going through the transition phase toward the adoption of the solutions offered under these systems [4] [5].

The e-Auction of Fancy Number was launched by different state transport departments, in collaboration with the NIC, has brought transparency into the system of allocation of vehicle registration numbers. The application has facilitated e-bidding for online booking of premium registration numbers by new-vehicle owners, thereby avoiding unwarranted pressure on officers for these numbers and contributing to additional revenue for the exchequer.

2.2. Compliant, Sustainable Solutions

In the next few decades, the global transportation sector will face some serious challenges related to demographics, urbanization, the pressure to minimize emissions in urban centers, and growth in fuel demand that will pave a way for electric/environmentally friendly vehicles, vehicle pooling, better public transportation systems, and other innovative, eco-friendly solutions.

Building a sustainable transport system is cheaper than a conventional one. Financial flows shift from operating costs (fuels) to investment costs (infrastructure for mass transit, efficient vehicles). This is particularly applicable for developing countries where the transport system is still being built [6].

Environmental Concerns: A lot of technological innovations are happening in the field of electric vehicles (EVs), making them more efficient, affordable, and adaptable for public and private transport.

Compliance with Rules: Compliance with traffic rules, like maintaining the speed limit, wearing safety accessories (seat belts, helmets, etc.), mandatory fitment of safety devices in vehicles (antilock braking systems [ABSs], electronically controlled suspension, airbags, etc.), compliance with emission norms, and vehicular fitness, and so on are becoming stricter. A combination of technology (for instance, cameras fitted with automatic number plate readers and speed detectors) and stringent regulatory guidelines (for instance, using high-security number plates, reflective tapes for commercial vehicles, or banning the use of tinted glasses, among others) are aimed toward better compliance of rules. Some countries are also linking traffic violations or noncompliance (like tinted glass windows) with higher insurance premiums as a deterrent [7].

2.3. Safety in Transport

Improving safety across all modes of transport to reduce fatalities, injuries, and crashes resulting from road accidents is catching up the attention of all concerned. Road safety is a major issue that the road transport sector is grappling with, as the number of road fatalities/accidents is growing. Road transport claims the bulk of transport-related fatalities worldwide, accounting for 97 percent of deaths and 93 percent of the costs. Bus occupants are 10 times safer than car occupants, with rail and air also considered to be safe modes of transport. Fatalities in urban areas of developing countries, like India, are highest [8]. During the calendar year 2016, road accidents in India claimed around 0.15 million lives and caused an injury to 0.5 million persons. Apart from the loss of lives, it is estimated that 3 percent of the gross domestic product is lost every year due to road accidents [9]. India, as a signatory to the Brasilia declaration, intends to reduce road accidents and traffic fatalities by 50 percent by 2022 [10].

This calls for stricter measures, preventive mechanisms, and responsive emergency management systems toward improving the safety quotient in road transportation, particularly. Some innovative solutions already being developed are:

VLTS (Vehicle Location Tracking System): Tracking Vehicular movement, along with the provision for a panic button, in public service vehicles is a big step toward ensuring road safety. It can track speed, direction, position, and any abnormal condition of a vehicle fitted with the tracking device. Passengers can also use the panic button that is linked to the emergency response system. The system can also be used as a preventive mechanism by facilitating analysis of driver behavior, identifying errant drivers, and, subsequently, tracking their movement to avoid likely accident cases.

OSVD (Over Speed Violation Detection): Checks on vehicle speed, RLVD (Red Light Violation Detection) for compliance with traffic signal rules, and so on are being implemented across India. Closed-circuit television (CCTV) cameras capable of reading vehicle number plates and equipped with such devices have been linked with enforcement systems to generate challans (traffic tickets) to errant vehicles.

Many safety devices like airbags, ABS, and others have now become mandatory fixtures in vehicles. Commercial vehicles are required to be fitted with additional safety devices and undergo stringent fitness tests. Type approval of vehicle models is mandatorily done by authorized testing agencies before any new model can be launched.

A new road safety scheme—IRAD (Integrated Road Accident Database), has been launched by the MoRTH, which will facilitate on-the-spot collection of accident data by police, which will help not only accident management and reporting but also root-cause analysis of parameters like faulty road design, lighting/weather condition, vehicle defects, driver error, and so on so that a generic and long-term fix can be devised for preventing or reducing further accidents. The system will also be integrated with various systems, including hospitals, police, transport, and so on, for advisory, insights, best practices, and emergency support related to road accidents [11]. The scheme is currently in the inception stage and will be a major boost toward improving road safety in India. Figure 10.3 illustrates the transformational journey of transport sector in India.

3. eTransport—Evolution of Transport Public Digital Platform

One of the most important IT initiatives undertaken by the MoRTH to modernize the management and operations of the transport sector is the eTransport Mission Mode Project, which is a comprehensive digital platform created with technical support from the NIC, facilitating all transport-related services through a centralized, web-based system operational across the country. It has successfully transformed the service delivery mechanism of various transport-related activities (vehicle registration, driving license, enforcement, taxation, permit, fitness, etc.) and has also empowered multiple stakeholders by ensuring improved delivery of services.

3.1. Project Components

Some of the key applications developed and implemented under this project include Vahan (for vehicle registration), Sarathi (for driving license), mParivahan (mobile app), e-Challan (enforcement solution), PUCC (pollution compliance system). The extent of transformation achieved is remarkable, cutting across the governance, social, economic, and environmental, as well as technological, areas.

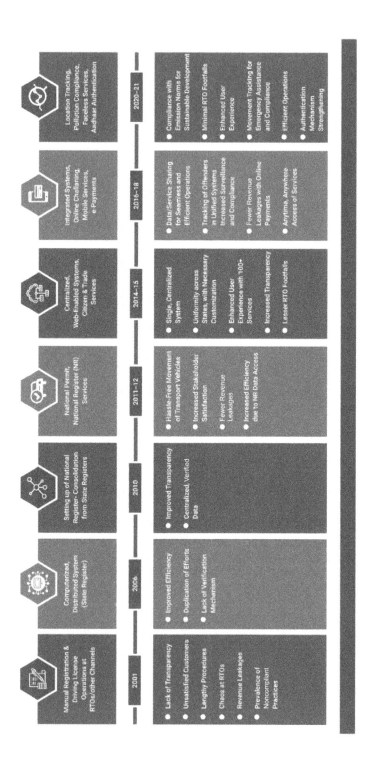

FIGURE 10.3
Transformational Journey of Transport Sector.

Vahan and Sarathi have extended their reach to 1300-plus RTOs, 30,000-plus dealer points, across 33 states/union territories, covering their diverse systems and processes under a common, unified system. Together, these applications contribute annual revenue of about INR 600 billion to government exchequers of various states. More than 100 online citizen/trade services are operational and facilitate online service requests, document upload, ePayment, appointments, and so on. Many of them are completely contactless eliminating the need for visiting an RTO by citizens. On average, 60,000 vehicles are registered, 80,000 licenses issued, 25 million SMS/OTP generated, 100,000 online applications, and 100,000 online appointments are booked daily. For the latest information, please visit the latest dashboard [12].

CASE STUDY 1: VAHAN AND SARATHI: ONLINE APPLICATIONS FOR TRANSPORT-RELATED SERVICES

Vahan and Sarathi

Vahan (vehicle in Sanskrit) is the application used by all transport officials across the country to carry out the processes related to registration of vehicles, the collection of road tax and fees, the issuance of permits for commercial vehicles, and carrying out vehicular inspection and fitness, traffic enforcement, and other associated functions.

The registration of new vehicles by automobile dealers is also facilitated by Vahan. Approximately 30,000 dealers are using the Vahan system for the registration of new vehicles.

Sarathi (driver in Sanskrit) is the application used by transport offices across the country to process and issue various types of licenses like learner licenses, driving licenses, conductor licenses, international driving permits, and so on. There are other associated functions in Sarathi like management of driving schools, online tests for learner licenses, the integration of automated driving test tracks, and the like.

Vahan and Sarathi together provide 100-plus online services for citizens, facilitating requests for various services for vehicles, permits, fitness, taxes, driving licenses, and so on. Many of these services are currently being provided in a completely contactless manner.

Vahan is linked to various external stakeholders like insurance companies, vehicles, and component manufacturers, the National Crime Records Bureau, banks, the postal department, and so on to facilitate an integrated solution and cross-linked validation on various services.

Originally, Vahan and Sarathi applications were implemented in decentralized mode with stand-alone instances implemented at individual RTO locations. In 2015, the centralized, web-enabled version for the whole country was rolled out and all the distributed systems were

migrated to the new system, which comprises a common data repository and an application for all states while allowing state-specific diver-
sities and variations through an intelligent configuration engine.

The consolidated Vahan and Sarathi systems are available under the
umbrella portal of eTransport [13].

After the core activity of process automation at the RTOs and other transport establishments has been achieved through the adoption of basic digital
technology, the emphasis has now moved to citizens and other stakeholders
in the sector. Applications and services are being offered through an online,
contactless manner to ensure ease in getting services. Stakeholders in the
ecosystem are connected through the sharing of data and the integration of
services.

Transport National Register created through the consolidated data comprising 290 million vehicles and 180 million driving licenses is a very critical
repository that is shared to authorized stakeholders through various modes,
including APIs. For the latest information, please refer to the dashboard [3].

The National Permit Application empowers the transporter community by
enabling online government authorization for free vehicle movement across
the country, improving the ease of doing business. More than 10 million permits have been issued online, generating revenue of INR 170 billion. For the
latest information, please refer to the dashboard [12].

Online Check Post Application provides a convenient option for payment
of interstate entry tax without any barriers. Several mobile-based initiatives
have also been launched under the eTransport project. e-Challan is a comprehensive traffic ticketing solution that has been adopted by transport enforcement officers and traffic police in 26 states [13]. The solution equips the traffic
police officers with handheld devices running e-Challan app for easier and
quicker issuance of challans and accepting ePayments. The system is also
linked with speed detection cameras that allow the issuance of traffic violation notices without human intervention.

CASE STUDY 2: E-CHALLAN: TRAFFIC
ENFORCEMENT SOLUTION

e-Challan

e-Challan is a comprehensive traffic enforcement solution, facilitated
for transport and traffic police departments. It is an end-to-end automated system, comprising POS-based issuance of traffic violation

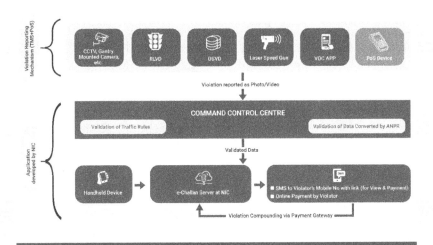

FIGURE 10.4
e-Challan Unified with Integrated Traffic Management System.

Challans (tickets), electronic collection of penalty amount, digital interface for all the stakeholders, and other related activities.

Additionally, under the purview of Smart Cities and ITMS, the e-Challan System is integrated with feeds from CCTV cameras (for red-line violation, speeding violation, etc.) and other devices like laser speed guns, gantry-mounted cameras, and the like to effectively track and penalize traffic offenders [14]. The e-Challan system is also linked to virtual courts, which is an online, faceless judicial system, enabling seamless and hassle-free adjudication of traffic violation cases.

As of January 2021, 50-plus million challans have been generated, across the 25 implementing states/union territories [13].

Altogether, the e-Challan initiative has ensured a complete shift of traffic enforcement operations from primarily being manual to a technology-driven system that is efficient, comprehensive, transparent, rule-compliant, and user-friendly through digital enablement. Figure 10.4 illustrates the e-Challan unified with Integrated Traffic Management System.

In line with the developments in the rest of the world—India is also catching up with the technological innovations, best practices, and user-friendly processes through ITMS interventions in public transport, eco-friendly transport practices/fuels/vehicles, measures to enhance road safety, and so on for efficient and hassle-free delivery of citizen services.

Emphasis is now being given toward the improvement of road transport efficiency through the development of a clean, safe, and sustainable road transport system. Improvement in road safety is one focus area, under which major policy initiatives are underway, including mandatory installation of a range of safety devices/features in motor vehicles, the modernization of enforcement system, a new system for accident reporting and management systems, a tracking mechanism for public service vehicles, and so on. Similarly, a focus on clean fuel, the adoption of the latest international emission standards, stringent compliance norms of pollution checking, and so on demonstrate the commitment toward environmental concerns.

PUCC is a web-enabled application used by about 30,000 pollution-checking centers across 24 states for certifying vehicular emission compliance (PUCCs) as per standards and norms set by the Motor Vehicle Act/Rule [13]. It facilitates real-time integration of the pollution status with various allied systems and stakeholders.

For citizens, a handy mobile app to cover various transport-related services and information has been developed and launched under the eTransport Project. mParivahan is a widely popular app for the citizens that allow multiple services and tools related to the transport sector, including virtual driving licenses and vehicle registration certificates, among others, to be available through a common platform.

CASE STUDY 3: MPARIVAHAN: A CITIZEN-CENTRIC TRANSPORT SOLUTION

mParivahan

mParivahan is a mobile app developed for citizens and transport operators providing anytime, anywhere access to all transport-related services such as driving licenses, vehicle registration, taxation, fitness, vehicle permits, and so on. The app can be used throughout the country, covering all driving license and registration certificate holders, and its key stakeholders are citizens and enforcement agencies. It comprises a mobile-based platform serving much of the user base, with its availability on both Android and iOS platforms.

The app has undergone a 180-degree shift from the earlier process as it saves the citizens from the hassle of carrying physical documents/cards, for verification/inspection purposes. The virtual driving license and virtual registration certificate facilitated through this app are legally acceptable, in place of physical documents. The embedded, encrypted QR code provides a verification mechanism for enforcement officers. The app has the functionality of easily locating the nearby RTOs through the RTO guide feature in the map and provides a convenient option for searching any vehicle or license. Limited parameters

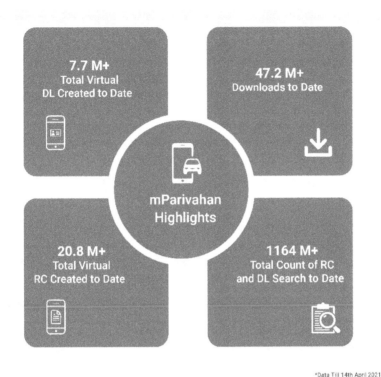

*Data Till 14th April 2021

FIGURE 10.5
mParivahan Highlights [13].

from vehicle and driving license registries are fetched and displayed on a real-time basis. The app has a high user-friendliness quotient as citizens need minimal guidance/training on the usage of various features. Figure 10.5 showcases the key highlights of mParivahan app.

Another mobile app—mVahan—has been launched to facilitate departmental officers to carry out various functionalities, starting with vehicle fitness and inspection conveniently and efficiently.

Manufacturer-specific solutions to cover the entire spectrum, namely, the homologation application for automobile and component manufacturers, to ensure smooth execution of type approval of vehicles before they enter the market (inventory of 140 million), 981 registered manufacturers, approximately 38,000 models [15]; the Speed Limiting Device application for approval and fitment of speed-limiting devices in transport vehicles; and compressed natural gas (CNG) maker applications for the fitment of genuine CNG kits in vehicles.

There are other recent initiatives like IRAD (Integrated Road Accident Database) for quick and accurate collection and processing of accident data from the field level. This World Bank–funded project aims at compiling detailed accident parameters for better accident management and analysis and engages all stakeholders on a single platform.

VLTEAS (Vehicle Location Tracking and Emergency Alerts System) with a GPS-enabled tracking device fitted in public service vehicles aims to enhance road and passenger safety. Under the eTransport project, the VLT device fitment process, as well as the tracking and monitoring through a command-and-control system, is facilitated to different states in India.

CASE STUDY 4: VEHICLE LOCATION TRACKING SYSTEM: TRACKING VEHICULAR MOVEMENT

Vehicle Location Tracking System

In the interest of public safety, the Government of India has mandated equipping all public service vehicles, namely, buses, taxis, and the like, with vehicle location tracking devices (VLTD), along with the provision of an emergency (panic) button, which may be used by citizens if any such need arises.

Command-and-control centers are being set up across the country to monitor and track all such VLTD-fitted vehicles. These systems are fitted with GPS tracking devices capable of sending continuous machine-to-machine signals on location, speed, acceleration, altitude, and other parameters as per the defined standards. The panic button equipped in these vehicles will be directly linked with the National Emergency Response System. The system will be integrated with the Vahan system in the eTransport project, ensuring the accuracy of data and the convergence of operations.

The VLT system provides real-time tracking of vehicles enabling users to track the location of their vehicles on the map, retrieve status information about their vehicle, and view the path traveled by a vehicle earlier, along with the generation of various other meaningful insights. The system also has a provision of panic buttons in vehicles, acting as a safety mechanism for the citizens. It also ensures the safety of vehicles gone missing, inadvertently deviating from the route. While the vehicle gets tracked continuously, as an added measure, the panic button may also be pressed by the vehicle driver/staff for required support.

Subsequently, VLT System ensures rule compliance, as the tracking mechanism involves geo-fencing. It identifies any deviation from the route, over-speeding, and the like and issues appropriate alerts/penalties for noncompliant vehicles.

3.2. Project Evolution

The eTransport project had a modest beginning in 2001 with the automation of RTO-based processes and services in a few states. By 2006, this extended to almost all states and covered most of the RTOs in India. Figure 10.6 illustrates the evolution of eTransport Project, its key components and the stakeholders involved.

In 2010, a Central Repository was created by connecting the distributed RTO systems across states through a data network. The Transport National Register comprises 290 million vehicle registration records and 190 million driving license records, including related information, undergoing a regular update. For the latest information, please visit the dashboard [12] [13].

The system was converted into a centralized, web-enabled platform in 2015–16, and the legacy data from all the distributed RTO-based systems were migrated to create a consolidated entity. Over the next few years, the system transformed from primarily a medium for online registration certificate– and driving license–related services to a comprehensive public digital platform. A multitude of upstream and downstream integrations with many internal and external stakeholders, along with an array of solutions around the entire life cycle of vehicle and license services have significantly enhanced the service delivery and user experience for multiple users. The integrated eco-system connects the common eTransport platform with various other entities such as automobile and component manufacturers, fitment centers, car dealers, pollution-checking kiosks, banks, insurance companies, transporters, private fitness centers, automated driving test tracks, driving schools, high-security registration plate, FasTag (a highway tolling system), e-Way Bill (a GST tracking system), Security agencies like the police, NCRB (National Crime Records Bureau), National Intelligence Grid (NATGRID), eDistricts, Common Service Centres Unified Mobile App for UMANG, and DigiLocker.

The continuous data and service exchange facilitated through these integrations endows the project with voluminous data, which is then analyzed to generate insights for decision making and monitoring by the authorities. Furthermore, it allows the preparedness required for adapting to upcoming trends and benchmarking with the best practices.

3.3. Project Beneficiaries

Any technology-led initiative or scheme is aimed at ensuring efficient delivery of services to the citizens. The computerization of various operations has transformed the traditional cumbersome processes, thereby ensuring increased transparency, ease of use, and readily available online services. The need for citizens and transporters to visit RTOs has been significantly reduced with the widespread adoption of the digital payments system, web-based service requests, online document upload, document verification, online appointment, and so on. Transport officials and staff across the country now have the benefit of working with a modern, integrated system

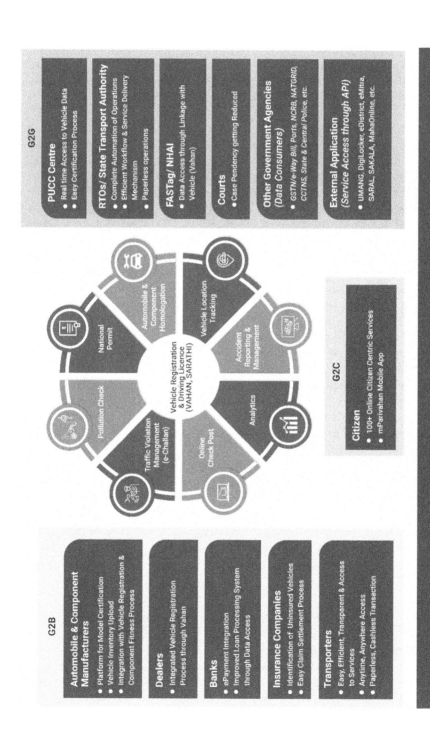

FIGURE 10.6
Project Evolution.

that has given a boost to their productivity. These IT-led initiatives have also contributed to the revenue of the states by provisioning new revenue streams (e.g., Fancy Number Auction) and reducing leakages (through ePayment, etc.). Compliance with rules and acts has increased significantly due to the adoption of applications like e-Challan Traffic Enforcement Solution, the Integrated Pollution Control System, vehicle tracking systems, and so on. The top authorities comprising the ministry and state transport departments are making use of the data-driven dashboards, which will help them make informed decisions and thereby formulate better policies. With multiple stakeholders, the transport ecosystem has emerged as a public digital platform where the exchange of data and services has grown tremendously, thus creating a constructive synergy.

4. Impact Delivered

The eTransport applications like Vahan, Sarathi, e-Challan, and others have transformed the transport sector by facilitating citizens with ease of getting services, increasing government revenue, making the RTOs more efficient and responsive, and bringing in overall transparency and compliance to the system. More than 100 services have been made online, many of them completely contactless, which reflects the synergy of technology intervention and process reengineering coming together to make a transformative change [13]. New initiatives have been undertaken in the areas of GPS-based vehicle tracking, accident reporting systems, the ITMS, automated driving test tracks, and fitment centers, among others. An important transformational impact has been witnessed in the area of governance in terms of better compliance with norms, transparency in systems, better data integrity through information exchange, provisioning of data-based decision support system, and the like.

There is an increased convenience to citizens that has been facilitated through anytime, anywhere capabilities such as ePayments, mobile apps, online processes/services, contactless interaction, and so on. More business opportunities and conducive working environments have been created through seamless, connected systems, which have empowered the stakeholders in the transport sector.

In terms of economic benefits, government revenue has increased due to plugging of leakage (checks and balances on the system, ePayment, etc.) and creation of additional revenue streams (like Fancy Number Auction, online check posts, data monetization, etc.).

A positive impact can also be experienced around increasing pollution and environmental concerns, with the enforcement of Bharat Stage VI (BS-VI) emission norms; promotion of electric and CNG vehicles; strict compliance with the PUCC; new scrapping policy to weed out old, polluting vehicles; and so on. Last but not the least, the social impact of the eTransport initiative is also a significant achievement. Due to the increase in transparency, citizen focus, and efficient online systems, the satisfaction level of end users has also improved. Technology and changed business processes together have ensured faster service, fewer hassles, and more options for citizens, which has significantly enhanced the perception of the whole sector.

5. Conclusion

The last decade of 2011–20 has been a period of tremendous growth in terms of the increasing number of vehicles, increase in citizen amenities, enhanced government revenue, increase in goods and passenger transport volume, and so on. On the other side, there have been challenges and shortfalls, like increasing environmental pollution, a raging number of accidents and related deaths, less public transport compared to the demand, and the like.

To address the growth and challenges, governments at the central and state levels have embarked on the journey of massive transformation of the transport sector through a combination of technology adoption and process reengineering. The extensive adoption of technology in providing better services to the citizen, bringing transparency in the system, ensuring better compliance of rules and environmental concerns, and building a connected ecosystem has addressed many important challenges of the transport sector in India. The amended CMVA and CMVR have also reflected this sentiment in incorporating many game-changing norms and practices in the regulatory system. Many of the services are now provided through online channels, some of which are completely faceless, thus minimizing the physical visit to the Transport Department Offices. On the other hand, emerging technology is increasingly being used in device-based traffic violation monitoring by transport enforcement, police, and Smart City authorities in ensuring better compliance of traffic rules and promoting road safety. Transport data collected through various applications in real time have paved the way for better reporting/analytics and controlled sharing among stakeholders for developing and enhancing many other external applications/systems.

The transport sector is an important contributor to the economic, social, environmental, and technological journey of a country. It is on the trajectory of realizing the larger objectives of nation building, keeping in view the scope of improvement in multiple avenues and challenges to be dealt with simultaneously.

The transport sector is at a crossroads, where the demand for fast-paced development is juxtaposed with the need to serve responsibly. Therefore, efforts should be channelized to bring in transformational changes in the processes, technology, and mindset behind the system, that is, a sustainable approach, warranting a greener environment, efficient systems, and minimal transport-related fatalities.

References

[1] "Road Transport System," *The Economics Times*, 28 August 2006. [Online]. Available: https://economictimes.indiatimes.com/industry/transportation/shipping-/-transport/road-transport-sector/articleshow/1930947.cms.

[2] Jean-Paul Rodrigue, "Urban Transport Challenges," in *The Geography of Transport System*, New York: Routledge, 2020, Ch. 8.4. [Online]. Available: https://transportgeography.org/?page_id=4621.

[3] Ministry of Road Transport & Highways, "Vahan Dashboard," Available: https://vahan.parivahan.gov.in/vahan4dashboard/.

[4] Deepak Halan, "How Intelligent Traffic Management Systems Enable Smarter Use of Transport Networks," *electronicsforu.com*, 28 June 2019. [Online]. Available: https://electronicsforu.com/market-verticals/automotive/intelligent-traffic-management-systems.

[5] UITP, "India: Public Transport in the Region," 2021. [Online]. Available: https://india.uitp.org/articles/indian-bus-operators-using-intelligent-transport-management-system.

[6] Sustainable Mobility for All, "Global Mobility Report 2017: Tracking Sector Performance," Washington, 2017. [Online]. Available: https://sustainabledevelopment.un.org/content/documents/2643Global_Mobility_Report_2017.pdf.

[7] RATESDOTCA, [Online]. Available: www.kanetix.ca/resources/will-tinted-windows-affect-your-auto-insurance-rate.

[8] Jean-François Gagné, "Global Transport Outlook to 2050: Costs of the Transport Sector Under Low Carbon Scenarios," 2015. [Online]. Available: https://sustainabledevelopment.un.org/content/documents/23490411Globaltransport.pdf.

[9] Ministry of Road Transport & Highways Transport, "Road Transport Yearbook (2015–16)," 1 February 2018. [Online]. Available: https://morth.nic.in/sites/default/files/other_files/Road_Transport_Year_Book_2015_16.pdf.

[10] Prachi Mishra, "Overview of Road Accidents in India," 28 March 2017, PRS Legislative Research. [Online]. Available: www.prsindia.org/policy/vital-stats/overview-road-accidents-india.

[11] World Health Organization, "Violence and Injury Prevention: Road safety in India," [Online]. Available: www.who.int/violence_injury_prevention/road_traffic/countrywork/ind/en/.

[12] Ministry of Road Transport & Highways, "Sarathi Dashboard," Available: https://sarathi.parivahan.gov.in/SarathiReport/DashBoardGr.do.

[13] Ministry of Road Transport & Highways, "Parivahan Sewa," Available: https://parivahan.gov.in/.

[14] Grant Thornton Bharat LLP, "Smart Transportation—Transforming Indian Cities," 12 May 2016. [Online]. Available: www.grantthornton.in/insights/ articles/smart-transportation—transforming-indian-cities/.

[15] National Informatics Centre, "Homologation Vahan Sewa," [Online]. Available: https://vahan.parivahan.gov.in/makermodel/vahan/dashboard.xhtml.

11

Open Government Data

A Way to Knowledge Discovery, Innovation, and Transparency

Alka Mishra, Durga Prasad Misra, Sunil Babbar,
and Sitansu S. Mahapatra

1. Introduction

The world is rapidly transforming into a digital ecosystem. Citizens and businesses use their modern gadgets to interact with each other, transact business, and deal with various government activities. With the increase in digitization, the focus has shifted to the open-source concept [1] and the socioeconomic value it can bring to the development and dissemination of information within a mixed economy comprising commercial, open-source, and hybrid solutions [2]. In the various sectors especially education, traditional models of publication are being challenged by the uprise of the new trend related to the open-access [3] movement.

Governments around the world are becoming more transparent by dynamically publishing relevant and comprehensive data as well as information and services on the web and mobile. This has opened new avenues in increasing access for data, which can further be analyzed, reused, and combined with other data by citizens free of cost. With open data, citizens are more informed about the day-to-day functioning of their governments. It also increases the level of transparency in tax collection, government spending, decision-making, the implementation of schemes and laws, and so on. The availability of information and data in a free and open format increases the participation of citizens and governments for improved social development and management.

Union and state governments in India collect, process, and generate a huge volume of data in its routine functioning, which are lying in silos and are hard to put for effective use. Evidence-based strategic planning is essential for socioeconomic development, and all this depends on the availability of up-to-date and quality data. Asset and potential values of data are extensively recognized at all levels. Data collected or produced from public funds, when made publicly available and maintained over time, witness a significant increase in their potential values, which could further be realized to its true potential. It helps in building a complete statistical viewpoint of the country and maximizes the use and reuse of data. In terms of social benefits, these data increase the accountability and transparency of the government bodies and help in better efficiency and effectiveness in service delivery, citizen participation, and social inclusion. The availability of data in a machine-readable format initiates innovation in business, the creation of new commercial products and services, efficiency in governance activities and service delivery, and so on. Figure 11.1 represents the various stakeholders involved in Open Government Data Ecosystem in India.

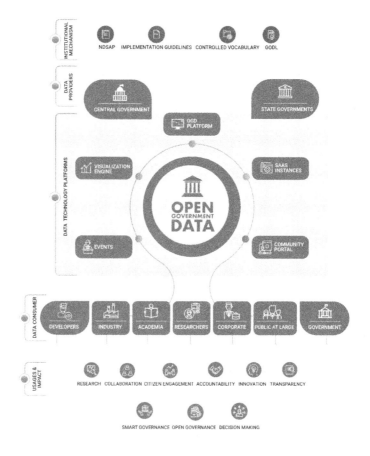

FIGURE 11.1
Stakeholders of Open Government Data Ecosystem in India.

2. Open Data—International Scenario

In December 2007, 30 thinkers and activists of the internet held a meeting in Sebastopol, north of San Francisco, intending to define the concept of open public data and have it adopted by the US presidential candidates [4]. Among them were two well-known figures: Tim O'Reilly and Lawrence Lessig. The first is familiar to the techies: This American author and editor is the originator of many vanguard computer and internet movements; he defined and popularized expressions such as open source and Web 2.0. Lawrence Lessig, a professor of law at Stanford University (California), is the founder of Creative Commons licenses, based on the idea of copyleft and free dissemination of knowledge [4].

In Sebastopol, Tim O'Reilly's contribution to open government shed new light on the relation between the opensource movement and the emerging principles of open data: In his own words, 'we must apply the principles of open source and its working methods to public affairs' [4].

In 2007, the result exceeded their expectations. A little over a year later, President Barack Obama took office in the White House and signed three presidential memoranda. Two of them concerned open government, of which open data was one of the pillars. These presidential memos explicitly set the culture of open source at the heart of public action by claiming its founding principles: transparency, participation, and collaboration [5]. Gradually the movement had taken shape, and many leading economies started their open data activities. In July 2013, Group of Eight (G8) leaders signed the G8 Open Data Charter, which outlined a set of five core principles on how data can support transparency, innovation, and accountability. Many nations and open government advocates welcomed the G8 charter, but there was a general sense that the principles could be refined and improved to support broader global adoption of open data principles [5]. In the months following, the Open Government Partnership's (OGP's) Open Data Working Group initiated activities to establish more inclusive and representative open data principles, including several multinational groups [5].

The International Open Data Charter (ODC) was launched at the margins of the 2015 United Nations General Assembly after a global consultation led by key representatives from OGP governments, including the United Kingdom, Canada, and Mexico, and civil society organizations, such as the World Wide Web Foundation, Open Data Institute, Open Knowledge Foundation, the Center for Internet and Society, and the Initiative for Latin American Open Data. It established six key principles, including that data should be open by default, timely, and interoperable [5]. Till now, the ODC has done collaborations with more than 100 governments and organizations working to provide data, based on a shared set of principles.

India was always working hand in hand with the international development in open data. In 2012, the foundation stone of open data was laid in India with a bilateral collaboration with the United States. A defined institutional mechanism, awareness among the data providers, state-of-the-art technology platform, calculated impact, and a wider stakeholder base have given India an edge to make the open data ecosystem more matured over these years.

3. NDSAP

There was an increasing demand by the Indian data consumers and community that data collected using public funds should be made readily available to all. They believed that efficient sharing of data among data owners and inter- and intragovernmental agencies along with data standards and interoperable systems was extremely important in a country like India. Hence, there was a need to formulate a policy with respect to national data sharing and accessibility, which could provide an enabling provision and platform for proactive and open access to the data generated through public funds available with various ministries/departments/organizations of the Government of India.

The NDSAP, gazette notified on 17 March 2012, was released by the Department of Science and Technology, where the Ministry of Electronics and Information Technology (MeitY) was mandated to implement the policy through the NIC. The policy coverage is for all the ministries, departments, and organizations of the Union government.

The objective of the policy is to facilitate access to shareable data and information owned by the Government of India in both human and machine-readable forms through a network all over the country in a proactive and periodically updatable manner. According to the preamble of the NDSAP, there has been an increasing demand by the community that data collected with the deployment of public funds should be made readily available to all, for enabling rational debate, better decision-making for progressive research and analysis, and use in meeting civil society needs [6].

The policy has also defined data classification, type of access, technology, legal framework, implementation strategy, and so on. The policy aims at the promotion of a technology-based culture of open data management and community engagement by creating the Open Government Data (OGD) Platform India [7].

4. Institutional Mechanism

The NDSAP earmarks a clear-cut way toward the initiation and the consequent implementation of open data principles enabling data sharing through a dynamic platform. After notification of the policy by the Department of Science & Technology (D/o S&T), the NDSAP Implementation Guidelines were framed after a multistage consultation with the central and state-level data managers, and an inter-ministerial task force was set up for this purpose. A separate policy for content moderation and approval was designed to make the content flow more robust and make officials accountable at various stages of the data publishing life cycle. Subsequently, the cabinet secretary to the Government of India steered to create the administrative setup for the policy implementation at all central government ministries and departments, that is, to create an NDSAP Implementation Cell and nominate a senior officer as the chief data officer (CDO) or nodal officer for implementation of the policy in their respective ministry/department/organization.

To cater to the contribution of data sets, the CDO can nominate several data contributors who would be responsible for the identification, cleaning, preparation, and contribution of the datasets along with their metadata. A dedicated project management unit (PMU) was set up at NIC headquarters for coordination and management of various activities of the project.

To acknowledge and encourage the CDOs, an Open Data Champion Award category was instituted in the Digital India Awards where platinum, gold, and silver awards are being presented to the CDOs according to their performance with respect to the contribution quality, quantity, and usage quotient.

5. Evolution of the OGD in India

The foundation of the OGD in India started with the NDSAP policy. It was further strengthened through a bilateral collaboration with the United States. The initial version of the product, OGPL, was developed and launched by India and the United States jointly in March 2012. The OGPL leveraged the best practices and features of India's 'India.gov.in' and the 'Data.gov' of the United States. The NIC from the Government of India and General Services Administration of the United States executed the development of the OGPL [8].

Launched with the name Data Portal India, it was the citizen-facing front end of the OGPL, which provided single-point access to all the datasets and apps as well as services. A beta launch was done on 1 October 2012 with only four datasets from two departments. Gradually it evolved to a full-fledged portal and was released on 1 August 2013 [8].

With the inclusion of more functionality, an improved version of the portal was introduced in February 2014 and named the OGD Platform—India with 7,000 datasets contributed by 66 departments [9]. In 2017, a new responsive and accessible version of the platform was developed in compliance with the

Guidelines for Indian Government Websites (GIGW). During these years, India was ranked among the top 10 countries in various international open data rankings.

Since its launch, community engagement activities were always a part of the OGD ecosystem. This includes feedback, events, challenges, workshops, hackathons, and so on. These engagements created a demand for a legal framework for data usages which led to the conceptualization of Government Open Data License (GODL) to fulfill that demand.

With increasing sensitization activities, few states and an urban local body (ULB), Surat, requested their exclusive data portals. To cater to the demand, OGD SaaS was launched. States such as Sikkim, Tamil Nadu, Karnataka, Kerala, Punjab, and Odisha have created their own dedicated data portals. Surat Municipal Corporation was the first ULB to create its dedicated portal. The Smart City Mission has taken this initiative forward and started the Smart City Data Portal for all 100 Smart Cities in India.

During these years, the team faced numerous challenges, such as adopting new technologies, withdrawal of community support in some open-source tools, scarcity of trained manpower, and so on. However, with dedicated efforts by the core team, adopting matured open-source technologies and minimum dependency on proprietary tools helped the platform overcome the majority of the technical challenges whereas other challenges were taken care of through collaboration with various stakeholders.

6. Conclusion and Way Forward

In its latest Open Data Barometer Leader's Edition survey, the W3C foundation outlined a few recommendations. These are specific ways that governments can improve their open data governance. Some of these recommendations are long-standing but have yet to be put into place and are necessary to solve crucial systemic issues. The recommendations include (a) put 'open by default' into action, (b) build and consolidate data infrastructure, (c) build open data skills across government, (d) update technical infrastructure, and (e) publishing with a purpose [16].

In the Indian context, these recommendations are highly relevant, and by adopting these recommendations, the OGD Platform India can potentially touch new highs and become a pathfinder for knowledge discovery, innovation, and transparency.

Proactive decision-making can only be achieved when the government and public authorities themselves consider publishing information as a responsibility without being requested by the public. This will enable citizens to track the use of public resources, spending, government expenses, actions, and more. It will lead to increase accountability of the government and implicitly subjected to social audit in India.

With Digital India at its peak, it is very easy to publish reliable information and make it available anywhere through the web. Citizens can have access to datasets openly and give their feedback for decision-making in various verticals of government. Several activities to provide seamless access to data for citizens are underway, which can be a catalyst to the empowerment of citizens, specifically the marginalized groups.

With open data now a decade old, it is time to move ahead and commit toward opening all-around government data by establishing a strengthening requisite institutional mechanism. This means developing strong policies, practices, and governing bodies and embedding these across all levels of the government. It means making open data core to governing—not just a side project.

In the next five years, the initiative is going to focus on guiding government departments for data publishing through open APIs through an API management solution. This will help in updating and maintaining the granularity of the datasets with minimum human interventions. In the long run, this will shape the ecosystem and give a positive impact on the social and economic value of open data.

A data exchange platform is also in the pipeline. This exchange would leverage data shared by the government and the community through a unified mechanism to spur data-driven research and commercial activities apart from moving toward data-driven governance. For example, the pollution numbers will affect property prices, restaurant reviews will mention official sanitation ratings, tollbooth data could be used to determine prices for nearby hoardings, and so on. The revolution across the industries and economies fueled by data from government and community is expected to contribute to the modern world in the way that the industrial revolution contributed during the past century.

The upcoming platform is expected to be a collaborative and participatory effort by all stakeholders, though driven and funded by the Government of India. Support from academic and research institutions, industry and corporate bodies, entrepreneurs, community, and thought leaders will make the platform more beneficial. The platform will become a driving force for the Indian data ecosystem consisting of databases from Digital India initiatives and projects and will attempt to leverage the India Stack. The Data Exchange Platform can potentially be developed into a central repository of various components of the open data and establish an exchange-cum-innovation ecosystem, making it a critical meta-database for integration and dissemination.

6.1. OGD Platform Technology

OGD Platform enables the proactive dissemination of government resources such as datasets, apps, and tools in an open or machine-readable format. The platform has been set up to provide collated access to resources (datasets, apps, and APIs) under catalogs published by different government entities in machine-readable formats. It also provides a search and discovery mechanism for instant access to desired datasets. OGD Platform also has a strong citizen engagement mechanism. The platform also allows citizens to express their requirements for specific resources and seek clarification or more detailed information from respective CDOs.

So far, most of the central ministries/departments/organizations have nominated nodal officers to drive this initiative, and most of them have started publishing open data on the platform. The statistics of published catalogs, datasets, and their usage can be accessed at the OGD India Platform website [7]. A ministry/department/state contributes and publishes resources in open format (CSV, XLS, XML, ODS, JSON) either directly or through web services on a predefined workflow in the data management engine. About 25 percent of datasets have been published through APIs/web services. The platform provides a government-to-government (G2G) service to all ministries/departments to contribute and manage the datasets. It also disseminates the government-to-citizen (G2C) service by allowing the citizens to consume datasets.

The OGD Platform has been developed and managed completely using Opensource Stack and has a responsive web layout design that helps seamless access of the platform on the web and mobile. The platform has state-of-the-art data discovery features such as search by synonyms, sector, jurisdiction, ministry/department/state, free keywords, data types, and the like. Suggestions and requirements of data can be submitted by citizens/community to help prioritize data sharing by participating ministries/departments. Anyone can also endorse already submitted suggestions. Citizens can directly write to the CDO (data provider) seeking any further clarification/information on the released resources or related requirements. The OGD Platform further enables better discovery and usage of government datasets through visualizations and development of apps, mashups, and so on.

The platform also has a provision for an update alert service that can be subscribed for catalogs. It also has custom widgets to share, link, and consume a filtered set of catalogs (ministry/department/organization as well as sectors, etc.). Over the years, the OGD Platform, with its associated subsystems, has evolved to support the open data ecosystem in totality, namely, with the following. Figure 11.2 represents the Open Government Data Timelines in India.

Visualization Engine: The OGD Platform enables better discovery and usage of government datasets through visualization and development of apps, mashups, and the like. The Visualization Engine [10] has the facility to create maps as well as different chart options like radar, bar, line, area, pie, and column, among others. Maps up to the district level, along with longitude and latitude coordinates, can also be created.

The engine also allows users to create visualizations by using available APIs and their datasets. Embedding and downloading facility of the

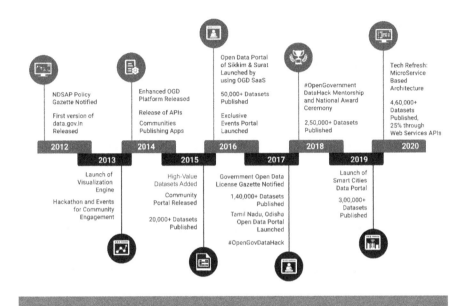

FIGURE 11.2
Open Government Data Timelines.

visualization is also available. The OGD PMU, along with states and Smart Cities, has regularly published visualizations on this engine, which can be browsed at the visualization gallery.

Community Portal: The dedicated Community Portal [11] works as a connecting link between the data providers and the consumers. Community members can share their knowledge through the contribution of blogs, infographics, visualizations, apps, and so on, and Datasets available on the OGD Platform can be used to create all these. Even the communities of SaaS instances extensively use this portal.

Event Portal: Community engagement is the key for field research on the released data, innovative consumption for social development right from the grassroots level by facilitating accessibility for all. Events play a vital role in this. OGD organizes regular events for various stakeholders whereby the dedicated Event Portal [12] facilitates the management of all events online. The portal provides end-to-end support to conduct hackathons, challenges, meetups, and so on.

6.2. Case Study: Smart Cities Open Data Portal

The Smart Cities Mission (SCM) in India was initiated by the Ministry of Housing and Urban Affairs (MoHUA) to transform 100 cities into Smart Cities. The mission has a plan to spur economic growth and to improve the quality of lives of residents through local infrastructure development and digital transformation. Various systems and processes, along with IoT devices, are deployed in these Smart Cities for improving the overall efficiency. A huge amount of data is being generated as a by-product of these systems. Making these data open for public use has a huge potentiality in creating meaningful business intelligence in operations and better service delivery to the citizens. Going forward, this data can help establish city-level data governance and SCM plans as the Data-Smart Strategy.

The Smart Cities Open Data Portal [13] is a step toward the culmination and effective execution of the Data-Smart Strategy. The portal is a single-window source for datasets of different Smart Cities. All the 100 Smart Cities are onboarded, and their CDOs contribute to datasets in the portal. These datasets are in a machine-readable format, and a majority of them are contributed through APIs.

With the publication of such datasets, it is expected that this data would be used to generate actionable insights not only by the local government bodies but also by other stakeholders such as research institutes, start-ups, academia, and industries. The data could help in developing products and services that would improve the lifestyle and governance in the urban scenario.

To give it a better institutional mechanism, a Data Maturity Assessment Framework has also been developed by the MoHUA. The Framework is envisaged to build a healthy competition among smart cities by conducting quarterly/half-yearly assessments through Systemic and Sectoral Maturity indices.

7. Stakeholders Engagement

Stakeholder engagement is one of the key components of the OGD ecosystem. The platform facilitates G2G and G2C engagement to encourage data publishing and consumption. The key stakeholders supplying data are ministries, departments, states, ULBs, and Smart Cities. Similarly, the stakeholders consuming the data include government departments, communities, academia, developers, start-ups, industries, businesses, corporates, media institutes, research organizations, individuals, and nongovernmental and not-for-profit organizations, among others.

Ministries/departments and states are the backbone for the data contribution operation. Sensitizing and knowledge-sharing sessions are organized for the government departments for generating value of data. Separate workshops are being organized for CDOs and data contributors regularly to keep them informed regarding the new developments in the data space. A compendium of case studies on data-driven decision-making was published for giving thrust to data usage [14].

Activities related to the engagement of data consumers are also being conducted at regular intervals. Challenges, hackathons, meetups, and seminars are organized for communities such as app developers, researchers, academia, students, start-ups, industry players, and others. Many national and regional events are also organized in association with industry, academia, community, and government.

Several applications have been developed by the community using the open datasets available on the OGD Platform. The process is getting matured day by day with more datasets available through APIs. This helps apps update in real time with micro-level data. Various applications were made using popular datasets such as Pin Code Directory, Mandi Prices, Air Quality Index (AQI), Air Sewa, Udyog Aadhar, HMIS, Company Master, Education Survey, Hospital Directory, and others.

8. GODL—India

With data-driven innovative applications in the market, there was an increasing demand from the communities, industries, and start-ups regarding a legal backing for usages of datasets available on the OGD Platform. In order to address this demand, the government has formed a committee with members from government departments and the open data community. The committee has studied global scenarios and licenses and drafted the GODL—India.

This license has been developed to give a legal framework and backing to the data consumers wishing to use and build on top of the public data. The license also gives assurance of what can be and can't be done with the data, both commercially and noncommercially [15].

As per the GODL, all users are provided a worldwide, royalty-free, nonexclusive license to use, adapt, publish (either in original or in adapted and/or derivative forms), translate, display, add value, and create derivative works (including products and services), for all lawful commercial and noncommercial purposes [15].

References

[1] Open Knowledge Foundation, "Open Data Commons: Legal Tools for Open Data," [Online]. Available: www.opendatacommons.org/.

[2] Paul Miller, Rob Styles and Tom Heath, "Open Data Commons: A License for Open Data," *LDOW*, 22 April 2008, p. 369. [Online]. Available: http://ceur-ws.org/Vol-369/paper08.pdf.

[3] Wikipedia, "Linked Data," [Online]. Available: http://en.wikipedia.org/wiki/Linked_Data.

[4] Simon Chignard, "A Brief History of Open Data," *Paris Tech Review*, 29 March 2013. [Online]. Available: www.paristechreview.com/2013/03/29/brief-history-open-data/.

[5] Open Data Charter, "Building Global Open Data Principles," [Online]. Available: https://opendatacharter.net/our-history/.

[6] Government of India, "National Data Sharing and Accessibility Policy (NDSAP) of India," *The Gazette of India*, 27 March 2012. [Online]. Available: https://data.gov.in/sites/default/files/NDSAP.pdf.

[7] Government of India, "Open Government Data Platform-India," 31 January 2021. [Online]. Available: https://data.gov.in.

[8] Neeta Verma, Alka Mishra and D. P. Misra "Open Government Platform: An Open Source Solution to Democratizing Access to Information and Energizing Civic Engagement," *Informatics*, July 2012. [Online]. Available: https://informatics.nic.in/uploads/pdfs/bf8ad9e4_lead_story.pdf.

[9] D. P. Misra and Alka Mishra, "Open Government Data (OGD) Platform India," *Informatics*, April 2014. [Online]. Available: https://informatics.nic.in/article/298.

[10] Government of India, "Visualize.data.gov.in," [Online]. Available: https://visualize.data.gov.in.

[11] Government of India, "Community.data.gov.in," [Online]. Available: https://community.data.gov.in.

[12] Government of India, "Event.data.gov.in," [Online]. Available: https://event.data.gov.in.

[13] Government of India, "Smartcities.data.gov.in," [Online]. Available: http://smartcities.data.gov.in.

[14] National Informatics Centre, "Data Driven Decision Making—Compendium," [Online]. Available: https://data.gov.in/sites/default/files/Compendium_Data_Driven_Decision_Making_NIC.pdf.

[15] Government of India, "Government Open Data License—India," *The Gazette of India*, 31 January 2018. [Online]. Available: https://data.gov.in/sites/default/files/Gazette_Notification_OGDL.pdf.

[16] Open Data Barometer, "Report from Promise to Progress," 23 January 2021. [Online]. Available: https://opendatabarometer.org/leadersedition/report.

12

eOffice—An Innovation in Governance

Rachna Srivastava and Kapil Kumar Sharma

> Good governance is perhaps the single most important factor in eradicating poverty and promoting development.
>
> —Kofi Annan

1. Introduction

Files are an important asset of the Government of India (GOI), and therefore, the efficient management and processing of files are fundamental to the core of governance. Much before the formation of ministries/departments (portfolio system) in the GOI, government business was disposed of by the governor-general of the council, later renamed as cabinet secretariat in 1946 [1]. The cabinet secretariat is responsible for the administration of the Government of India (Transaction of Business) Rules, 1961 and Government of India (Allocation of Business) Rules, 1961 facilitating smooth transaction of business in ministries/departments [2]. With an increase in the complexity in the government initiatives, it was important to have well-defined processes and procedures for handling secretarial work, which could be followed by government employees across various ministries/departments and other government organizations. The Department of Administrative Reforms and Public Grievances (DAR&PG), as a nodal agency in the field of 'Organization and Methods', has documented various procedures for the performance of secretarial work by the functionaries in various ministries/departments of the GOI in the form of the *Central Secretariat Manual of Office Procedure* (*CSMOP*) with the objective to create awareness of these processes and practices, especially at the cutting-edge level and to sensitize new entrants inducted at different levels. First published in March 1955, the *CSMOP* is revised from time to time to take care of the evolving situation [3].

The effectiveness of government organizations and employees can therefore be measured by their ability to dispose of matters, mainly receipts and cases, among others, with speed and quality, in compliance with the procedures prescribed for the purpose. One of the objectives of all government activities is to fulfill the needs of the people and promote their welfare without unnecessary delay. At the same time, those who are accountable for fair business practices must ensure that public funds are handled with utmost care and prudence. Therefore, in each case, it is important to keep an appropriate record of not only what has been done but also why it has been done. These records serve as evidence, precedent, reference, and material for training too.

1.1. Transaction of Government Business in India

The efficiency of an organization depends largely on the evolution of adequate processes and procedures and the ability of its employees to follow them. The procedures prescribed in the *CSMOP*, therefore, form the backbone of process management in the Central Secretariat.

Information received from various types of communications (letters, notes, etc.) is known as a DAK. Once a DAK/letter is diarized, and a unique receipt/diary number is allocated; then it becomes a receipt. A DAK/receipt is generally received in the central registry, given an identification number, and gets distributed to different sections/officers through peons/messengers and riders between various ministries/departments. The concerned section is required to take actions, like drafting a reply, opening a file, or putting the DAK in a file, creating notes, and so on, and further submits those actions to the officers for approval. Files now flow through the hierarchy in the department, where officers can record their decisions in the form of note and attach supporting documents as correspondence in the file. After approval, the letters/file are dispatched as per directions. After the action on a file is completed, it is marked as closed and moved to the record room.

Files and receipts are one of the most important assets in any organization. Governments produce and manage immense volumes of documents (files/receipts/office memoranda), which are being dealt with in the organization on a daily basis and play an integral role in decision-making process. Physical file management has always been a part of the functioning of the government. The manual system of movement/distribution of these documents has several challenges for effective functioning/monitoring. The challenges are difficulty in searching, retrieving, and tracking when needed. The storage of the files is another challenge, both in terms of storage and secure preservation. In addition to this, keeping record of these paper documents, their movement and safety involve lots of time, money, and efforts, which, in turn, decreases the efficiency and productivity of an organization.

Normally, files/receipts take up to 10 days to move across different levels, depending on the urgency, but it is largely determined by the employees handling the movement of these paper documents. File movement time is much higher for interdepartmental transactions by dispatch riders due to

scheduled times of dispatch vehicle or related issues. Furthermore, there were chances of leaking information/copying/tearing or misplacing papers.

Similarly, in the case of any new circular or notice that needs to be circulated to all employees, section, or to the selected group of officers of ministry(s)/department(s), it requires a lot of paper movement by creating multiple photocopies of concerned paper resulting in delay and at times not reaching to the concerned.

As the entire system is paper-based, it becomes vulnerable to destruction by other means such as fire, flood, insects, rats, or fungus. Protecting the files kept in record rooms from wear and tear and any misuse is a major challenge. At times, receipts are received printed on thermal paper that fades and ultimately vanishes over time, making the documents unreadable. Physical files may be lost forever. The searching, tracking, retrieving, and storing of receipts and files were very cumbersome.

2. Digital Transaction of Government Business in India

Writing letters and paperwork, adding up columns of figures, computing and sending out bills, and keeping precise financial records were all part of an office job in the past. All the writing and copying had to be done by hand using a pen and paper. For a duplicate copy of a document, one simply rewrote. Letters were often copied twice: one for the record and the other copy to mitigate the risk of misplacement of the original.

The advent of typewriters, the 'writing machine', along with carbon paper, made full-time handwriting obsolete. Typing was faster than writing by hand and provided far more readability and uniformity. However, the amount of time that the clerks spent in writing and copying remained the same while the number of documents produced increased.

With the onset of computers, an electronic format, a new information medium, was introduced as an alternative to paper. This new medium did not replace the paper format and led to the emergence of printers and scanners. Although documents can be read, authored, transported, stored, and retrieved, both formats existed side by side. The persistent paper document remained an important asset of office life, despite the computer and later the internet.

Over a period, many versions of office productivity applications were introduced to ease the functioning of offices. Initial versions of such applications were primitive but still provided editing and formatting capabilities. These products were widely accepted by officials for typing noting drafts, circulars, letters, office memorandums with the release of better versions with features like cut-and-paste, autocorrect, and autoformat, among others. With the help of computers and office productivity applications, the files/letters, noting, and the like can now be easily created, edited, and saved on computers, but the management of files and their processing were still manual. The entire system of file processing and decision-making was slow and lacked transparency leading to delays in the delivery of citizen-centric services.

2.1. Office Automation Solutions

Seeking a way to address the aforementioned issues, the immediate need was to have a system where an authorized employee can locate the required documents and/or files in the shortest possible time, update and share them with other relevant users and eventually store them with proper reference. With the emphasis on effective tracking of files/receipts and their movement and most importantly, recording the movement of files/receipts, the NIC [5], the GOI developed the Office Procedure Automation (OPA) application in 1997. The OPA was a client-server-based application and had to be installed on each official's computer. Although few departments adopted it, the client/server deployment mode made it somewhat difficult to manage.

With the internet revolution around the world, the OPA was redesigned and redeveloped into the File Tracking System (FTS) software, a web-based application, in 2000, which helped in tracking the movement of files and receipts. The use of the FTS in all central government organizations was mandated by the Cabinet Secretariat in 2000. However, soon user departments started seeking customization, enhancements, reports, and so on. As a result, different flavors of the FTS were released, most notably the File Data Management System for the Prime Minister's Office and the Document Management Information System for the Department of Personnel and Training, among others.

Although these tracking systems helped in tracking the files, the physical nature of a government file in a paper format remained. There were delays, and at times, it came to notice that the status of the file/receipt was not being updated by sections, resulting in gaps between the physical location of the file and the FTS.

To address the shortcomings of the FTS and to bring in the much-needed standardization across the government, the GOI, in recognition of the long-felt need for efficiency in government processes and service delivery mechanisms, had thus included eOffice as a core Mission Mode Project under the NeGP. In 2006, the NeGP was approved by the Cabinet and the DAR&PG was made the Line Department responsible for the implementation of eOffice across the government ministries/departments [6].

The objective of the eOffice system was not only to define the complete file creation and related processes but to also bring in transparency and accountability, reduce delays, and, most important, to save paper. The electronic creation of files was quite a revolutionary change as it would change the way of working in government offices and involved concepts like digital signing.

In 2009, eOffice was conceptualized with the aim to improve the functioning of government through more efficient, effective, and transparent inter- and intra-government transactions and processes. In the same year, a beta version of eOffice was released. This version was expected to be a fully functional filing system that would remove the need to maintain paper records completely. With the introduction of the eOffice system, the processes and procedures laid in earlier manuals (relating to physical paperwork) were carefully examined and reengineered by introducing the *Central Secretariat Manual of eOffice Procedures* (*CSMeOP*). In the 15th edition of the *CSMOP—2019—*eOffice procedures have been incorporated [7]. Figure 12.1 depicts the transformational journey of Filing System in India over a period.

Since most government ministry(s)/department(s) opted to migrate their in-house tracking system to standard eOffice system, few ministry(s)/department(s) further desired to start with electronic files on some identified subjects. Hence, a hybrid model was conceptualized that worked as both a tracking system and electronic filing with the facility to perform electronic diarization, file creation, noting, and Draft for Approval in a single system.

Many organizations adopted the electronic mode of eOffice with a vision to achieve 100 percent electronic movement to save paper and time. Organizations that opted for hybrid mode of eOffice were slowly moving to the electronic mode by adopting different transitional approaches such as 'all-new files to be created in electronic mode only from a cutoff date' or 'old files which are in tracking mode were evaluated for conversion to electronic within a defined time frame'. These were also the organizations who have initiated the use of Digital Signature Certificate (DSC) by officials while writing the note in a file, to add legal sanctity to the note. In 2016, eSign (Aadhaar-based signing) was introduced in eOffice as an alternative to DSC-based signing.

It was during 2014 when state governments like Kerala and Maharashtra came forward to implement eOffice in their states, and eOffice was maintained as a single code base only. State-specific customizations were undertaken with utmost care ensuring the single-code base philosophy of eOffice Product. It is the same eOffice product that was rolled out in the Ministry of Telecommunication and Digital Infrastructure, Government of Sri Lanka, in January 2018 [8], in a short period of a week only, as a testimony to the generic nature of the eOffice product. The standardized eOffice product can be adopted easily in Commonwealth countries as our filing system originated from the common governance. Figure 12.2 depicts the evolution of eOffice in the last 25 years.

As a by-product of the eOffice application, which was producing large volumes of documents, circulars, notices, and the like, the KMS became an integral part of the eOffice suite. The first version of the KMS and eOffice Portal was launched in 2002, by the NIC, under the name of IntraNIC, which provided for a comprehensive document repository, and the portal served as

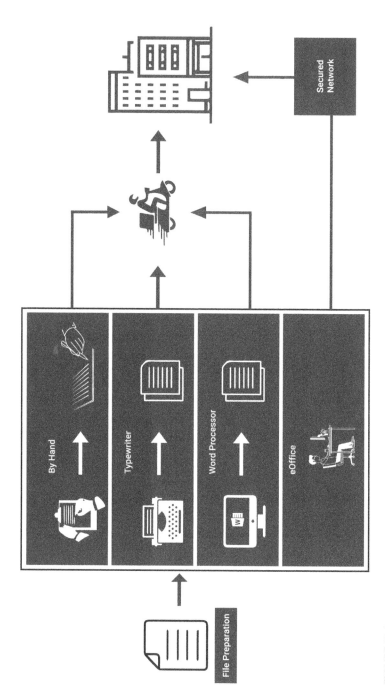

FIGURE 12.1
Transformational Journey of Filing System in India.

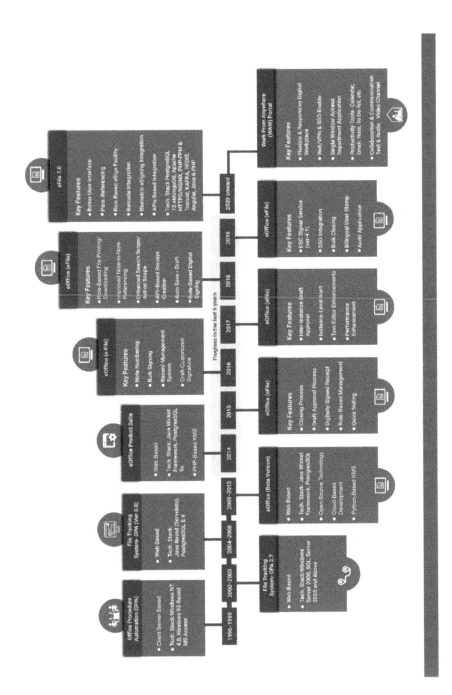

FIGURE 12.2
The eOffice Evolution.

a gateway, integrated with most of the in-house applications, offering a single window for government employees to access all the information like notices, circulars, pay slips, GPF statements, and so on. The first version of IntraNIC (KMS and Portal) was developed in Microsoft SharePoint technology and proved revolutionary as it was the first of its kind product from the government to its employees with a purpose to provide all the needed documents in a single place.

The objective of eOffice was to provide transparency, accountability and reduce the delays in the decision-making in the filing process, but similar was the need in other aspects of employee functioning, resulting in the development of applications for leave and tour automation, annual performance appraisal reporting, and so on. eOffice was all about facilitating government employees to execute their functions in the channels of the governmental hierarchy and created the inventory of employees' data in the PIMS, which forms the core data across each of the eOffice applications.

As the data center and virtualization technologies emerged as game changers in the field of infrastructure provisioning to leverage the cloud technologies and to support smaller organizations, eOffice was made cloud-enabled in 2012. The implementation of eOffice experienced a huge push in 2014, and the Digital India Program accelerated this whole journey.

During the COVID-19 pandemic in 2020, the implementation of eOffice across the country increased significantly. It was difficult to continue to work with traditional paper-based file systems during a complete lockdown state, without significant delays in the functioning of any government office. Also, there was fear of novel coronavirus infection through physical paper/files, which may be transmitted among messengers/dispatch riders and others. During the period of lockdown, eOffice emerged as a game changer by facilitating unfettered and secured access to the files to government officials. One of the major factors that have contributed to the growth of eOffice was the availability of interdepartmental file transfers through eOffice. As soon as the lockdown was announced, government officials could access eOffice over the secure channel through WebVPN at any time and from anywhere.

2.2. eOffice—A Digital Workplace Solution

eOffice is a product suite comprised of several applications for transforming the day-to-day official work-related activities of a government organization [4]. It aims to achieve simplified, responsive, effective, and transparent paperless working in government offices. The components of eOffice are as follows. Figure 12.3 showcases the key components of eOffice and are explained in the subsequent sub-sections.

2.2.1. *File Management System (eFile)*

eFile is a workflow-based system (refer to Figure 12.4 for a broad workflow of eFile creation) that extends the features of existing manual handling of files

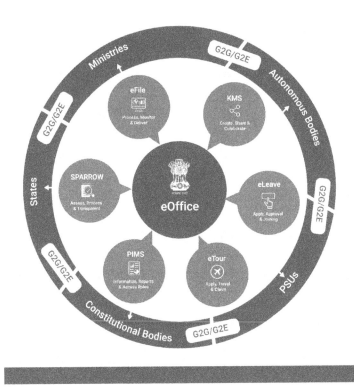

FIGURE 12.3
eOffice Product Suite.

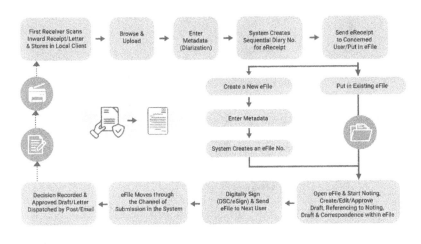

FIGURE 12.4
Broad Workflow of Electronic File Creation.

in addition to a more efficient electronic system. It is a product aimed to bring efficiency to office work and is based on the *CSMeOP* of the DAR&PG, GOI. The system comprises different sub-modules that are interlinked to manage the official workflow of the entire life cycle of a document/DAK from the moment it is received by the organization till the time it is disposed of with the proper set of actions. It involves all stages of working in a file, including the scanning, diarization of inward receipts, creation, movement of files, and, finally, the closing of files/receipts.

2.2.2. KMS

The KMS component of eOffice brought the concept of a central repository of documents in an organization. It provides for users to create and manage electronic documents in the workflow, along with versions (tracking history) that can be easily viewed, searched, shared, and published. It logically organizes the content and standardizes content creation and presentation across an organization. Figure 12.5 depicts the process flow of KMS.

2.2.3. Leave Management System (eLeave)

eLeave is a centralized system for the maintenance of leave records. It is a simple intuitive workflow-based system to apply for leave online, track the status of applied leave, details of leaves taken, leave balance, and so on. The approval of leave is enabled through the hierarchical channel of submission in a predefined workflow. The leave rules are configured as per the existing government rules. It helps employees in the tracking of their leaves with short message service (SMS) and email-based alerts.

FIGURE 12.5
KMS.

2.2.4. Tour Management System (eTour)

eTour is a system that facilitates the management of employee tour programs from the time of applying for the tour to the final settlement of bills. This system ensures that all tour requests are properly accounted for. Employees can apply, cancel, approve/reject, and view tour records. For employees, the system allows them to easily view their tour details at any given point and request tours online. For managers, tour approval no longer involves trails of paperwork. The system provides complete trails of an employee's tour and plans.

2.2.5. PIMS

The PIMS is a workflow-based system for maintaining the details of every aspect of an employee record including employee identity, educational qualifications, skill set, contact details, posting and location, the CGHS, the Central Government Employees Group Insurance Scheme, nomination, Leave Travel Concession, Salary Details, House Building Advance, record verification details, and more. The PIMS allows users to enter and update the employee personal data and employment records according to the access and role privileges. The PIMS is also available on self-service access through which users can view, check, and update their information and submit the same to the admin, which is further validated before it is changed in the employee's record.

2.2.6. SPARROW

SPARROW is a web-based application for processing of APAR. Employees can fill in their APAR, which is further reported and reviewed by the official hierarchy. The system provides a dashboard facility that enables the service controlling authority to monitor the status such as officers posted, pendency at various levels, and APARs processed and closed. SPARROW helps in reducing delays in submission and processing of APARs and ensures transparency by tracking the movement of APAR. The system has also streamlined the Departmental Promotion Committee process by providing various data analytics reports such as grading, domain specialization reports, and so on.

3. Transformational Journey of a Service

eOffice aims to contribute significantly to transforming the core of the government's functioning which would eventually improve transparency, efficiency, accountability, and faster decision making. The following methods were adopted for smooth, successful, and sustainable implementation of eOffice across different kinds of government organizations with a huge user base, varying from the lowest level to the highest.

3.1. Change Management and Capacity Building

Changing the perception/mindset of people at all levels to change the traditional ways of the physical file movement system has been a challenge. To overcome this challenge, capacity-building programs on eOffice, for various categories, like users, master trainers, employee master details, managers and product administrators, and system administrators are conducted by the NIC regularly.

3.2. Multilevel Support Mechanism

As the eOffice product has been rolled out in nearly all the central government ministries/departments, several state secretariats, districts, and public-sector undertakings, the support to users becomes extremely critical. A multilevel support system has been set up for the implementation of eOffice across the country. The on-site rollout team at the L0 level is set up by the implementing user department for providing hands-on/troubleshooting support to the end users. This team can further escalate/coordinate with the next level (Service Desk). At Level 1, a Service Desk, set up by the NIC is the common platform to register any issue. Apart from the bugs and issues, an eOffice Support Portal is also in place, through which the users can register their feedback or change request. NIC Teams in NIC State units and ministries/departments form the Level 2 support layer. Finally, it is governed by the NIC eOffice Project Division at NIC headquarters at Level 3.

3.3. Adoption of Emerging Technologies

The adoption of emerging technologies is of paramount importance because it has the potential to address the challenges that were earlier not resolved by traditional technologies. eOffice adapts to the ever-changing ecosystems around it with changes in the technologies, frameworks, operating systems, browsers, and changes in government policies and processes in the form of new releases and version upgrades.

3.4. Government Process Reengineering and Preparation of Standard Operating Procedures

The efficient functioning of the government systems to a large extent depends on the evolution of adequate processes and procedures, and the ability of its functionaries to follow them. Physical file system–based processes and procedures were carefully examined and re-engineered by introducing the *CSMeOP* in the 15th edition of the *CSMOP—2019*—by the DAR&GP [7].

3.5. Monitoring and Promotion

The DAR&PG, in coordination with the NIC, is regularly monitoring the implementation of eOffice in all central government ministries/departments. To recognize and promote the implementation of eOffice, Certificates of Appreciation are presented by the DAR&PG to central ministries/departments who have implemented eOffice successfully (with eFiles greater than 80 percent of their total files).

3.6. Integration with External Systems

Most of the user departments already had their domain-specific-related workflow-based applications and dashboards in place. After the implementation of eOffice in a department, the next requirement was for the integration of eOffice with existing workflow-based systems (external systems) because approvals were being done in eFiles only. eOffice has become the feeder to other eGovernance systems by providing interfaces to external applications through read/write APIs. Figure 12.6 illustrates the integration of eOffice with other external systems.

The government has been putting great emphasis on improving productivity in its internal processes and increased transparency in the decision making and bringing in citizen's participation as part of the inclusive Governance in the country. An automated eOffice attempts to achieve this with an extension of the system to citizens through the Citizen Interface to facilitate their knowledge about the status of action taken on their grievances, applications, petitions, and Right to Information. Telemetry APIs are available that can

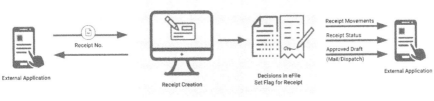

FIGURE 12.6
Integration with External Applications.

be easily consumed and integrated within departmental dashboards for providing progress reports, monitoring, and information/reports, resulting in managing the productivity at the individual/section/department level, thereby bringing in positive change in the administrative system.

4. Impact and Outcomes

eOffice is currently being adopted across the Government ministries and departments in India as 'ONE INDIA ONE PRODUCT'. As of this writing, eOffice has been implemented in 647 organizations, which include 275 central government institutions and 372 at various state governments. So far, eOffice has been used by 0.62 million (620,000) users generating 20.7 million eFiles and 66 million eReceipts leading to a total of 385 million transactions (*numbers as of 10 February 2021*).Quick Decision-Making and Faster Delivery of Services eOffice is accessible from anywhere anytime ensuring that the decision-making is delayed. This 24/7 accessibility even from remote locations (while on tour, leave, or away from the office) has made the working environment more flexible and increased the productivity and efficiency of the organization leading to faster delivery of services.

4.1. Reduction in Malpractices and Red-Tapism

The speed and efficiency enable informed and quicker decision-making within government offices, which results in better public service delivery and reduces malpractice and red-tapism. All transactions in eOffice are captured with audit trails and are tamper-proof. Unproductive, unintended touchpoints/dealing hands and personal priorities/discretions for any file movement are eliminated to a large extent.

4.2. Accountability and Transparency

eOffice has instilled transparency in the system of office procedures, as files/receipts can be easily searched, retrieved and action can be taken on forthwith. eOffice also provides an effective monitoring mechanism to monitor the performance of individuals, the pendency of files, files cleared, and files worked on, leading to increased accountability and responsibility of staff at all levels.

4.3. Environmentally Friendly and Support to the Go-Green Initiative

With the implementation of eOffice, organizations are gradually transitioning to a less-paper office, which has helped in reducing green wastage and

FIGURE 12.7
Benefits of eOffice.

saving trees. Apart from the paper sheets, infrastructure cost toward procurement of printers, cartridges, cupboards, office spaces, and transport expenditures are also saved.

4.4. Resilience to Disasters

eOffice provides for much-needed resilience against disasters as files are preserved in servers with disaster recovery measures in place. The digital environment of eOffice also safeguards the documents and files from other common disruptive factors like insects, rats, fungus, damage to the files, and fading of printed text in documents over the years. Benefits of eOffice are shown in Figure 12.7.

5. Case Studies Highlighting Impact Delivered

5.1. Collectorate Jagatsinghpur, Odisha [9]

The eOffice product suite has been made fully functional in Jagatsinghpur, a coastal district in Odisha, prone to natural disasters. The entire collectorate, district-level offices, subdivision, and block/Tehsil-level offices have no physical movement of files. Daily, an average of 40 to 50 files are approved by the district magistrate without any restraint. This has resulted in the effective delivery of services in several social sectors, including security pensions like old age and widow pensions and a stipend for divyangjans, being very much applauded across the entire district. The movement of files is tracked, and any cause of delay is taken up seriously by the collector. With the launch of eOffice touchscreen kiosk [10], people can track the status of their applications and the movement of official files. Visits to government offices for queries relating to services or filing complaints have been reduced substantially.

5.2. Greater Hyderabad Municipal Corporation, Telangana (GHMC) [11]

The implementation of electronic filing in the GHMC has resulted in increasing the speed of filing applications and has also facilitated the movement of files at all times. The officials can now dispose of the files marked to them at any time while working from anywhere.

Before implementing eOffice, there were personal priorities/discretions in the movement of files. This has been greatly reduced post-implementation of eOffice. Moreover, deleting/replacing the notes, tearing of files, photocopying of important papers, and so on cannot be even thought of. The citizens are aware of the movement of their application, and their perception toward eOffice is very positive due to enhanced transparency, accountability, and quick decision-making, resulting in better public service delivery.

5.3. Mantralaya, Maharashtra [12]

The need to opt for a paperless environment in the government of Maharashtra emerged when an unforeseen firebreak incident occurred on 21 June 2012, in Mantralaya, Mumbai, resulting in the loss of an immense number of files/documents belonging to 18 departments. Maharashtra decided to go paperless after this incident by introducing eOffice.

According to a study [12] undertaken by the government, it could quantify the rate at which the number of pages/files in a paper-based file system grows in an office and the average time to retrieve them. A letter had to be recorded in dozens of registers and generally took 41 movements before it is answered. It is estimated that only 12,500 sheets of paper can be made from a fully grown tree and an average of 210 billion sheets of paper is sent annually by fax, translating into 'green damage'.

5.4. Konkan Railway Corporation Limited (KRCL) [13]

A study related to return on investment on several parameters, such as infrastructure and real estate, manpower for file handling, savings in the use of paper, and efficiency parameters, was carried out by KRCL. As a result of this study, it was found that after implementing eOffice, KRCL had saved a huge sum of money every year. The cost toward infrastructure and real estate in terms of cupboards, office space, and physical security (custodian) is 100 percent saved, as the data generated in eOffice is stored in servers and audit trails for every transaction being done are maintained.

Before implementing eOffice, the file movements were done through individuals, and almost every day, one person was required to travel from Ratnagiri to Mumbai and vice versa for delivering important files for approvals at KRCL Headquarters in Mumbai. After implementing eOffice, the need for traveling to move files inter-regionally is not required.

6. Conclusion and a Way Forward

The eOffice product suite is an extremely challenging product on account of the ever-changing ICT and operating environments, with a large user base, varying from lowest levels to the highest, in different kinds of government organizations. The feedback and change requests from them enriched the product in an unparalleled way. Over a period, the eOffice product suite has eventually evolved as a matured platform with applications providing for a much-needed efficiency in the government in a generic and uniform manner.

Going forward, eOffice will explore the use of AI to identify decisions as precedence for future cases/subjects to quickly arrive at decisions and achieve 'observance of precedent'. In addition to this, Smart Noting powered by machine learning to offer suggestions to recipients will also be explored. Enhancements by reengineered processes and building in smart chatbots to assist while working in eOffice would also be worked on. The use of speech-to-text in Indian languages is another area of work envisaged.

At present, the decisions taken on files are unstructured, and one has to read all the contents of the file (previous notes and correspondence) to arrive at a decision. As the structured approval process for government files is a complex domain and will add another dimension to government functioning, therefore, eOffice would also attempt to work in this area. A central knowledge repository and archiving government files with linkages to the National Archives, the ultimate resting place for government records, is also on the wish list.

References

[1] Cabinet Secretariat, "Origin," [Online]. Available: https://cabsec.gov.in/aboutus/origin/ [Accessed 8 February 2021].

[2] Cabinet Secretariat, "Functions," [Online]. Available: https://cabsec.gov.in/aboutus/functions/ [Accessed 8 February 2021].

[3] Department of Administrative Reforms & Public Grievances, "Central Secretariat Manual of Office Procedure," 13th ed., 23 September 2010, New Delhi, pp. 1–250. [Online]. Available: https://darpg.gov.in/sites/default/files/CSMOP-13.pdf [Accessed 19 January 2021].

[4] National Informatics Centre, "eOffice: A Digital Workplace Solution," 2020, pp. 1–129. [Online]. Available: https://eoffice.gov.in//downloads/eOfficeBook2020.pdf [Accessed 20 January 2021].

[5] "National Informatics Centre," [Online]. Available: www.nic.in/ [Accessed 25 February 2021].

[6] Department of Administrative Reforms & Public Grievances, "The e-Office Framework: A Way Forward for the Government," 2 December 2011, New Delhi. [Online]. Available: https://darpg.gov.in/sites/default/files/The_e-Office_Framework_0.PDF [Accessed 20 January 2021].

[7] Department of Administrative Reforms & Public Grievances, "Central Secretariat Manual of Office Procedure: Enabling the March Towards the Digital Secretariat," 15th ed., 2019. [Online]. Available: https://darpg.gov.in/sites/default/files/CSMOP2019/mobile/index.html#p=1 [Accessed 20 January 2021].

[8] "India's NKN, Sri Lanka's LEARN Connect with High Capacity Net," *Outlook: News Scroll*, 15 January 2018. Available: www.outlookindia.com/newsscroll/indias-nkn-sri-lankas-learn-connect-with-high-capacity-net/1230701 [Accessed 22 February 2021].

[9] "Lockdown: E-office in JSpur Dist Comes Handy," *The Pioneer*, 3 April 2020. [Online]. Available: www.dailypioneer.com/2020/state-editions/lockdown--e-office-in-jspur-dist-comes-handy.html.

[10] "E-office Kiosks to Be Installed in Jagatsinghpur," *Local Wire*, 28 June 2020. [Online]. Available: https://localwire.me/e-office-kiosks-to-be-installed-in-jagatsinghpur/ [Accessed 20 January 2021].

[11] Y. Satyanarayan Murthy, "Success Story of eOffice in the Greater Hyderabad Municipal Corporation (GHMC), Telangana," *Informatics: An eGovernance Publication from NIC*, July 2015, pp. 14–16. Available: https://informatics.nic.in/uploads/pdfs/56082549_E-Office.pdf [Accessed 20 January 2021].

[12] Government of Maharashtra, "Case Study on Implementation of eOffice in Mantralaya, Mumbai," [Online]. Available: www.egovernance.guru/wp-content/uploads/publications/casestudies/case-study-eoffice-mantralaya.pdf [Accessed 20 January 2021].

[13] Bindu Muralidharan, "Implementation of eOffice in KRCL: An Innovative File Management Solution," June 2016. [Online]. Available: http://cips.org.in/mmp/documents/Workshops/2016/June/eOffice1-3/3/eOffice_BinduMuralidharan.pdf [Accessed 20 January 2021].

13

Transforming the Ambit of Indirect Taxation through Technology

P. V. Bhat, Nagesh Shastri, H. L. Ravindra,
Sunita P. Bennur, and Suresh C. Meti

1. Introduction

The new Goods and Services Tax (GST) system was started with the policy of 'One Nation–One Market–One Tax'. This system has brought the concept of uniform taxation throughout the nation so that tax rates are moderated and the whole nation becomes a single market. In addition to providing online services, the new regime brought self-monitoring among the taxpayers. It also strengthened internal accountability and brought transparency in the processes.

'Indirect taxes' includes various taxes collected by the state and central governments. The important and new one is the 'GST'. The government has brought major reforms in the taxation system from 1 July 2017 throughout the country. The various indirect taxation systems were merged, and a new 'GST' system has replaced all of them [1]. Each instance of supply liable for VAT previously is now levied under the GST. There would be millions of such transactions each day. The challenge is to ensure that each supply trans-action gets accounted for completely. In the previous regime of indirect taxes, procedures and systems for tax collections were essentially complex, man-ual, and paper-based. Furthermore, the monitoring of such a large number of taxpayers and each of their transactions became a stupendous task. The tax department tried to impose several types of controls that worked to some extent, but they also created hardships for the taxpayers. Thus, the old sys-tems and procedures had completely outlived their utility.

Major technology reforms in the indirect taxation processes started taking place from 1991 onward. These reforms can be categorized into three peri-ods. The first one was between 1991 to 2004, which has been characterized by central taxes by introducing the Modified VAT (MODVAT) Service Taxes, a simplification of taxes [2]. During this time, MIS systems were developed. The central government had built the SERMON (System for Excise Revenue and Monitoring) to monitor and manage the central excise duties. The state tax departments had also adopted various IT initiatives to computerize the records of the taxpayers and generate the MIS reports.

The next one was between 2005 to 2016 by states, by implementing the VAT system [3]. Initially, the tax departments built the IT systems with a workflow-based system to capture the processing of the various applications. This was the time when internet technology took off and introduced websites. ePayments and e-filing of returns were major initiatives taken by the departments.

Finally, the center and the states have collaborated to implement the GST since 2017 [4]. The online services are strengthened further and ensured that the services are delivered in a stipulated time. In this period, all GST services were made online, including grievance redressal. Some of the services were moved to an auto-approval mode if they have not been approved by the competent authority within the stipulated time. One of the long-pending requests of the taxpayers for making an online refund process was also implemented, and finally, the refunds are transferred to the bank account of the taxpayers.

2. Indirect Taxes in India

The taxation of commodities also has a long history in India. Kautilya, a great Indian statesman in the Mourya Kingdom, more than 2,000 years ago anticipated classical economic thought in international trade, taxation, and labor value. Kautilya wrote 'Arthashastra', an epic treatise on the art of good governance and views on increasing the monarch's wealth and realm. Kautilya's discussion of taxation gave expression to three principles: Taxing power should be limited, taxation should not be felt heavy or excessive, and tax increases should be graduated. Kautilya recognized that the ideal tax system should embody the following: easy to calculate, inexpensive to administer, fair (equitable in its burden), non-distortive of economic behavior in its impact (neutral), and, in general, not inhibit economic growth and development.

Indirect taxation contributes significantly toward government revenues. Indirect taxes in India are administered by the central, state, and local governments (municipalities) (refer to Figure 13.1) [5]. Previously, the Central Taxes Department administered excise duty, customs, and service taxes. These taxes were brought into effect during different time periods to increase the tax base and reduce the tax burden. Furthermore, the Central Sales Tax Act was enacted for the levy, collection, and distribution of taxes on the sale of goods during interstate trade or commerce.

The legislation was available to the states, to enact laws for levying and collecting tax on the transactions of sale or purchase of goods. Accordingly, state governments were administering the Sales Tax Act, right from the commencement of said enactment. The multipoint tax system was prevalent in the state until the early 1980s. Turnover tax, additional tax, and resale tax,

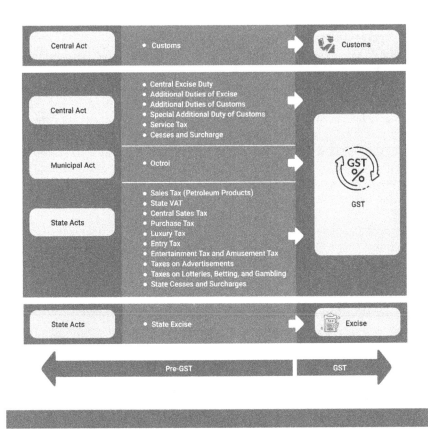

FIGURE 13.1
Indirect Taxes before the GST.

among others, were also being levied and collected during different periods in addition to basic tax.

In addition to sales tax, the states have also enacted multiple acts to increase the tax base and collection. These include the Entertainments Tax Act, the Purchase Tax, the Betting Tax, the Octroi Act, the Entry Tax Act, the Luxuries Tax Act, the Advertisement Tax, and others.

The concerted efforts of the States paved way for the introduction of the Value Added Tax System during 2005–2006 in place of the conventional Sales Tax System [6]. One of the many reasons underlying the shift to VAT in the country was to have a uniform system of commodity taxation all over the states. In the earlier sales tax, a structured tax was not levied on all the stages of value addition or distribution. The VAT system widens the tax base by levying tax on the sale of goods at every point of sale and makes the levy of tax transparent and removes cascading. In the VAT system, the tax paid on inputs purchased within the State is rebated against the goods sold. The municipalities (local governments) were also enabled to collect the taxes for entry of goods in their jurisdiction as Octroi.

During 2000–2001, the central government and all the governments of states and union territories had started working toward the implementation of the GST system by removing the existing complex tax system [4]. After arriving at a consensus, the GST was implemented uniformly throughout India from 1 July 2017 and has subsumed eight central taxes and nine state taxes, thereby bringing uniform taxation for the goods and services through-out the nation [7] [1]. The GST is levied as a dual tax—Central GST and State GST—and it is administered equally by central and state authorities [4]. The government has formed a company called 'GST Network—GSTN' to support and implement the end-to-end IT solutions for the GST system [8]. Figure 13.2 depicts the hierarchy of GST setup in India.

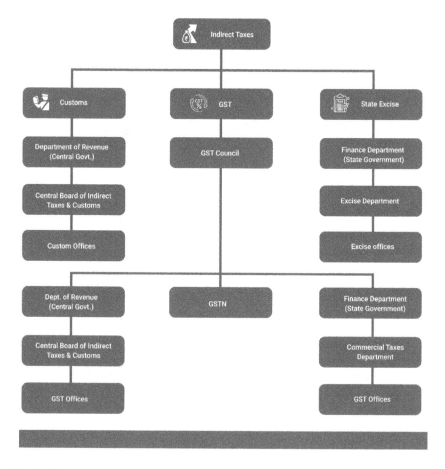

FIGURE 13.2
Hierarchy of the GST Setup.

3. Global Trends in Indirect Taxation

The indirect taxes across the countries are a complex scenario. The taxes are based on the acts of the local governments as per their suitability. For a country like India, it was a very complex tax structure due to the hierarchical democratic setup.

Global companies have to adapt to all such scenarios. As it requires a robust digital system to handle the complex tax compliances at the global level, it has become inevitable for companies to build digital ecosystems. To complement the dependency of the companies on robust digital systems, the governments of many countries have started computerization of their tax systems. The tax departments established faceless digital environments through which the taxpayer could carry out most compliances through the digital systems only. The taxpayers themselves are encouraged to punch in the data directly into the government tax systems, and there will be no or minimal data entry mistakes as the onus of providing correct data is on the taxpayer. New tax reforms in any country are happening with a focus on ICT-based development.

The new digital systems are being designed in such a way that a piece of information now needs to be entered once and can be used multiple times, thereby reducing a lot of efforts in data entry, mistakes in data entry, and so on. Recent trends across the globe depict increased adoption of e-invoicing systems. Many countries, including India, are implementing this new game-changing system in a phased manner and have put up the road map for coming years. e-invoicing helps the taxpayer in meeting most of the tax compliance with one single transaction. Businesses can exchange invoices digitally among themselves as well as with statutory organizations and financial institutions, and this will help in quicker payment cycles, input tax credits, and the like. From the tax authority's perspective, this will reduce fraudulent activities and ensure easy monitoring of compliance.

The governments are trying to provide a seamless interaction mechanism for the companies having businesses across the globe by adopting standard invoice structures. With this, the businesses can easily exchange the invoices digitally with their counterparts across the countries that are in a machine-readable format as well as meet the respective government compliance requirements. Digitally signed invoices provide the added advantage of digitally verifying the contents of the invoices. Countries have been accepting the standards such as Pan-European Public Procurement Online (PEPPOL) used by the European countries and Universal Business Language—an XML-based standard for the business documents such as invoices [9]. The countries are setting up or facilitating the exchange of invoices among the stakeholders including the tax authorities in electronic form. India has adopted a derivative of the PEPPOL with minor changes to meet the local requirements.

The countries are focusing on improving the overall experience of the taxpayers through simplification of the taxation system, tax rates, faceless digital systems, and providing simplified ways for compliance with the help of robust IT systems. Singapore is one of the successful South Asian countries in implementing indirect taxes [10].

The global focus is on using business intelligence, AI, and machine learning tools to analyze data for policymaking, derive the tax structure, and predict tax collection, in addition to detecting tax evasion and fraud.

4. Reengineering the Processes Using IT

Over the years, the departments dealing with indirect taxes have taken up several e-initiatives. Reengineering of the processes has been taken with the focus on user convenience and user experience in paying the taxes and improvement in the tax compliance and collection. It is also aimed at strengthening the internal transparency and accountability in the governance and enhancing the efficiency of the officers [3]. The following sections explain a few of the important ones.

4.1. Online Registration, Payments, and Filing of Returns

The taxpayers complete their registration, file the return, make payment of tax, collect, and submit the forms to carry out the business activities. All these processes were manual, and taxpayers were made to visit the tax offices multiple times to do the same. As all the data were stored in paper format, it used to take time for processing and approval by the officer as well. The entire model of delivery of services was changed and the interface between the taxpayer and the tax department was made through the 24/7 online systems services. The specific services provided under this are described in the following.

To overcome the difficulties of the taxpayers, a single-window system of online filing with supporting documents, status checking, and downloading of registration certificates was introduced. The tax officers carried out the processing and approval activities online through a back-office system. All the taxpayers are enabled to file the returns electronically through a web-based service, with a unique username and password. A system of e-payment and automatic reconciliation was introduced. The taxpayer can view the tax liabilities through the website and make the payment online to the government. The statutory forms that were previously availed manually by the taxpayer only after the approval by the tax officer have now been made available online. The facility for raising the grievances is also made online, and the status and response of the officer for the grievance can be viewed in the portal.

4.2. Online Refund Process

Sometimes, the taxpayer will have an excess credit on the ledger due to input tax credit, export, or double payment. Under these circumstances, there is a provision in the act to claim the excess amount as a refund. Previously, the taxpayer had to prepare the refund request with all supporting documents and submit it to the tax office. After verifying the claim of the taxpayer, the officer used to pass an order for refunding the claim. Based on this order, the taxpayer had to go to the Treasury to get the refund amount, which will be given in a check form. This entire process was extremely time-consuming and entirely dependent on the tax officers.

An online refund process has been introduced wherein the taxpayer mentions the refund amount being claimed, along with the reason, and submits the supporting documents for the claim [11]. This will be verified and processed online in the back-end system by the tax officers, and the refund amount is directly transferred to the bank account of the taxpayers in a time-bound manner.

4.3. End-to-End Automation

Five principles of Right to Services are implemented:

- Online information status
- Online request
- Auto-verification and approval
- On-time delivery
- On-line delivery

The GST system increased the tax base and the input of tax credit claims. Managing the same without an ICT system was an almost impossible task. Hence, the governments had planned the rollout of GST with a strong ICT system. The GSTN organization has been formed to build and implement all the IT requirements under the GST [8]. All the services to the taxpayers are now provided online. Registration, payment, and returns are made online along with the workflow-based system for processing these requests. Most of these services are delivered within the stipulated period by the officers [12]. The refund processes are made completely online with a faceless system. The input tax credits of the taxpayers are processed based on the transactions of the suppliers and further displayed to the users. This has resulted in self-monitoring by the taxpayers for availing the input tax credits.

4.4. Self-Generated Permit to Move Goods

Previously, the tax department issued blank copies of permits to the taxpayers in the form of delivery notes. The taxpayers or transporters need to carry a permit to move the goods from one location to the other. Before moving the goods, the delivery note was filled with details of the invoice, goods, and delivery location. During the movement, the delivery notes were inspected and collected at the check posts by the tax officials. These were then reconciled and verified with the books of accounts of taxpayers to know if the tax was paid correctly by the taxpayers or not.

A new online system has been introduced which is user-friendly and avoids taxpayers from visiting the offices for delivery notes. With the advent of this new system, the check posts have been abolished, thereby reducing the transportation time by the vehicles [13]. The system is environmentally friendly and contributes to a declining carbon footprint. This system has also led to an improvement in the efficiency of the officers of the tax department. The system is promoting self-policing in the trading community, thereby making everyone accountable for the transactions. This has led to an improvement in the tax collection by the department. Thus, this digital transformation has proved to be a successful initiative for the taxpayers, transporters, government, and all other stakeholders in the system.

E-WAY BILL

'e-Way Bill', a new paradigm, is the digital transformation of the paper-based permits in the indirect taxation system. It was introduced on 1 April 2018, a year after the introduction of the GST. The taxpayers can use this online system to generate the permit (known as an e-Way bill) and receive a unique reference number that can be verified by the officers online using the mobile app. The transporters can carry only the e-Way bill number without needing to carry e-Way bill hard copy [14].

Online permits for the movement of goods existed in some states in the pre-GST regime. In Karnataka, it was called 'e-Sugam'. e-Way Bill is an improved version of e-Sugam that facilitates taxpayers, transporters, and recipients. As shown in Figure 13.3, it is double-sided as the recipients can accept or reject the e-Way bill generated on their GSTIN. The e-Way bills can be generated using various modes like web, APIs, offline tools, mobile apps, short message service (SMS), and Suvidha providers. Likewise, officers are enabled for verifying the e-Way bills using the web, mobile apps, and SMS-based services.

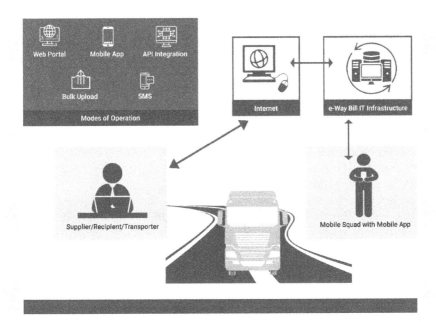

FIGURE 13.3
e-Way Bill Process.

The system is available 24/7 and is highly responsive. The easy, simple, and user-friendly interface is catering to the diverse needs of all the sections of the business community. About 3.5 million taxpayers are using the system. On a daily average, 2.4 million e-Way bills are generated [15]. The interface with other external departments such as National Securities Depository Limited, Vahan, and the GST has ensured that the system is up to date with verified information related to Permanent Account Number, vehicle number, and GSTIN, respectively.

4.5. Tax Analytical System for Better Compliance

GST return filing is based on self-assessment and reporting, however, there will be a considerable number of cases where the transaction details are suppressed or not reported by the taxpayers to reduce or avoid tax liabilities. Another way of tax evasion is by illegal claims for Input Tax Credits (ITCs). Hence, it becomes the responsibility of the concerned authority to identify such tax evasions and leakages and recover the taxes that are due on the taxpayer. Due to a large number of transactions of returns filed and statements, it is practically not feasible to manually scrutinize every return and detect tax suppression or evasion. Hence, an IT tool is required for the tax authorities to detect and act on such irregularities.

GST PRIME

'GST Prime' is an analysis tool that has been developed and implemented as a standard product for all the state GST departments to identify the tax evasions, ineligible ITC claims, and other irregularities.

The system analyzes basic details of the taxpayers, various returns, statements, payments, e-Way bills, generates intelligent and easy-to-understand analytical reports and graphical representations, and detects possible fraudulent cases.

So far, GST Prime has been implemented in 15 states [16]. The departments have improved the tax collection using ABC analysis of the defaulters provided in this tool. The officers are using the 360-degree view of the taxpayer and the various mismatches in ITC reports, based on various statements, provided in this tool. It has helped monitor the performance of the offices and officers in terms of tax collection and overall compliance.

4.6. Transparent and Accountable Assessment of Taxpayers

In the VAT regime, the states introduced the self-assessment system, wherein the taxpayers had to calculate the tax liabilities and pay the tax along with an expected return to the tax department. These returns were supposed to be assessed by the tax officials. As the number of taxpayers was large and returns were filed monthly, it was difficult to scrutinize all of them. The tax department officers were made to select taxpayers randomly, based on their judgments, and further do the scrutiny of respective returns. As it was a completely manual process, there was no proper maintenance of records of the audit orders, demands raised, and the collections made. The taxpayers could not verify the audit and demand orders issued by the tax officers. Hence, an IT-driven audit system was required wherein the selections of cases were objective; orders issued by the officers are digitized, transparent, and accountable.

4.7. Connected Ecosystem for Registration of Invoices

E-INVOICING SYSTEM

GST e-invoicing system is a system of reporting the invoices being issued by the taxpayers to their customers, on the government portal on a near-real-time basis, and obtaining a unique Invoice Reference

Number. The e-invoicing system facilitates the taxpayers to integrate their Enterprise resource planning (ERP) systems for the exchange of information between machines using APIs.

The standardized e-invoice format, based on an international standard (UBL/PEPPOL), has led to machine readability, enhanced interoperability, and uniform interpretation between various stakeholders mainly the suppliers, recipients, transporters, government, and financial institutions [9]. Onetime reporting of invoices has reduced the reporting of the same GST returns and e-Way bills. There is a substantial reduction in transcription errors as the machine-readable e-invoices data get exchanged with the tax department for compliance and to the buyer to prepare the inward supplies (purchase) register. The system is ensuring faster credit of ITCs and a substantial elimination of fake invoices [17].

In a value-addition chain, the GST allows the taxpayers to take an ITC on purchases made by them. Previously, fake invoices were in circulation and used by the taxpayers to make false ITC claims. Also, the taxpayers were suppressing the sales by not accounting in the tax returns and evading the tax payment. The e-invoicing system has been introduced worldwide to handle many such challenges. Figure 13.4 illustrates the life cycle of an e-Invoice.

COMPREHENSIVE AUDIT SYSTEM

In Karnataka, during the VAT regime in 2015, several factors were identified for selecting the audit cases, and then a comprehensive audit system was developed. The cases were allotted to the officers proportionately based on their designations. These cases were scrutinized and earmarked if it was a fit case. Accordingly, assignments were given to officers to conduct the audit on a round-robin basis. The taxpayers could also verify the audit assignment and order passed by the department using the online system. Liabilities by the taxpayer were recorded on the system and were further pursued for collection activity. The taxpayers made the payments online, and the ledgers were automatically adjusted.

To validate the orders passed, a peer-review system was adopted in the audit process. This improved the quality of the orders. Any appeal by the taxpayers was accepted online, and all the proceedings were recorded including that of appeals made in the High Court and the Supreme Court. A similar system has been instituted in the GST regime also.

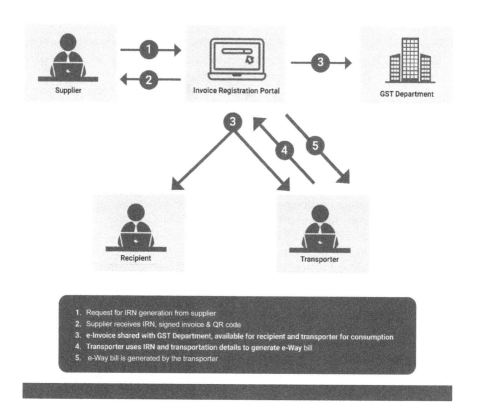

FIGURE 13.4
Life Cycle of an e-Invoice.

4.8. Fraud Analytics

e-Way Bill ensures movement of goods and is generated while roadways being the mode of transport. For this mode of transport, it is mandatory to update the registration number of the vehicle carrying the goods in the e-Way Bill system. There will be every possibility that e-Way bills could be generated, but transactions never happened, or the transactions are recycled on the same e-Way bill to transport the goods multiple times, among other methods, to evade tax. To mitigate such challenges, the government has made it mandatory for every commercial vehicle to have a Fastag (radio-frequency ID [RFID] device) for digital payment of toll charges. Along with this, e-Way Bill Analytical Reports provide intelligent analysis and helps in detecting frauds based on various parameters. The analytical and mismatch reports are used by the tax administration to identify and curb fraudulent activities. Furthermore, the data exchange between various systems has helped in finding out the variations in reporting by the taxpayers and detecting the tax evasions.

With this, the movement details of the vehicle are captured as it passes through the tolls. This information, along with e-Way Bill data, helps in tracking every e-Way bill on the move. Hence, frauds involving e-Way bills can be closely monitored.

5. Transformational Journey

As the challenges faced by the tax department were multifarious, the strategy also had to be multipronged. First, to change the image of the tax department from a regulatory body to a service provider and enable 'ease of doing business', all the services of the departments were made electronically available to the taxpayers on a 24/7 basis. Second, the law was also amended to ensure that these services are delivered in a time-bound manner. Third, the business process reengineering approach in the tax department has resulted in dramatic improvements in performance through a radical redesign of its processes. A new paradigm shift in administration has been brought through new systems and procedures to introduce self-policing. The check posts were removed, and random checks were introduced for making the movement of goods hassle-free and allowing the truckers and suppliers to furnish the information before the movement of goods. The audit, inspection, and assessment activities have been made online to bring accountability and transparency to the internal processes of the tax department. The tax officers could focus more on data analytics by leaving the repetitive work for IT-enabled systems. Figure 13.5 depicts the major milestones of transformation in the taxation ambit in India.

6. Impact Delivered

The implementation of various digital initiatives has proved to be of benefit to the taxpayers, the transporters, and the tax departments. These initiatives have improved the index of 'ease of doing business' and have increased the establishment of businesses by the taxpayers. The tax-related services are online and are available 24/7. This provided the convenience of applying and availing the services anytime and anywhere. It also led to reduced footfall to the tax offices by the taxpayers.

In the previous system, returns and statements were collected in hard copy, and the details were entered by the officials. Manual systems are often prone to human errors, and thus, it is natural that mistakes may happen while doing the data entries. Now, the capturing of voluminous data from

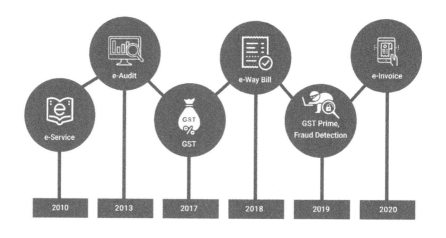

FIGURE 13.5
The Pillars of Transformation.

the taxpayers is done at the primary source, which is accurate and captured in time. These technological interventions have also helped in various types of insightful analyses that are helping in making informed decisions.

The new system has reduced the manual activities done by the official to a large extent. Activities such as data entry, preparing the statements and notices, and the like are now being handled by the system, providing time to the officers to work on various data analysis and decision-making tasks. The IT-based system is completely environmentally friendly and saves tons of paper on the filing of returns, statements, forms, and so on. It is also saving fuel and wear and tear of trucks and is providing free movement of goods/logistics by the removal of check posts and the self-generation of permits [13].

The introduction of faceless online services has changed the perception of the government with the taxpayers. It has encouraged increased compliance of registration, return filing, tax payments, and improvement in the overall tax collection. Over a period, the tax base has risen substantially in India. The reengineering of the processes with the reduction in steps and online validations has led to simplicity and ensured the quality of the data captured in the system. This also brought transparency in the system, enhanced accountability, and increased efficiency of the officers. This has further eliminated the subjectivity/discretionary power in approval of transactions [3].

The IT system has helped in easy and effective monitoring of the filing of the taxpayers, action taken by the officers. Top management was able to make appropriate decisions on restructuring the tax and the policies as and when it is required. With extensive data from various sources in the system, the government is leveraging these data for building analytical systems to detect tax evasion and fraud by using advanced data analytics. Figure 13.6

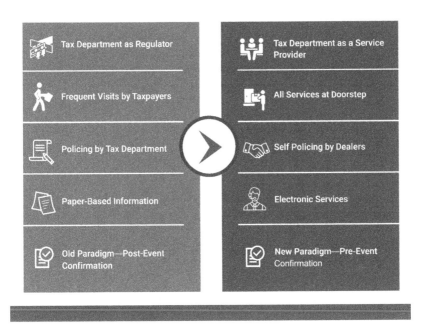

FIGURE 13.6
Impact Assessment.

showcases the impact assessment of technology interventions in the taxation system in India.

7. Conclusion and a Way Forward

Over a period, a phased introduction of e-services has enabled the tax department to achieve the set objectives of reimagining the tax practices and providing ease of services to the taxpayers. There has been improved service delivery by the reduction in human effort, paperwork, cost, and time required for availing the services. With digital systems, there is a significant reduction in response time, errors, visits to office premises, and denial of service delivery at any point. Increased accessibility, the ease of using the system, and heightened transparency are other advantages.

In parallel, the tax department officers are now spending time on advanced project management activities that require human interventions. There is improved and paperless service delivery with automated workflows, calculations, peer reviews, instant, and digitized data availability. The readily available MIS reports have also enabled better mechanisms for the detection of tax evasions.

Since the data are now available in digital format, it is very easy to build digital intelligence systems. AI, machine learning, and data analysis tools and technologies are now helping overcome the limitations the query-based database analytical system had and is also facilitating predictive analytics with the help of previous data. Simple and graphical representations of the outcomes of the analysis are easy to understand by the authorities at every level and help them in making informed decisions.

As the e-invoicing system has a wider taxpayer base, it is being implemented in a phased manner by the GST Council. In the first phase, a taxpayer with a turnover of more than INR 500 billion was enabled for business-to-business and export invoices. In the second phase, the taxpayers with turnover above INR 1 billion [18] are being enabled and gradually other taxpayers will be covered. This is being done to increase awareness and preparedness and infuse confidence in the taxpayers in a staggered manner. Once these milestones are covered, the business-to-citizen transactions will be enabled.

References

[1] Central Board of Indirect Taxes and Customs, "Goods and Service Tax (GST) Concept & Status," 1 August 2019. [Online]. Available: www.cbic.gov.in/resources//htdocs-cbec/gst/GST-Concept%20and%20Status01072019n.pdf.

[2] M. Govinda Rao, "Tax Reform in India: Achievements and Challenges," *Asia-Pacific Development Journal*, vol. 7, no. 2, December 2000.

[3] National Institute for Smart Government, "Government Process Re-engineering," 2012. [Online]. Available: www.meity.gov.in/writereaddata/files/GPRH170512.pdf.

[4] Central Board of Indirect Taxes and Customs, "First Discussion Paper On Goods and Services Tax In India," 10 November 2009. [Online]. Available: www.cbic.gov.in/resources//htdocs-cbec/gst/1st-discn-paper-new.pdf.

[5] P. K. Naseema, "History, Constitutional Framework and Evolution of Indian Tax System and Goods and Service Tax- A Study," *Bharati Law Review*, 2016, pp. 1–9. [Online]. Available: http://docs.manupatra.in/newsline/articles/Upload/197FAA37-956C-4573-8F58-20464016819D.pdf.

[6] M. Govinda Rao and R. Kavita Rao, "Trends and Issues in Tax Policy and Reform in India," in *Indian Policy Forum, 2005–2006*, vol. 2, New Delhi: Sage Publication, 2006, pp. 55–122.

[7] "Goods and Services Tax Council," [Online]. Available: www.gstcouncil.gov.in/.

[8] "Goods and Services Network," [Online]. Available: www.gstn.org.in/.

[9] PEPPOL, "PEPPOL 'BIS' Specifications—An Overview," [Online]. Available: https://peppol.eu/what-is-peppol/peppol-profiles-specifications.

[10] Surbhi Gupta, "Goods and Services Tax (GST): A Comparative Study of Select ASEAN Countries," *VISION: Journal of Indian Taxation*, vol. 4, no. 1, 2017, pp. 79–102. doi: 10 1 7492 4 01 9995.

[11] Central Board of Indirect Taxes and Customs, "Report of the Joint Committee on the Business Processes for GST on Refund Processes," August 2015. [Online]. Available: www.cbic.gov.in/resources//htdocs-cbec/gst/Report_on_GST_Refund%20Process-082015-new.pdf.

[12] "Goods and Services Tax," [Online]. Available: https://gst.gov.in.

[13] NDTV, "GST Ground Report: An E-Way Bill Means 10 Hours Less On 2000 Km Journey for This Truck Driver," 4 July 2018. [Online]. Available: www.ndtv.com/india-news/gst-ground-report-an-e-way-bill-means-10-hours-less-on-2000-km-journey-for-this-truck-driver-1877432.

[14] Goods and Services Tax, "e-Way Bill System," [Online]. Available: https://ewaybillgst.gov.in/.

[15] E-Way Bill System: https://ewaybillgst.gov.in/EWB2YrJourney.pdf.

[16] GST Prime System: https://gst.kar.nic.in/gstprime/videos/videos.html.

[17] Goods and Services Tax, "e-Invoice System," [Online]. Available: https://einvoice1.gst.gov.in.

[18] e-Invoice System: https://einvoice1.gst.gov.in/Notifications/notfctn-61-central-tax-english-2020.pdf.

[19] Ministry of Electronic & Information Technology, "Mission Mode Projects," [Online]. Available: www.meity.gov.in/content/mission-mode-projects#:~:text=A%20mission%20mode%20project%20(MMP,records%20or%20commercial%20taxes%20etc.

[20] Department of Administrative Reforms & Public Grievances, "2011–12 Awards Presented on 21st April 2013," [Online]. Available: https://darpg.gov.in/relatedlinks/prime-ministers-awards-excellence-public-administration.

[21] Ministry of Electronics and Information Technology, "Saaransh: A compendium for Mission Mode Projects under NeGP," January 2011. [Online]. Available: www.meity.gov.in/content/saaransh.

14

Transformational Journey of Indian Immigration and Visa Services

Jitender Kumar Yadav and Anand Swarup Srivastava

1. Introduction—Immigration and Visa Services

Immigration and visa services are rendered to safeguard the borders from illegal immigrants while facilitating the tourism and economy of the country. For this, countries are leveraging technology to improve efficiency and enable efficient dissemination of information regarding immigration and visa requirements, processes, and timelines so that potential travelers seeking services are not deterred from the outset.

Over the last decade, Indian immigration and visa services have seen phenomenal progress in IT enablement, process automation, process reengineering, service delivery, and strengthening security at all touchpoints such as Indian missions abroad, ICPs, FRROs, and FROs in India. It has benefited travelers and stakeholders alike in terms of ease of services, enhanced transparency, and better compliance with rules and regulations. This has led to the reduction in the processing time of visa applications from the traditional three months to almost three days now. Furthermore, the travelers' clearance time at ICPs has also been reduced to 1.5 minutes from the traditional 5 to 6 minutes. The key initiatives such as e-Visa, Visa on Arrival, e-FRRO (Foreigners Registration), and Immigration Control System (to monitor and regulate international borders and facilitating entry and exit of bona fide travelers) have witnessed a significant impact across the service delivery, foreigner facilitation, security, and safety.

As India happens to be one of the largest growing economies in the world, besides being the second-most populous, it has been witnessing a continuous increase in total international traffic (foreigners and Indians) every year. This had resulted in the arrival/departure of nearly 70 million passengers through ICPs in 2018, which was 8.51 percent higher than the passenger traffic in 2017. More than 93 percent of international traffic in 2018 was handled by the ICPs at various international airports, a testament to the significance of air traffic. Furthermore, among international airports, Delhi and Mumbai handled more than 45 percent of the total international traffic [1].

DOI: 10.1201/9781003111351-14

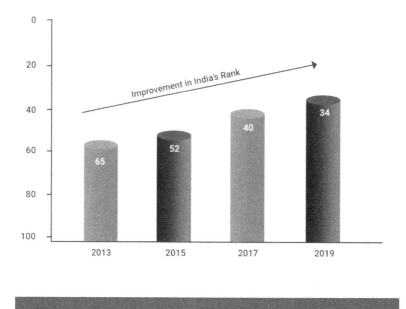

FIGURE 14.1
India's Global Travel and Tourism Index.

In the era of globalization and the increasing movement of people, governments are confronted with the challenge of balancing national security and immigration concerns, on one hand, while promoting economic activities and fostering political relations, on the other [2]. India has seen a progressive growth in passenger movement, which could be seen from the numerical data released by the Ministry of Home Affairs (MHA) on its website [1]. Furthermore, India has also succeeded to attract foreign students to study in India with its liberalized visa regime as the ease and expense of obtaining a student visa greatly influence international student enrollment.

As per the travel and tourism competitiveness report published by World Economic Forum, India has shown enormous improvement (refer to Figure 14.1) in its rank from 65th in 2013 to 34th in 2019. Furthermore, India has been ranked 33rd in air transport infrastructure, an important indicator given the country's scale of development, and reasonable ground and port infrastructure [3].

2. Institutional Structure

As depicted in Figure 14.2, the MHA is the nodal ministry that deals with the policies and administration of visas, immigration, citizenship, overseas

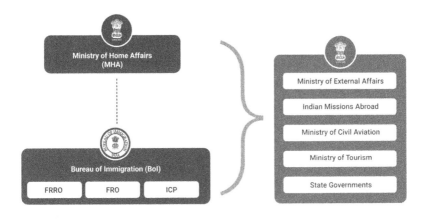

FIGURE 14.2
Major Stakeholder Intervention.

citizens of India, and other related services in India. The operational responsibility lies with the Bureau of Immigration (BOI) headed by a commissioner, which was set up in 1971 to undertake immigration functions at airports, seaports, and land and rail check posts and render visa-related services to foreign visitors staying within the country. Presently, there are 86 ICPs all over India catering to international traffic. Out of these, 37 ICPs are functioning under the BOI, while the remaining are being managed by the respective state governments [4].

Visa-related services to foreigners staying within the country are provided through jurisdictional FRROs/FROs established in district headquarters and state home departments. More than 694 FROs, 12 FRROs, and 21 state home departments have been interconnected for rendering smooth visa-related services within the country.

The Ministry of External Affairs, also known as the Foreign Ministry, is responsible for the conduct of foreign relations for India. The ministry functions through more than 190 Indian embassies established across the world for facilitating immigration and visa-related services to foreign tourists and strengthening bilateral relations with other nations. The ministry also regulates the issuance of passports to Indian nationals through 37 Passport Offices spread across the country.

The Ministry of Civil Aviation is the nodal ministry assigned for the formulation of national policies and programs for the development and regulation of civil aviation and for devising and implementing schemes for the orderly growth and expansion of civil air transport [5].

The Ministry of Tourism is the nodal agency for articulating national policies and programs for the facilitation, as well as the strengthening, of tourism in India along with augmenting tourism infrastructure and assurance of quality standards by tourism service providers. The Ministry of Tourism works in close coordination with the MHA and the Ministry of External Affairs for visitor facilitation in ease of travel and stay in India.

3. Global Scenario and Trends

Countries across the world are focusing on leveraging technology for improving the efficiency of their immigration and visa services in terms of visitor facilitation and border management. India, too, is catching up with the technical innovations, best practices, and user-convenient processes in delivering services efficiently and smoothly. Recently, the U.S. Customs and Border Protection unveiled the first biometric terminal at Atlanta International Airport followed by Singapore, the United Kingdom, and Hong Kong, which are shaping the passenger experience through biometrics-related projects. Furthermore, robots are becoming a common sight at airport terminals. Countries such as the United States, South Korea, and Germany are adopting humanoid robots to engage with customers and optimize efficiency. Countries like the United States, Singapore, the United Kingdom, Switzerland are exploring blockchain's potential to help improve passenger identification processes by reducing the need for multiple ID checks [6].

3.1. Innovative Technology and Infrastructure

The evolution and application of digital technologies are transforming the delivery of immigration, visa, and hospitality services across the world. Countries are leveraging technologies in various ways, from allowing online submission of visa applications, streamlining delivery systems, supporting end-to-end electronic visa processing, delivering electronic travel authorizations, and automating border entry processes, to name a few [7]. Figure 14.3 depicts the various technology solutions adopted globally in the immigration and visa services.

Automated border control e-Gate—e-Gate allows an automated border passage by authenticating an electronic machine-readable travel document (e-MRTD), establishing that the passenger is the rightful holder of the document, querying border control records, and automatically determining eligibility for border crossing according to predefined rules, which is composed of a self-service system and an e-gate. The end-to-end e-Gate process usually takes up to a minute for passenger clearance [8].

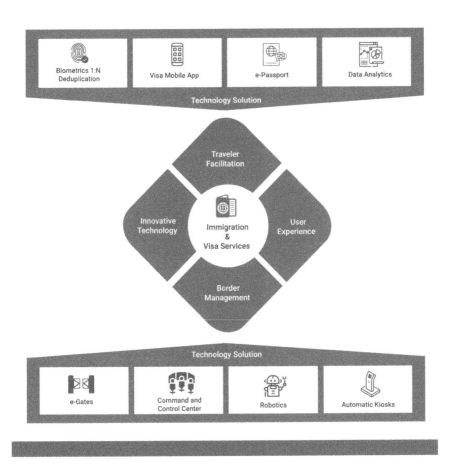

FIGURE 14.3
Innovative Technology Solutions Adopted Globally.

Biometrics 1:N deduplication—Individuals' identities have traditionally been verified by biographical and demographical information such as passports. Biometric data, such as facial recognition, is used at 'smart borders' around the world to identify the person and run security checks. To ensure that each person in a database is unique, systems use biometric identification to perform a duplicate biometric enrollment check. This involves comparing a template generated from an enrolled biometric against all or a subset of templates stored in the biometric database to detect a duplicate registration (a 1:N search), after which the new template is added to the database. The increased use of biometrics signals not only a shift to more sophisticated technology but also an approach to identification based on individual characteristics rather than on nationality [9].

Data analytics—Border agencies have started to collect data from multiple points rather than only from traditional sources such as visa applications and border-crossing points. The application of data analytics on these data would enrich immigration authorities and security agencies with proactive insights for risky travelers intending to enter or cross borders. Over a period, a large volume of travelers' data has been collected by immigration authorities that need to be utilized for intelligent decision-making by immigration and visa authorities. Furthermore, the application of predictive analytics on historical data for supervised inductive learning shall be explored to train various discriminative models and evaluate these models using simple statistical validation methods for better insights to immigration authorities [10].

Automatic kiosks for the facilitation of trusted travelers/passengers—Automatic kiosks use digital biometric ID management technology to automate the journey from secure check-in to on-time boarding. The use of the automatic kiosk facilitates the travelers in saving time during check-in, immigration, baggage clearance, feedbacks, grievance redressal, and so on at airports. Immigration authorities are giving a large thrust on passenger's facilitation, including the reduction in passenger clearance time at all touchpoints.

Mobile app–based visa services—Mobile applications have become one of the easiest available sources of services that enable interactive engagement and instant online and offline access to users. Most countries are exploring the possibility of rendering visa services on a mobile app for passenger facilitation. A few countries have already launched their mobile app for visa information dissemination, status inquiry, and tourist packages. The Immigration Department of Hong Kong recently deployed its mobile app for providing end-to-end visa-related services to foreign tourists like appointment booking, visa application services, land boundary control points waiting time, application status inquiry, submission of documents, and other services [11].

Considering the volume of foreign tourists' footfall in India, Indian immigration authorities have proposed to launch a mobile app containing all Indian visa and immigration services whereby tourists would be facilitated with end-to-end visa services from obtaining an Indian visa for entering the country to visa services rendered within the country, such as visa extensions, conversions, and many more.

Integrated command-and-control center (CCC)—A CCC is considered the core for managing disasters and responding to inconsistent conditions and various operations in an area. It is also referred to as 'situation room', where the overall operations of an organization like monitoring, controlling, and commanding are carried out. CCCs serve the purpose of collecting vital information, important communications, and connected systems. It further helps in sharing decisive commands, warnings, and alerts flawlessly in huge numbers.

Airports and immigration premises are major border control areas that require constant monitoring and instant response in case of any disaster or unscrupulous activity. Indian immigration authorities are exploring possible solutions for the implementation of an emergency response system at immigration areas for better profiling of the passengers and real-time responses to the alerts.

e-Passport—A biometric passport or e-Passport consists of an embedded electronic microprocessor chip containing biometric information that is used to authenticate the identity of the passport holder. It is based on contactless smart card technology, including a microprocessor chip embedded in the front or back cover of the passport. More than 100 nations currently issue e-Passports, and over 490 million e-Passports are in circulation. e-passports add a layer of security to traditional nonelectronic passports by embedding an electronic chip in the passport booklet that stores the biographical information [11]. Digitizing passports and visas helps in streamlining and simplifying passport and visa issuing, renewing, revoking, verification, and validation processes [12].

Robotics—AI and machine learning–based robots can learn and expand their knowledge, and humanoid robots can provide more relevant information to passengers and additional operational benefits to immigration authorities and airlines. Robotics may play a crucial part in strengthening the relationship with passengers in the times to come.

3.2. Compliant and Sustainable Solutions

With more than a billion people moving across the borders for tourism and trade, the need for more efficient and cost-effective visa processing has moved to the forefront of the national agendas of many countries. To cater to the needs of future cross-border travel, the Indian immigration authorities are emphasizing the facilitation of immigration and visa services with a wider focus on implementing real-time travel services like e-Visa and Visa on Arrival and the use of contactless immigration services like automatic kiosks, e-Gate, and biometrics-based identity authentication.

3.3. Secure Border Management

Foreigners landing on Indian soil are subject to national security checks regardless of ethnicity or national origin. The BOI performs profiling of the travelers through an intelligent immigration control system. Visa overstayers are not conceptualized as threats to security in the discourse on par with other categories of irregular migrants; visa-goers and other travelers are, too, increasingly subjected to a rationale of surveillance and risk [13]. These security checks match information about unscrupulous elements involved in serious crimes and links with terrorism. Immigration authorities across the globe normally rely on the following mechanism for security checks:

Intelligent Document Scanners: Intelligent document scanners are designed with security features as per the International Civil Aviation Organization norms to detect the use of fraudulent travel documents by passengers at immigration checkpoints.

Biometrics Enrollment and Verification: Biometrics is one of the safest identities of a person which cannot be manipulated by any means, thereby maintaining the uniqueness of the person. The biometrics traits of the traveler (fingerprint and iris) are captured at the entry point during an immigration check and the same is verified with the database while check-in/checkout at ICPs.

Negative List: Each country maintains a database of unscrupulous passengers to restrict their entry into the country. The biographic and biometric traits of these passengers are matched against a negative list before rendering any immigration or visa-related service to them.

4. Transformational Journey of Indian Immigration and Visa Services

The trends and scenarios in immigration and visa services act as stimulants/drivers for the ongoing transformational drive, largely addressing concerns and focus areas such as compliance with Foreigner's Act, Rules and Regulations; integrated systems; efficient and transparent systems; and long-term and sustainable solutions. As shown in Figure 14.4, over a period, the Indian Immigration and Visa Services have transformed significantly in India.

Some of the revolutionary solutions comprising the overall immigration and visa framework and various components have been captured as case studies in this chapter.

The entry, stay, and exit of foreigners within India are governed by the Passport (Entry into India) Act 1920 and 1950, the Foreigners Act 1946, and the Registration of Foreigners Rules, 1992 [14]. Till 1992, the Indian immigration and visa services were provided annually to foreigners entering India, which was taken over by the setting up of the first Immigration Clearance System in 1993 at Delhi Airport and was further extended to other major airports. Subsequently, a consular issuance system was implemented at HCI Colombo in 2001, which was further extended to 30 more Indian missions by 2009.

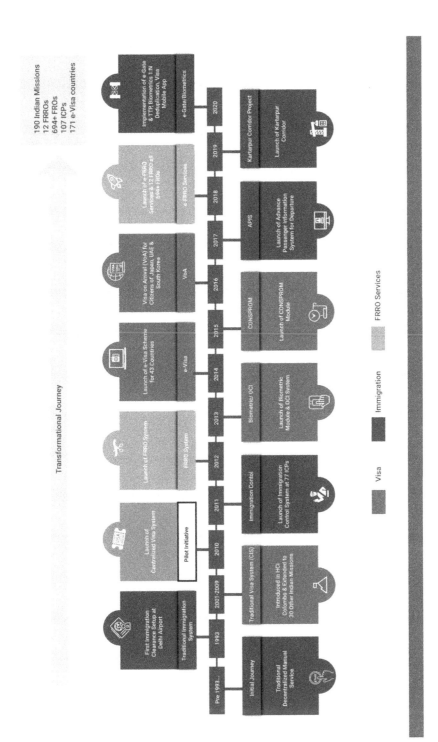

FIGURE 14.4

Evolution of Indian Immigration and Visa Services.

IMMIGRATION CONTROL SYSTEM

The first Immigration Control System was set up at Delhi Airport in 1993 to facilitate speedy passenger clearance. Over the last 25 years, immigration clearance has seen substantial progress in passenger facilitation and security, which has been strengthened and integrated with other databases for intelligence-led profiling of passengers by immigration authorities. The Immigration Control System is operational at 107 ICPs across the country, which includes 34 airports, 35 land posts, 26 seaports, 5 rail posts, and 4 river posts for facilitating immigration authorities in speedy passenger clearance. These larger ICPs have more than 40 immigration check counters to deal with the passengers whereas smaller ICPs have on an average 10 counters, which comes to approximately 1,200-plus immigration counters across all the ICPs.

Out of 107 ICPs, 28 airports and 5 seaports have been designated for availing e-Visa facility by travelers. These ICPs (107) cater to daily passenger traffic of approximately 0.24 million (240,000) passengers, which include 0.165 million (165,000) Indians' arrivals and departures and 65,000 foreigners' arrivals and departures. The ICS application has also been integrated with the biometrics enrollment and verification facility for identity authentication of travelers.

The modernization and upgradation of immigration and visa services were identified in 2010 and undertaken by the MHA under the NeGP, with the core objective to develop and implement a secure and integrated service delivery framework that facilitates legitimate travelers while strengthening the security measures. Figure 14.5 depicts the Indian Immigration and Visa Services Framework.

E-VISA SERVICE

The introduction of the e-Visa service by the Government of India in 2014 has completely transformed the Indian visa services over the traditional way of Indian visa issuance through Indian missions abroad, which had longer processing times and procedural delays due to the distributed processing framework by all stakeholders. e-Visa service facilitates in seeking Indian visa for a short duration to visit for recreation, sightseeing, casual visit, short duration medical treatment, casual business visit, and so on. It is a completely faceless, cashless, and paperless service, provided through the applicant's email within 72 hours of online application.

FIGURE 14.5
Indian Immigration and Visa Services Framework.

The travelers have been facilitated by an online portal for filling the e-Visa application form with the photo and document upload facility along with the provision of online visa fee payment. The final decision on the application is communicated to the traveler on their registered email ID in the form of Electronic Travel Authorization (ETA). The traveler needs to print a copy of the ETA and travel to the designated Indian airport/seaport.

As a part of the liberalization of the visa regime, the Government of India further extended Visa on Arrival facility to the nationals of Japan, South Korea, and the United Arab Emirates at Delhi, Mumbai, Kolkata, Chennai, Bengaluru, and Hyderabad airports. The service facilitates the nationals of these countries in planning their journey to India on a real-time basis and further strengthening the bilateral relations among all three nations. The passengers from these countries are required to fill an application form on arrival at an Indian port and present the same to the 'visa officer' at the visa counter on arrival. The format of physical form is also made available to the airlines for onboarding the flight.

Centralized Visa Issuance System—*The paper visa of any country is issued from the embassy in the concerned country; similarly, an Indian visa* *is issued through Indian embassies spread across the world. These embassies are scattered in wider geographical locations that have been connected through a secured, centralized, and integrated application for rendering visa-related services. Applicants are facilitated with an online visa application through the central portal, indianvisaonline.gov.in, which is further made available to all concerned agencies through a centralized channel for processing. The immigration and visa authorities in India and Indian embassies abroad have been provided with access to a centralized visa issuance system for processing visa-related services. Previously, it took three months for processing and granting visa applications, which has now been reduced to almost three days. Furthermore, an online application, Consprom, has been implemented at outsourcing agencies attached with Indian missions abroad for accepting the visa applications and forwarding them to Indian missions for processing.*

Thus, a centralized visa issuance system was introduced in 2010 followed by an integrated immigration control system in May 2011. The identity authentication of foreigners within the country was a big concern for immigration authorities, which was resolved by the introduction of the FRRO module in 2012 and the biometrics enrollment application in 2013. Furthermore, in 2014, a completely cashless, faceless, and paperless service was launched in the form of 'e-Visa' followed by Visa on Arrival facility in 2016 to facilitate foreigners seeking on-demand Indian visa service.

Complimentary to the objective of facilitating travelers, an e-FRRO application was introduced in 2018 and subsequently used in the Kartarpur Corridor Project in 2019. Presently, the emphasis is on strengthening security by the introduction of an automated border control system (e-Gate) at airports and biometrics 1:N deduplication at all touchpoints.

E-FRRO SERVICE

Indian visa-related services like visa extensions, visa conversions, exit permits, and the like for foreigners during their stay in India are provided through FRROs and FROs across the country. Previously, foreigners were supposed to visit the FRRO/FRO physically with their documents, which was a cumbersome process. The introduction of e-FRRO service in 2018 in India has eliminated the need for the physical visit of foreigners to the FRRO/FRO, to a large extent, thus providing faceless, cashless, and paperless visa services to foreigners staying in India. Figure 14.6 *showcases the various functionalities of eFRRO Service in India.*

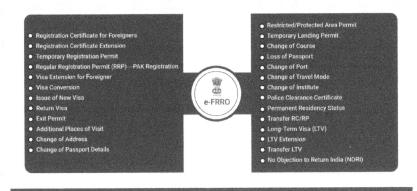

FIGURE 14.6
e-FRRO Service.

5. Impact Delivered

Governance: The computerization of immigration and visa services has provided a connected platform free of redundancies ensuring transparency in the process and systems. The decision support systems have also been strengthened for informed decision-making and monitoring through near-real-time dashboards and data analytics tools for better compliance with the rules and regulations. The vertical and horizontal integration of the stakeholders and immigration functions has established a connected platform for state authorities, immigration, and law enforcement agencies. Streamlining and reorganizing operating procedures have reduced the cost and service delivery timeframe, setting accountability on an organizational level.

Stakeholders: The introduction of centralized online application platforms such as e-Visa, e-FRRO, Overseas Citizen of India Service, and others has not only added convenience to foreigners in seeking anytime/anywhere service but also ensured the accountability toward efficient enforcement of immigration and visa rules. Furthermore, the use of dashboards, SMS alerts, online channels, and social media has made the beneficiaries more connected, informed, and involved.

The implementation of 100 percent contactless and faceless online visa services has reduced visa processing and passenger clearance time to a larger extent.

More than 90 percent of visas are issued within three days of visa application submission in Indian missions abroad for non-Prior Reference Check (PRC) countries. Under the e-Visa service, 70 percent of cases are being disposed of within 24 hours, and all cases are disposed of within 72 hours. The average time for clearing the passenger aircraft has been reduced to 30 minutes on arrival.

Economic impact: The efficient facilitation to travelers directly attracts foreign visitors to the country, which benefits the trade and travel industry through foreign investments for economic growth. Direct benefits include economic support for hotels, retail shops, transportation services, entertainment venues, and attractions, while indirect benefits include government spending on related infrastructure, plus domestic spending.

Security: The availability of near-real-time high-risk travelers' data to immigration/visa authorities facilitates intelligence-led decision-making. The augmentation of biometrics-based identification of authentic travelers and software-aided passenger profiling for identifying risky travelers at each touchpoint have strengthened the security agencies in India.

6. Conclusion

Efficient immigration and visa services are the major catalysts for attracting foreign visitors to the country, which, in turn, is an important contributor to the socioeconomic development of a country.

In developing countries like India, tourism is considered to be one of the major sectors fueling economic growth, as it contributes directly to the national income and generates huge employment opportunities. It has become a rapidly growing service industry with a great potential for further expansion and diversification. India has seen a drastic growth in foreigners' footfall over the last five years. Aiming at large-scale impact, it becomes imperative to enable the facilitation of the tourists at all touchpoints right from visa services to immigration services.

The role of the technology in facilitating international travel is well accepted, the potential of technology solutions to produce tangible results such as the reduction in the length of the application form and number of documents required, availability and accessibility of information in multiple channels, better workload and resource planning, and outsourcing of administrative tasks are worth mentioning.

Liberalized immigration and visa policies, strengthening the ICPs (entry and exit points for foreigners and Indians), and secure and efficient border management systems are the major key areas demanding attention. Recognizing the pivotal role of passenger facilitation in tourist footfall, Indian immigration authorities are also exploring the implementation of mobile visa services through mobile applications. Tourists would be facilitated with anywhere, anytime visa application and other visa-related services through an integrated mobile app for all Indian visa-related services.

The security and efficiency of the visa and immigration services can be heightened using latest technologies for identification of the travelers and facilitation in reducing the time spent in the visa and immigration process. The technology initiatives under the project are preparing India to compete with the other neighboring countries in becoming a favorite destination for foreigners with a wide plethora of reasons to visit, whether it be for tourism, business, medical tourism, and/or education, among others. India has witnessed a drastic improvement as it ranked 34th in the Global Tourism Index published by World Economic Forum in 2019.

Furthermore, in anticipation of the competition from the other nations, Indian immigration authorities have started working on passenger facilitation through global technologies such as automatic border control, biometrics 1:N deduplication solutions, automatic kiosks, data analytics, integrated CCCs, and a mobile app for visa facilitation.

Adaptability to changing technological landscape with time and understanding the needs of customers are imperative to success in the service sector. Thus, Indian immigration authorities shall explore all possible applications of existing and emerging technologies for providing a seamless experience of immigration and visa-related services to travelers.

References

[1] Ministry of Home Affairs, "e-Visa Dashboard," [Online]. Available: https://consprom.nic.in/boi_dashboard/ [Accessed 27 August 2020].

[2] Ministry of Tourism, [Online]. Available: http://tourism.gov.in/annual-report [Accessed 27 August 2020].

[3] World Economic Forum, [Online]. Available: https://reports.weforum.org/travel-and-tourism competitiveness-report-2019/rankings/ [Accessed 27 August 2020].

[4] Bureau of Immigration, [Online]. Available: https://boi.gov.in/ [Accessed 28 August 2020].

[5] Ministry of Civil Aviation, [Online]. Available: www.civilaviation.gov.in/ [Accessed 24 January 2021].

[6] Future Travel Experience Innovation and Startup Hub, [Online]. Available: www.fte-hub.com/ [Accessed 27 September 2020].

[7] OECD, [Online]. Available: www.oecd-ilibrary.org/sites/f528d444-en/index.html?itemId=/content/component/f528d444-en [Accessed 26 August 2020].

[8] ICAO, [Online]. Available: www.icao.int/publications/Documents/9303p2_cons_ en.pdf [Accessed 18 August 2020].

[9] OECD, [Online]. Available: www.oecd.org/investment/globalforum/40302909.pdf [Accessed 28 August 2020].

[10] Sharmila Vegesana, "Predictive Analytics for Classification of Immigration Visa Applications: A Discriminative Machine Learning Approach," 2018. [Accessed 10 February 2021].

[11] ICAO, "Security and Facilitation," [Online]. Available: www.icao.int/Security/ FAL/PKD/Pages/ePassportBasics.aspx [Accessed 24 January 2021].

[12] S. Panchamia and D. K. Byrappa, "Passport, VISA and Immigration Management Using Blockchain," 23rd Annual International Conference in Advanced Computing and Communications (ADCOM), IEEE, Bangalore, 2017, pp. 8–17. doi: 10.1109/ADCOM.2017.00009.

[13] Frida Hansen, "[Thesis] Discrepancies in European Union Policies Towards Illegal Immigration: The Securitisation of the Visa-Overstayer and the Irregular Migrant," Uppsala University, 2020. [Online]. Available: www. diva-portal.org/smash/get/diva2:1477702/FULLTEXT01.pdf [Accessed 10 February 2021].

[14] Ministry of Home Affairs, "Foreigners Division Acts," [Online]. Available: www.mha.gov.in/MHA1/ACtRule.html [Accessed 27 August 2020].

Glossary

Aadhaar	A verifiable 12-digit identification number issued by Unique Identification Authority of India to the residents of India.
Annavitran	Means Distribution of Food Grains. The Annavitran Portal hosts the data of distribution of food grains through e-PoS devices within a state.
Arthashastra	The Hindi word for economics.
Antyodaya	A Hindi word that refers to uplifting of the weakest section of the society.
Atmanirbhar Bharat	A Hindi word which means 'Self-reliant India', an initiative launched during the COVID-19 pandemic.
Ayushman Bharat	A health protection scheme to provide health insurance to citizens. *Ayushman* means 'healthy' and *Bharat* means 'India'.
Bharatkosh	Non-Tax Receipt Portal (NTRP) providing one-stop services to deposit any fees/fine/other money into the government account.
Challan	A document in physical or electronic form issued by any authorized officer in government to a person acting in violation of the act.
DigiLocker	An online service aimed at providing paperless governance to the citizens.
Doordarshan	An autonomous public service broadcaster founded by the Government of India.
Gramin	Means 'rural'.
Gram Panchayat	The local self-government organization in India of the Panchayati Raj System at the village or small-town level.
Gram Sabhas	The forum of the Gram Sabha people use to discuss local governance and development and make need- based plans for the village. Gram Sabha is the primary body of the Panchayati Raj System and is, by far, the largest.
Har Khet ko Pani	Every agricultural field is to have irrigation water.
Khatauni	An abstract based on the Khasras (land details) of a village that lists out all the holdings of an individual or family in that village.
Kisan	Hindi word for farmer.

Lok Sabha	The House of the People, the lower house of India's bicameral parliament.
MeghRaj	The cloud computing infrastructure of the Government of India—'GI Cloud' that has been named as 'MeghRaj'.
Nyaya	Sanskrit word which means justice.
Panchayati Raj	Local government in the Indian subcontinent. The word *raj* means 'rule' and *panchayat* means 'assembly'.
Pradhan Mantri Krishi Sinchayee Yojana	Prime Minister Agricultural Irrigation Scheme formulated by the government with the vision of extending the coverage of irrigation and improving water use efficiency in a focused manner.
Rajya Sabha	Rajya Sabha or Council of States, the upper house of the bicameral parliament of India.
Rojgar	Means employment.
Samagra Shiksha	Integrated scheme for school education extending from preschool to class XII to ensure inclusive and equitable quality education at all levels of school education.
Sarathi	Software package for the creation of a complete computerized database of drivers' licenses, conductors' licenses, driving school licenses, and fees.
Sarva Shiksha Abhiyan	A flagship program for the achievement of the Universalization of Elementary Education in a time-bound manner.
Suvidha	Means facility or support.
Swayam Prabha	A group of 34 DTH channels devoted to telecasting of high-quality educational programs on 24/7 basis using the GSAT-15 satellite.
Taluka	The subdistricts of a district.
Tehsil	An administrative area in parts of India. Districts are divided into Tehsils, and Tehsils is further divided into blocks.
Vahan	A vehicle, such as wagons, bicycles, motor vehicles, railed vehicles, or watercraft, that transports people or cargo. Vahan is also an Integrated Solution for Vehicle Registration System.
Vedic Gurukul System	A residential schooling system popular in ancient India. Gurus trained their students with meditations, yoga, and other standards.

Vedic Period	Named for the Vedas, the oldest scriptures in Hinduism, which were composed during the period 1750–500 BCE.
Zila Parishad	District council or Mandal Parishad or district panchayat, the third tier of the Panchayati Raj system and functions at the district levels in all states. A zila parishad is an elected body.

Index